Gramática Apasionada:

Reminiscences of a Love Affair with the Spanish Language

By

James K. Gavin

© 2000, 2003 by James K. Gavin. All rights reserved.

No part of this book may be reproduced, stored in a retrieval system, or transmitted by any means, electronic, mechanical, photocopying, recording, or otherwise, without written permission from the author.

ISBN: 1-4033-6904-6 (e-book)
ISBN: 1-4033-6905-4 (Paperback)

Library of Congress Control Number: 2002111835

This book is printed on acid free paper.

Printed in the United States of America
Bloomington, IN

Para and por (in chronological order) Robin, Molly and Emma

As a sneak preview of the sequel to this book,
due out in September, 2022,
(working title – <u>*Gramática Geriatra:* How to Remember Some of the Grammar You Forgot</u>),
I am pleased to offer this
Pre-dedication.

To all of my many Spanish teachers:

To mention a few: David, a *yanqui* who didn't go home, and Anita, the reason he didn't; Mac, anthropoid anthropologist, and Carmen, his most significant Central American discovery;
Gabriela, *la gaviota chilena*; Hazel, color perceptiveness ebony; Patricio, color tequila green;
Estif, still a PCV after all these years, and Evelyn, *belleza de Borinquen*;
and last but certainly tallest, Juan, *co-jugador de basquetbol y verbos.*

Table of Contents

Preface – explains how this book fits into the overall strategy for learning to speak Spanish.. ix

Glossary of Terms – gives definitions of common grammatical terms used in this book xiii

Note: all chapters of this book are not equally suitable for all stages of learning. For that reason there are suggested levels of appropriateness in parentheses beside the title of each chapter in the Table of Contents. Numbered 1 to 4, they correspond to four broad stages in the learning process:

1. Beginner, 2. Lower Intermediate, 3. Advanced Intermediate, 4. Advanced.

Chapter One	What to Expect When You Inflect....................................... 1 is a reality check that discusses the learning process and the expectations that adults bring to the task of learning to speak a second language. (1, 2, 3, 4)	
Chapter Two	There's No Time Like the Present.. 6 imposes order on the seemingly chaotic conjugation of the present tense, inclusively reducing all possibilities to four groups of verbs. (1, 2, 3)	
Chapter Three	Shakespeare Didn't Get It... 20 reviews the correct uses of the two Spanish verbs meaning 'to be.' (1, 2, 3, 4)	
Chapter Four	Re: Dictionaries .... 33 warns of the danger of too much reliance on an English/Spanish dictionary. (1, 2, 3, 4)	
Chapter Five	A Tale of Two Tenses.. 37 looks at the uses of the two past tenses, preterit and imperfect. (2, 3, 4)	
Chapter Six	Achieving Conjugational Bliss.. 51 presents the conjugation of the two past tenses, preterit and imperfect, with special attention paid to the reputedly intractable preterit tense. (1, 2, 3, 4)	
Chapter Seven	All About Me, Thee, and Your Grace .... 63 discusses familiar versus formal address - *tú* vs. *usted*. (1, 2, 3, 4)	

Chapter Eight	Jiffylex .... 70 demonstrates how to generate an extensive vocabulary through the existence of cognate words. (1, 2, 3, 4)	
Chapter Nine	Uneeda Verb .... 83 talks about ways to develop an effective verb vocabulary. (2, 3, 4)	
Chapter Ten	Don't Go for the *Gusto* .... 97 addresses the problems that inevitably accompany the use of the important verb *gustar*. (2, 3, 4)	
Chapter Eleven	An Alternative to Conjugation.. 104 talks about the importance of attitude and other intangibles when attempting to communicate in Spanish. (1, 2, 3, 4)	
Chapter Twelve	Now You Too Can Speak Perfectly (and Imperfectly)................... 110 reviews the uses of the present and past participles in both English and Spanish. (2, 3, 4)	
Chapter Thirteen	The Killer Bees of Spanish Grammar.. 118 defines and explains the uses of direct, indirect, and reflexive object pronouns. (2, 3, 4)	
Chapter Fourteen	Words 'R' Us... 135 dwells upon words as interesting objects in themselves. (1, 2, 3, 4)	
Chapter Fifteen	Junk Is My Middle Name .... 146 presents and demystifies the subjunctive. (3, 4)	
Chapter Sixteen	It Takes Two to *Tenga* .... 156 lists and gives examples of the conditions that create the subjunctive mode. (3, 4)	
Chapter Seventeen	Add Some Stress to Your Life.. 173 explains the uses of the accent mark in both the written and the spoken language. (3, 4)	
Chapter Eighteen	It Cleans, Fixes, and Gives Splendor.. 180 gives a brief history of how the Spanish language evolved and discusses the importance of the Royal Academy of the Spanish Language in that process. (1, 2, 3, 4)	

Preface

This is a book about learning to speak Spanish, about learning how to learn, and about the Spanish language itself. There is a lot of grammar in it but it is not a complete grammar nor even a compendium of Spanish grammar. The intent of this book is to combine academic Spanish and linguistic common sense, the former as handmaiden to the latter. Put into one sweeping sentence, the purpose of this book is to help you learn to speak Spanish by correlating the practical knowledge acquired by one who learned to speak Spanish on the streets of South and Central America with those elements of Spanish grammar that he found most useful as he struggled toward linguistic proficiency.

The student of Spanish, like the newborn babe he or she once was, goes through a series of progressively more challenging developmental stages. The child learns to sit up, crawl, walk, talk, read, ride a bicycle, and so on. The details of this process are as varied and unique as each individual, but the sequence of stages itself is pre-ordained and inevitable. For the developing child the moment of mastery is epoch-making. The youngster who has just learned to walk or ride a bicycle is entering a new phase of his or her life. The pride and joy the child feels are evident to whatever fortunate adult was present and assisting at the event. The child goes forth from that moment with increased self-confidence as well as the extremely important reassurance that all the stumbling and falling and seeming failure along the way have ultimately brought a tremendous reward.

Just so does the student of Spanish crawl, toddle, walk, run and, perhaps one day, fly like Michael Jordan or Mikhail Baryshnikov.

For almost forty years I have been both observing and participating in this process as a student and teacher of Spanish. I had my first experience teaching Spanish less than three months after I began learning the language. I have been engaged in those two processes more or less continuously ever since. During these three-plus decades I have observed the same errors, problems, and linguistic traps occur over and over again at predictable stages of the learning process. Young or old, linguistically adept or steady plodder, each student must get over a series of obstacles that are set out in his path almost as precisely as the barriers in the 800 meter high hurdles foot race.

This book intends to help you clear those hurdles – those epoch-defining moments of triumph. The ground between those jumps, the nuts and bolts of Spanish grammar – agreement of nouns and adjectives, possessive pronouns, demonstrative adjectives, etc. – has been covered quite well by any number of Spanish grammar books and will not be dealt with here.

The emphasis of this book is on helping the student get past the big barriers that block his path. Among these are the problem of the two Spanish verbs meaning 'to be,' the use of the two past tenses, the subjunctive. (See the Table of Contents for the others). These are problems for which I have not found fully satisfying explanations and solutions in other places. This book assembles the observations, discoveries and insights gathered through three-plus decades of encounters with these recurring obstacles. Some of the stratagems herein are of my own devising, some came from conversations with colleagues and the study of other peoples books about grammar and language, many were simply stumbled upon in the very fluid context of teaching conversational Spanish for thousands of hours.

I have never taken a Spanish course. I have no academic credentials. But I did not simply wander off into the Andes Mountains and emerge years later with a long beard and a fully developed ability to speak Spanish. My first teachers were Venezuelan young people with whom I worked as a Peace Corps Volunteer for two years. I have also studied on my own. More importantly, I have had many good friends and have worked with skilled colleagues who have shared their enthusiasm for and knowledge of the language with me. I think of myself as 'friend-taught' rather than 'self-taught.'

My goal was never to obtain a Doctorate or Master's Degree, or even to pass a course. My interest is and my goal has always been to improve my own ability to communicate in Spanish. The distinction is significant.

The academic approach to learning Spanish consists of a formal and orderly acquisition of knowledge, the abstruse detail carries as much weight as the broad principle. In the academic approach to Spanish the difference between dormió and the correct durmió is one point on a final exam. As a practical matter the difference is zero, nada, zilch. Communication is achieved either way. The speaker/learner who is struggling to incorporate the preterit (simple past) tense into his speech does not need to know about durmió (i.e., stem changes in the preterit) until he has gained a comfortable level of confidence in conjugating and using the preterit. *This is not to suggest that I do not believe that the details matter.* Any student who has spent time studying with me would vehemently give the lie to that thought. The academic and the practical routes to learning Spanish will lead the student toward the same greatly desired, albeit elusive, destination, complete knowledge. One of the differences in the two approaches is deciding when to teach what

As a practical matter and, perhaps, by temperament, it is my tendency to look for ways to simplify. In the academic world there is little incentive to streamline. There are books that require four and five chapters to present the conjugation of the preterit tense, creating the impression of an incredibly complicated process. This book will put everything that the beginning or intermediate level student needs to know about the conjugation of the preterit tense in one clear concise chart that will occupy less than a page. A few additional pages will be required to inform the advanced student of the spelling and stem changes that occur in the preterit so that his knowledge will be complete.

Speaking the language begets improved ability to speak. In contrast, studying things that cannot be immediately used in speech delays the process of learning to speak. As a Peace Corps Volunteer I learned Spanish on the job. I needed to learn the things that would help me to communicate a little better right at that moment. Mine was a very pragmatic approach to learning. In the evenings or during siesta I studied those fragments of grammar that would help me to say what I wanted to say to somebody that evening or the next morning. I was not interested in acquiring a body of knowledge. I was trying to survive, make friends, do a job.

That is how and why I learned Spanish. That is the point of view from which I teach Spanish.

Being in the unusual position, as I have been and still am, of learning and teaching Spanish at the same time gives me something in common with the doctor who took out his own appendix. It gives one a unique perspective on both processes, including an especially close identification with recipient of the applied skill. The result is not a radically different approach to the task of learning to speak Spanish, rather a similar method seen from a different perspective - a non-academic point of view. This is an approach in which the emphasis is on learning to speak rather than on acquiring a body of knowledge.

This book is intended to complement the mix of cassette tapes, classes, dictionaries, grammar and exercise books that will be used in the course of learning Spanish. There is no 'one and only' book for acquiring a new language. I do believe this book offers perspectives on grammar and the philosophy of learning and speaking Spanish that will not be found elsewhere.

There is not one right way for all people to learn Spanish. There are many good methods of teaching and many talented people doing the teaching. An approach that works very well for Jill may fail Jack miserably. The serious student must shop around, try different approaches, find the one that best suits her or his temperament and style of learning. In my long teaching career I have worked within a number of different systems. I have picked and chosen among them. The result is a combination of what I have found to be the most effective elements from several of these systems coupled with ideas from my own experiences as a learner and teacher of Spanish.

I invite you to imbibe this unique pedagogical cocktail.

Glossary of Terms

We all learned to speak our native tongue long before we knew of the existence of such a thing as grammar. Many adults go on to become very articulate speakers of English without knowing much more about grammar than subject/verb, if that. But nobody can speak English (or any other language, for that matter) without an intuited knowledge of grammar. A huge vocabulary would be of no use if we did not know how to string all those words together in meaningful combinations. And that requires grammar. Grammar <u>is</u> the set of rules that governs the way we put words together to achieve communication. So, consciously or not, whether you like it or not, you are a grammarian.

You, my dear reader, would never say, "I have eating." Even if you do not know the grammatical labels, you do know that the helping verb 'have' requires the past participle of the verb, 'eaten,' "I have eaten;" or, alternatively, the present participle 'eating' goes with the helping verb 'to be,' thus either "I am eating," or "I was eating."

Conscious knowledge of this sort ~~was not~~ was not required to learn to speak your first language, nor is it a prerequisite to learning to speak a second language. But, if you will take a few minutes to acquaint (or reacquaint) yourself with some of the most basic grammatical terms, I guarantee that it will facilitate your progress toward speaking Spanish. The knowledge is already in your head – it is merely a question of categorizing and naming all that knowledge.

What follows here is not graduate level English. We are not going to evaluate the different theories about the proper use of the comma, nor will we parse sentences in these pages. But there is a basic terminology, the names for the building blocks needed to construct a sentence, that will be used in the chapters to come.

Please review this terminology now, or refer back to this glossary of terms as the need arises.

Adjective - an adjective is a word that describes a noun. 'Tall,' 'ugly,' 'smart,' 'blue,' 'foggy,' 'hard', and many other words are adjectives; or it is a word that qualifies a noun or another adjective such as 'the,' 'twelve' or 'few'. In English an adjective has only one form (rare exception: *this* house, *these* houses). In <u>Spanish an adjective must agree with the noun it refers to</u>, i.e. modifies, in number and gender. Therefore it may have two, four, or in a few cases, five different forms.

Agreement - there are two kinds of agreement in Spanish grammar. A verb must agree with its subject, e.g. <u>tú</u> <u>habl-as</u>, the verb ending <u>-as</u> goes with or agrees with the subject <u>tú</u> just as <u>-amos</u> agrees with <u>nosotros</u>. And an adjective must agree with the noun it modifies in number (singular or plural) and gender (masculine or feminine).

Clause - a group of words clustered around a finite verb form (a conjugated verb) making up one part of a complete sentence that has at least one other finite verb. The clause is that portion of the sentence that helps express the idea related to the finite verb at its core.

For example: The teacher believes that you are a good student. 'The teacher *believes*' is one clause; 'you *are* a good student' is another clause. Each clause has its own finite verb within the totality of the sentence. There are several kinds of clauses. For our purposes it is sufficient to be able to recognize the generic entity, a clause. It is a bit of knowledge that will be helpful as you study the subjunctive.

Conjugation - is the process of applying the correct verb ending to the proper stem of the verb to indicate time (present, future, past) and person (I, you, he, she, we, they).

Gender - as used in grammar is a totally arbitrary (with exceptions noted below) division of all things into two groups. All things, that is, all nouns are assigned masculine or feminine gender. This is a carryover into Spanish from Latin grammar, English gets along fine without it. Gender is sex-specific when referring to human beings, el hombre, la mujer; el niño, la niña; etc.; and in the case of a few of the animals most closely associated with human survival through the centuries, el caballo, la yegua; el toro, la vaca; el gallo, la gallina; to name three. All the rest is arbitrary. Even some of the names for the body parts most intimately associated with masculinity and femininity are assigned the opposite gender for grammatical purposes (I will not make a list!). The sexual identity of individual creatures in the vast animal kingdom, when there is a need to specify, is done by use of the terms el macho (the male) and la hembra (the female), not by using masculine or feminine grammatical forms. El mosquito and la ballena are the correct ways to refer to all members of these two species regardless of their sex.

Infinitive - is the basic form of a verb. It is the 'infinite' form of the verb, i.e. unbounded by time, making no reference to time. In English the infinitive is indicated by the preposition 'to,' to speak, to eat, to live, etc. In Spanish it is indicated by a terminal letter 'r,' hablar, comer, vivir, etc. To give this infinite form of the verb a time frame in English the 'to' is dropped and the verb is than combined with an auxiliary to express future (I will work tomorrow) or conjugated to the past by adding '-ed' (I worked yesterday). In Spanish the time frame is established by a much more elaborate system of conjugation or changes in the form of the verb. Standard Spanish dictionaries list only the infinitive form of the verb. Therefore conjugated forms of a verb must be converted back to the infinitive if the student wishes to look up the meaning of a verb.

Noun - is the name of a person, place, or thing (in Spanish nombre means both 'name' and 'noun') - tree, idea, boy, food, air, and noun are all nouns. 'Jim' is a noun, as is 'Cleveland.' In Spanish every noun is assigned masculine or feminine gender.

Number - as in the term 'number and gender' means 'grammatical number.' There are only two possibilities, singular (one of something), and plural (two or more of something).

Person or Grammatical Person - There are six grammatical persons: First person singular, first person plural, second person singular, second person plural, third person singular and third person plural.

The first person is the speaker. The speaker referring to him- or herself says "I" or "me," which is the *first person singular*, or "we" or "us" which is the *first person plural*.

The second person is the person or persons being spoken to, "you." If one person is being spoken to, he or she is the *second person singular*, if two or more people are being spoken to they are collectively the *second person plural*.

The third person is the person or thing being spoken about. "He," "she," "it," or any singular noun that is to be the subject of a verb, "car," "independence," or "dog," for example, is the *third person singular*. If two or more people or things are being spoken about or are to be the subject of a verb, they are collectively the *third person plural*.

This matters to us because in Spanish each verb has a set of six different ending for each tense. These six endings correspond to the six grammatical persons. There are also sets of pronouns that correspond to these same six persons.

All possible subjects for a verb fall into one of these six categories. So 'person' in this sense may also be a thing. If we are speaking of two houses, for example, they (the houses) are third person plural.

Pronoun – is a word that replaces a noun. For example: Your hair is beautiful. Is it naturally curly? In the second sentence the pronoun 'it' has replaced the noun 'hair.' Or: My brother is over there. Give the book to him. In the second sentence the pronoun 'him' has replaced the noun 'brother.' As will be seen, there are several sets of pronouns that will be needed for different grammatical contexts, subject pronouns, direct object pronouns, etc.

Stem of the infinitive - is the infinitive of a Spanish verb minus the -ar or -er or -ir. The stem of the infinitive contains the meaning of the verb. To conjugate regular verbs in the present and past tenses the appropriate verb endings are added to the stem of the infinitive.

Subject - is the doer of the action in a sentence (*he* wrote, the *tree* fell, bad *things* happen, *Maria* will go) or the person or thing in a state of being (*we* are tired, *it* is easy).

Verb - identifies an action or state of being - swim, think, try, study, stop, go, be. It is the word (or words) that tells what the subject is doing.

Gramática Apasionada
Reminiscences of a Love Affair with the Spanish Language

Chapter One

What to Expect When You Inflect

Make a list of the five best things that have happened to you in your lifetime.

The list might include events like falling in love, winning the state lottery, or a spiritual epiphany - life experiences that we might put in the 'bolt of lightning' category. But your list would undoubtedly contain a different category of items as well, things that demanded commitment and effort over a long period of time - a special friendship, parenthood perhaps, or some professional accomplishment.

It would take time to produce a thoughtful list. One item, falling in the second category, that would certainly be on my list is learning to speak Spanish.

Knowledge of Spanish has afforded me some very interesting employment: Peace Corps trainer, courtroom interpreter, translator of label text for the major museum exhibition "Mexico: Splendors of Thirty Centuries," traveling language consultant to the Educational Testing Service, advisor to minority students of New York University, director of an intensive conversational Spanish program at Ghost Ranch for twenty summers, and teacher to thousands of people ranging from giggling pre-schoolers to silvery-gray octogenarians.

These jobs provided income. I do not dismiss their importance in that regard. To paraphrase John Kenneth Galbraith - money matters, and the case to the contrary, though often made, has not proved persuasive. But learning Spanish did not make my top five because it put money in my pocket. It is on my list because it opened up worlds to me - literally (significant parts of three continents), figuratively (worlds of literature, song, poetry, history, art), and, most importantly, a world of people.

There are many windows through which we can look in on other people's lives. Language is the door through which we may enter their lives - and they ours. The modest incomes that I earned due to my knowledge of another language are long since spent. The substantial wealth acquired through the acquaintanceships that came about as I have been learning and speaking Spanish is gold bullion stacked permanently in my mind. <u>Campesinos</u>, Doctors of Letters, angry young men from the <u>barrios</u>, fellow Peace Corps volunteers, people of every stripe shared their view of the world with me, challenged my beliefs.

Describing the effects of these experiences on me is not the purpose of this essay. The point to be taken is that the effort invested in learning Spanish pays huge dividends.

James K. Gavin

One of the biggest obstacles facing the adult who wants to learn to speak Spanish is the problem of unrealistic expectations. Perhaps you have seen, read or heard advertisements for special language learning systems that promise you will speak Spanish in 27 days, 15 days, even five days. What is meant by "speak Spanish" is left undefined so there is little grounds for claims of false advertising. But as one who has taught in various sorts of intensive Peace Corps language programs with intelligent and highly motivated students, I state emphatically that nobody goes from knowing no Spanish to being a proficient and confident near-native speaker in a matter of days. Intensive Peace Corps programs (and other language teaching institutes, I am sure) can produce a solid survival level speaker in two or three months. However, anything resembling native proficiency will come only after years of effort.

Another kind of expectation must also be addressed. That is the expectation that adults have about the day by day learning of a new subject matter. False expectations will create frustration and a sense of failure. So let's talk about learning.

Most adults already have a well established idea of how to go about learning something new. You visit the library, you buy some books, perhaps you take a course. If you want to learn more early history of the United States, for example, a teacher or a book tells you about George Washington. Perhaps you see a picture of George astride a white horse or leaning out over the bow of a boat crossing the Delaware River. You read or are told many of his significant achievements. You write down key dates. If this were a course you would review your notes and take an exam. You would successfully demonstrate your knowledge of our first president. And thereafter you would retain most, if not all, of that knowledge. This is learning as most of us have experienced it.

But how do you go about learning to say, in Spanish, "George Washington was the first president of the United States?"

Here are some things you must already know or learn before you will be able to make that statement.

You must know the vocabulary, the Spanish words for 'first,' 'president,' etc. You must identify the verb - in this case 'to be.' Because there are two verbs meaning 'to be' in Spanish, you must choose the right one for this statement. Then you must select the tense needed, the past tense, but again you must choose. There are two past tenses in Spanish so you must know how to choose the right one for this situation. Then you must identify the subject and conjugate the verb to agree with it. There are four adjectives in the sentence each of which must agree in number and gender with the noun it modifies - in three cases you will choose from among four possibilities, and in one case from among five. There is also one preposition to deal with - in our example sentence it is a simple translation, but prepositions are not always that cooperative. Having done all this you must still understand Spanish word order before you can finally construct your sentence. The sequence of words will not be the same in Spanish as it is in English.

Up to this point you have only planned out the sentence. Now you must execute the plan, i.e. say the sentence.

So you must know how to pronounce Spanish. You must learn how to produce the Spanish sounds for 'r' and 'd.' They are not only different than their English counterparts, they are unlike any sounds we have in English. You must also deal with the vowels. The pronunciation of the Spanish vowels is actually easier and more orderly than in English. But in using 'a,' 'e,' 'i,' 'o' and 'u' you will need to overcome the habits ingrained during a lifetime of speaking English.

Therefore you must re-train the muscles that produce sound - the muscles that push air out of the lungs up through the larynx and mouth, the muscles that regulate and sometimes cut off that flow of air, the muscles that position the tongue, lips and jaw - all these must not only learn to work together to make new sounds (and new sounds for old symbols) but countless new combinations of sounds in a reasonably smooth and well paced sequence. This part of language learning is not an intellectual process; it is not cognitive learning. It is physical training, like learning to serve a tennis ball or to play "Moonlight Sonata." It requires the repetition of the muscle movements to the point where it would take a conscious effort <u>not</u> to do them correctly.

There is one more habit of speech that must be dealt with. The intonation of English speech is rather mono-toned. Spanish is spoken with a much more lively beat. To impose English intonation on Spanish is to smother the musical quality of the language; but also, in some instances, no matter how good your pronunciation otherwise is, it will render what you wish to say unintelligible.

These are some of the factors that must be considered before you can make the 'simple' statement, "George Washington was the first president of the United States," in Spanish.

And now we come to the most difficult aspect of this whole process.

Let us assume that you enrolled in that class about George Washington. You took an exam at the end of the semester. You read the questions, composed your thoughts for several minutes and wrote them down. I am sure that you got an excellent grade. But in a conversational situation the exam happens every time it is your turn to speak. You do not have even thirty seconds to compose your thoughts. If you want to tell us who the first president was, you must do all the planning and constructing of the sentence as outlined above and execute that plan in just a few seconds. In our native language we do all this organizing in a split second. Eight or ten empty seconds is an eternity in a conversational setting. It is an all but intolerable amount of time to wait for someone to speak. So your 'exams' are always taken under the pressure of very limited time.

What I have tried to demonstrate above is the vast amount of knowledge that goes into saying even the simplest things. And it is knowledge that must be sorted through and applied all but instantaneously.

Year after year students say to me, "I feel so stupid," "I cannot even say the simplest things right," "I make the same mistakes over and over again!"

When students feel "stupid" it is because they do not realize the complexity of the task they have undertaken. Most learning tasks we face are like doing a jigsaw puzzle - Washington was President, one piece of the puzzle; Jefferson was Secretary of State, another piece of the puzzle in place; protection of our coastline and shipping lanes from the British navy was a major governmental responsibility, one more piece; westward expansion into the unsettled territory beyond the Appalachians was a national purpose, another piece; and on we go. <u>One piece at a time</u> we put the puzzle together. <u>One piece at a time</u> we get a bigger and more complete 'picture' or understanding.

But learning to speak Spanish is not like putting together a jigsaw puzzle. It is like learning to juggle. And you are not even given a uniform set of objects to toss in the air. It is as though you were given a bowling pin, a plate, a top hat, and a horseshoe to juggle. And as is the case when juggling there is very little time allowed for making decisions. Specifically, you must handle grammar, vocabulary, syntax, and pronunciation - each a complex subject in itself, and must keep them all in the air simultaneously. If you drop any one of them you 'fail.' So it is very important to realize how unfair it is to judge yourself as though you were doing a jigsaw puzzle.

Of course you will make the same mistakes over and over again. If you are thinking about the verb you will forget to make some adjective agree with its noun. If you are focused on adjectival agreement you will probably misconjugate the verb. And if you do manage to get both of those things right you may stumble over some aspect of the pronunciation. To be able to put all the elements of a sentence together correctly and quickly takes, not hours or weeks, but months and years of practice.

Having read to this point you might well be thinking, "Why am I even thinking about trying to learn Spanish?" The answer: "Because it is fun!"

Learning Spanish made my top five because it opened up worlds to me. Those worlds did not suddenly open when I had attained a certain high level of mastery. The doors to those worlds start slowly opening almost as soon as you start learning. Like tennis, dancing or skiing, it is an activity that is fun at whatever level you are doing it. And there is always more to learn. You are always making progress – 'improving your game,' so to speak - and that is very satisfying. Learning a second language will be intellectually stimulating and personally rewarding for years to come.

There is a question implicit in the title of this essay. What should you expect when you inflect, i.e. conjugate verbs and make adjectives agree with nouns? The answer, straight and simple: you should expect to experience syntactical dissociation syndrome and repetitive inflectional discordance - even straighter and simpler, you should expect to make lots and lots of mistakes, and to make most of those mistakes over and over again. If you are judging yourself fairly that will not take the fun out of learning to speak Spanish.

You must be patient with yourself, but you must also be persistent.

<u>Paciencia y persistencia</u>.

Chapter Two

There's No Time Like the Present

Unless you were atypically attentive as a teen-ager during high school English class you probably think that there is a present tense, period. What else could there be? Present, past, future. Right?

Wrong.

There are three modes, or ways of speaking, in the present tense, the indicative, the imperative, and the subjunctive modes. We will leave the imperative and subjunctive modes for another time. In this chapter we will deal with the present indicative - what you have probably always thought of as the good ol' present tense.

For example: My name **is** Ima Latch.
I **live** in Door County, Wisconsin.
I **work** at the Acme Barrel Bolt and Hinge factory.
I **believe** that Spanish **is** the gateway to a life of romance and adventure.

Let us begin by looking at the present tense of English. Write the proper form of the verb 'to read' in the present tense to complete each of the following English sentences:

1. These days I _read_ the newspaper every morning.

2. These days you _read_ the newspaper every morning.

3. These days she _reads_ the newspaper every morning.

4. These days we _read_ the newspaper every morning

5. These days they _read_ the newspaper every morning.

You have just conjugated the verb 'to read' in the present tense. English has a very minimal conjugation to deal with. All you had to do was to add an 's' to the verb in sentence #3. Substitute any other verb, repeat this short exercise and you will do the same thing. You will add an 's' to the verb in sentence #3. The verb in sentence #3 would still require an 's' if you changed the subject from 'she' to 'he' or 'it' or 'my kooky neighbor.' We can say that the verb ending '-s' goes with or *agrees with* 'he,' 'she,' 'it,' and 'my kooky neighbor.'

Gramática Apasionada
Reminiscences of a Love Affair with the Spanish Language

Spanish has a much more sophisticated system of conjugation but the basic concept is the same. You change the ending of the verb to make it agree with its subject.

Whereas in English there is only one step involved in conjugating a verb, there are two in Spanish. Before adding the appropriate verb ending you must isolate or find the stem of the infinitive[1] of the verb. This is a very simple process - just drop the last two letters of the infinitive. Those two letters will always be one of the following, -ar, -er, or –ir.

For example: escribir is the Spanish verb meaning 'to write.' Drop the last two letters of the infinitive and you have the stem of the infinitive, escrib-. The stem carries the meaning of the verb, in this case 'write.' (You may have noticed the similarity of the stem of this verb, escrib-, to some English words related to writing like 'scribe,' 'scribble,' and 'scripture').

Having isolated the stem of the infinitive you may now proceed to step two: adding the appropriate ending to the stem. There was only one change to make in the English example but there are six possibilities in Spanish that correspond to the six grammatical persons[2]. However, because I learned, speak and teach Spanish as it is spoken on the New World side of the Atlantic Ocean you will only have to learn five endings for the six grammatical persons, the second and third persons plural will always be the same.

The verb endings for conjugation of the present indicative are as follows:

	-AR verbs			-ER and -IR verbs		
Stem +	-o	-amos	Stem +	-o	-emos or -imos
of the	-as	-an	of the	-es	-en
infinitive	-a	-an	infinitive	-e	-en

In our sample verb this becomes:

Escribo = I write
Escribes = you (singular and familiar[3]) write
Escribe = he writes (also, 'you' singular and formal[4])
Escribimos = we write
Escriben = you (plural) write
Escriben = they write

---

[1] See: Glossary of Terms.
[2] See: Glossary of Terms.
[3] The difference between the familiar tú and the formal usted is discussed in Chapter 7.
[4] The reason that the formal 'you' is conjugated in the third person is found in Chapter 7.

Please note that the English pronoun 'you' may refer to one person or to any two or more people to whom you might be speaking. Spanish makes a distinction between these two 'you's.' I used to say "you" and "you all" in class as a way of distinguishing between the English 'you (singular)' and 'you (plural)'. Then a student from Georgia pointed out to this Massachusetts Yankee that 'you all,' better said "y'all", can also be singular! This left me back where I had started with the more cumbersome and pedantic sounding 'you (singular)' and 'you (plural).'

It is the function of the Spanish verb endings to tell you the subject of the verb. For that reason the subject is frequently omitted when speaking Spanish. However, the verb ending tells *only* the grammatical person. It does not identify specific individual subjects of the verb, e.g. my house, José, the broken camshaft. The speaker must supply that information before he starts omitting the subject and he must continue to make sure that the references are clear as he goes on speaking.

Mi cuñado se llama Carlos.
My brother-in-law is called Charlie.

El vive en Denver.
He lives in Denver.

Es un buen amigo.
(He) is a good friend.

Besides being needed to clarify and to provide contrast, the spoken subject is sometimes used to provide emphasis in Spanish. In English this effect would be achieved by raising the voice. For example:

¿Quién quiere ir al cine?
Yo quiero.

The yo is redundant here, the verb ending -o is sufficient, but yo supplies emphasis. Read the same two sentences out loud in English:

Who wants to go to the movies?
I do.

Notice that you automatically raised your voice and gave extra stress to the pronoun 'I.'

Although it is often unnecessary and may sound redundant, it is never wrong to include the subject of the verb when speaking Spanish. If you are just starting to learn Spanish I suggest that you always include the subject. (I insist upon this with my own beginner-level students). Forming the habit of stating the subject is helpful for two reasons. First, you will learn to conjugate faster by always saying, and hearing yourself say, the yo and its related ending -o, the tú and its associated endings -as and -es, and so on - that reinforcement really does speed learning. Second, if you are out somewhere actually speaking Spanish—trying to communicate, and you misconjugate the verb (this will happen from time to time)—your listener is more likely to understand your intent. If you say just "quiere" meaning to say "I want" the person you are speaking to might understandably get rather confused. If you say "yo quiere" your listener will probably assume you meant to say "yo quiero" and you will be understood.

It will not be necessary to 'unlearn' this habit of stating the subject. As you gain proficiency in speaking Spanish—as you attain a certain comfort level with the language—you will start omitting the subject without even realizing it.

Spanish verbs are conjugated in the present tense as outlined above - the stem of the infinitive plus the appropriate ending. Probably 90% of the verbs in the language fall neatly into step and behave as they should. These obedient verbs are called regular verbs.

There are, however, a few verbs that do not behave as they are supposed to. We call these verbs irregular verbs. That is most of us call them irregular verbs. I once had an eighth grade student who always referred to an irregular verb as "one of those weirdo verbs."

Irregular Verbs of the Present Indicative

A very skilled linguist once said to me, "Don't look for logic in verb conjugation, look for pattern." That is good advice. We shall do that.

Most verbs *are* regular verbs. However, verbs become irregular primarily through heavy use. The more we use almost anything the more it gets worn down and beaten out of shape. This happens not just with old marble stairways and pickup trucks but with verbs as well. Therefore, unfortunately, the most basic verbs—to have, to go, to be (in its two Spanish incarnations), to say, etc., the verbs the student needs first—tend to be irregular. This leaves the beginning student with the impression that learning Spanish is going to be an unending series of encounters with irregular verbs. Such is not the case.

And more good news! Even in their irregularity or "weirdness" there is pattern. Irregular verbs are not a manifestation of a cosmic theory of random pervasive difficulty. There are only three ways that a verb can be irregular in the present tense.

Let The Weirdness Begin

First, a verb may be a stem-changing verb. As suggested by the name itself, you will make a change in the stem of these verbs.

If there is to be a stem change it will be the vowel of the last syllable of the infinitive stem that changes. There are only three kinds of stem-change[5]. An 'o' can turn into 'ue,' an 'e' can become 'ie,' or an 'e' may turn into 'i.' The stem change does not occur in the first person plural of the verb. As you are conjugating the verb you will revert to the regular stem of the infinitive for the <u>nosotros</u> form.

The endings used for regular verbs are also the endings for all stem-changing verbs. Therefore:

<u>recordar</u> (to remember)		<u>entender</u> (to understand)		<u>pedir</u>(to request)	
rec<u>ue</u>rdo	recordamos	ent<u>ie</u>ndo	entendemos	p<u>i</u>do	pedimos
rec<u>ue</u>rdas	rec<u>ue</u>rdan	ent<u>ie</u>ndes	ent<u>ie</u>nden	p<u>i</u>des	p<u>i</u>den
rec<u>ue</u>rda	rec<u>ue</u>rdan	ent<u>ie</u>nde	ent<u>ie</u>nden	p<u>i</u>de	p<u>i</u>den

Only verbs with an 'e' or an 'o' in the last syllable of the stem are candidates to be stem-changing verbs. But how can you tell if some new verb that meets one of these two criteria is, in fact, a stem-changer?

Piece of cake!

If the vowel in question was a long vowel in the Latin verb from which the Spanish verb is derived, it will be a stem-changer in Spanish.

Which brings us to the very important question of accent or stress. (Oh, by the way, if your Latin is so deficient that you cannot identify stem-changing verbs by the long vowel test you will just have to learn them as you go along. That is what most people, including myself, do). But let us get back to the accent.

In the present tense the accented syllable is always the next-to-the-last syllable of the verb form.

The accent patterns of English and Spanish speech are very different. It is natural that as an English-speaker you will impose the accent pattern of your native tongue on the new language. But it is very important that you learn the accent pattern of Spanish right along with good pronunciation of the vowels and consonants.

Much more so than in English, stress or accent carries meaning in Spanish. In Spanish if you stress the wrong syllable of a word you may totally change its meaning; e.g. <u>trabajo</u> (tra-BA-jo) is 'I work,' <u>trabajó</u> (tra-ba-JO) is 'he or she worked;' <u>cerro</u> (CE-rro) means 'hill,' <u>cerró</u> (ce-RRO) means 'he or she closed;' <u>abra</u> (A-bra) is the command form 'open,' <u>habrá</u> (ha-BRA) means 'there will be.' (Remember, 'h' is a silent letter in Spanish and has no bearing on the pronunciation of <u>habrá</u>); <u>ira</u> (I-ra) means 'anger,' <u>irá</u> (i-RA) 'he or she will go.' There are thousands of examples of this in Spanish. Here is an example of three

---

[5] There is also the unique case of <u>jugar</u>, 'u' changes to 'ue.'

shifts of the accent creating three separate meanings - continúo (con-ti-NU-o) means 'I continue,' continuó (con-ti-nu-O) means 'he or she continued,' continuo (con-TI-nu-o) means 'continual.' The accent does matter.

This can happen in English as well. Read the following sentence out loud:

On my daughter's birthday I want to present her present to her personally.

You will have noted that you said 'pre-SENT' and then 'PRE-sent.' The meaning changed when you shifted the accent from the first to the second syllable. But correctly placing the accent does not play the pervasively important role in English that it does in Spanish.

English is spoken in something much closer to a monotone than Spanish is. A typical English sentence goes:

Dah-dah-dah-dah-dah-dah-dah-dah-dah-DAT-deh.

The typical sentence in Spanish would be more like:

Dah-DAT-dah-dah-DAT-dah-dah-DAT-dah-DAT-dah-dah-DAT.

The point, again, is that the accent matters. As an English-speaker you are accustomed to a more suppressed system of stresses[6]. You must make a conscious effort to pick up the tempo when speaking Spanish - it is rather like the difference between dancing the two-step and the tango.

You may think that the main problem that you are going to have with the present tense will be sorting out all the endings and stem changes, not to mention other irregularities yet to be looked at. But that is not the case. You will learn those things. In the long run, the main problem that you will have is going to be getting the stress to fall on the correct syllable. If only I had one of those proverbial dimes for every time I have gone through a sequence similar to this:

Estudiante: "Todos los días yo caminó (ca-mi-NO)…
Profesor: "Momento, el acento del verbo no es correcto."
Estudiante: "Oh. Pues, yo cámino (CA-mi-no)…"
Profesor: "Todavía no es correcto."
Estudiante: "No? Oh, okay, yo caminó (ca-mi-NO)[7]."

There is something in the accent pattern of the present tense in Spanish that runs counter to the natural sense of linguistic rhythm of the English-speaker.

---

[6] For more on this subject see Chapter 17.
[7] The elusive correct form is camino (ca-MI-no).

Listed below are examples of one-, two-, three-, and four- syllable verbs in Spanish. Read them out loud. Try to hear and to <u>feel</u> the rhythm of the present tense in Spanish. Substitute other verbs and repeat the exercise. Do this a lot!

<u>Dar</u> (to give)		<u>Tomar</u> (to take)		<u>Aprender</u> (to learn)	
DOY	DA-mos	TO-mo	to-MA-mos	a-PREN-do	a-pren-DE-mos
DAS	DAN	TO-mas	TO-man	a-PREN-des	a-PREN-den
DA	DAN	TO-ma	TO-man	a-PREN-de	a-PREN-den

<u>Justificar</u> (to justify)		<u>Poder</u> (ue) (to be able)	
ju-sti-FI-co	ju-sti-fi-CA-mos	puE-do	po-DE-mos
ju-sti-FI-cas	ju-sti-FI-can	puE-des	puE-den
ju-sti-FI-ca	ju-sti-FI-can	puE-de	puE-den

<u>Encontrar</u>(ue) (to find)		<u>Recomendar</u>(ie) (to recommend)	
en-cuEN-tro	en-con-TRA-mos	re-co-miEN-do	re-co-men-DA-mos
en-cuEN-tras	en-cuEN-tran	re-co-miEN-das	re-co-miEN-dan
en-cuEN-tra	en-cuEN-tran	re-co-miEN-da	re-co-miEN-dan

With stem-changing verbs the change occurs when the vowel in question receives the spoken stress. Think of the accent as a hammer striking that vulnerable long vowel from the Latin and breaking it (it is much easier to snap a long pencil in two than a short one). For example, the hammer strikes the 'o' of <u>poder</u> in the first person singular, it shatters into 'ue.' When the hammer does not hit the 'o,' as is the case in the <u>nosotros</u> form (po-DE-mos), it does not break.

In the present tense, as you have been practicing above, it is the next-to-the-last syllable that receives spoken stress. Know that rule and put it into practice. There are, however, two groups of verbs that require special attention. The first of these is the first conjugation (-AR) verbs that end -<u>iar</u>, e.g. <u>cambiar</u> (to change) and <u>enviar</u> (to send). In their conjugation some of this group of verbs employ a written accent over the 'i' to break the diphthong (the vowel combination 'ia'). This creates a new next-to-the-last syllable featuring the stressed 'i.' Some of these –<u>iar</u> verbs do not break the diphthong so the stress falls automatically on the vowel of the syllable preceding the –<u>iar</u> ending.

If you would like to know more about diphthongs, stress, and syllabification see Chapter 17. If not, just do as you are shown in the following models.

-<u>Iar</u> verbs that use a written accent in present tense conjugation come out this way:

<u>Enviar</u>		
Envío	Enviamos	Other verbs that follow this pattern are:
Envías	Envían	<u>Esquiar</u> (to ski), <u>enfriar</u> (to cool), <u>espiar</u> (to spy),
Envía	Envían	<u>fotografiar</u> (to photograph).

en-VI-o   en-vi-A-mos
en-VI-as   en-VI-an
en-VI-a   en-VI-an

Verbs that do not employ the written accent follow this model:

<u>Cambiar</u>

Cambio	Cambiamos	Other verbs that follow this pattern are:
Cambias	Cambian	<u>Estudiar</u> (to study), <u>copiar</u> (to copy), <u>limpiar</u>
Cambia	Cambian	(to clean), <u>pronunciar</u> (to pronounce).

CAM-bio   cam-bi-A-mos
CAM-bias CAM-bian
CAM-bia   CAM-bian

The second, smaller group of verbs is made up of first conjugation verbs that end –<u>uar</u>. Again a written accent is used, over the 'u' in this case, to dissolve the diphthong ('ua') thereby creating a next-to-the-last syllable featuring the 'u.' Three of the more commonly heard verbs from this group are <u>continuar</u>, <u>evaluar</u>, and (appropriately enough) <u>acentuar</u>. In their spoken and written conjugation they follow the pattern of <u>enviar</u> shown above (con-ti-NU-o, con-ti-NU-as, etc.).

<u>Averiguar</u> (to find out), uses the model illustrated by <u>cambiar</u>. As the written accent is not employed the diphthong remains intact—therefore 'ua' constitutes one syllable—and the next-to-the-last syllable shifts one vowel further forward in the verb (a-ve-RI-guo, a-ve-Ri-guas, etc.)

And It Gets Weirder

Now let us look at the second thing that can happen to a verb to make it irregular in the present tense. Again there is a very clear pattern.

A verb will be irregular because the <u>yo</u> form, the first-person singular of the verb, is irregular.

These verbs are only one-sixth irregular. The other five grammatical persons are conjugated like any other regular verb. Just a few of these verbs suffer the double indignity of first-person irregularity and a stem change. They will be so indicated in the lists to be given below.

This is not a large group of verbs and there are sub-groups or patterns within the whole.

In the first sub-group to be studied a 'g' shows up from out of the linguistic blue. There are only ten verbs in this group.[8] But again, as is so often the case with irregular verbs, most of them are verbs that are frequently used. There will be one fully conjugated verb for each group. The irregular <u>yo</u> form will be given in parentheses with each of the other infinitives.

<u>Salir</u> (to leave)
Salgo   Salimos   <u>Traer</u> (traigo)   <u>Poner</u> (pongo)
Sales   Salen   <u>Hacer</u> (hago)   <u>Valer</u> (valgo)
Sale   Salen   <u>Caer</u> (caigo)   <u>Oír</u> (dealt with below)

The stem-changing members of this group are:

<u>Tener(ie)</u> (to have)
Tengo   Tenemos   <u>Decir(i)</u> (digo)
Tienes Tienen   <u>Venir(ie)</u> (vengo)
Tiene   Tienen

The second sub-group is larger but with the possible exceptions of <u>conocer</u> ('to know,' in the sense of 'to be acquainted with') and <u>traducir</u> (to translate) these are not among the first fifty verbs that the beginning level student needs to know. These verbs are easy to identify. They are the verbs whose infinitive ends <u>–cer</u> or <u>-cir</u>. They all place a 'z' before the final 'c' of the stem in the first person singular and conjugate like regular verbs the rest of the way. A few examples are:

<u>Traducir</u>
Traduzco Traducimos   <u>Ofrecer</u> (ofrezco)   <u>Conocer</u> (conozco)
Traduces Traducen   <u>Producir</u> (produzco)
Traduce   Traducen   <u>Merecer</u> (merezco)

As was mentioned above, most of the verbs in this group are not in the high-frequency use category. However, these verbs will enrich (<u>enriquecer</u>) and embellish (<u>embellecer</u>) your vocabulary.

The last sub-group of verbs in the irregular <u>yo</u> category is the smallest. There are only four. These are the mavericks. They share no common characteristic in their first person singular irregularity. They are:

<u>Ver</u>
Veo   Vemos   <u>Saber</u> (sé)
Ves   Ven   <u>Dar</u> (doy)
Ve   Ven   <u>Caber</u> (quepo)

---

[8] There are a number of compound verbs formed by adding a prefix to some of the verbs in this group; for example <u>contener</u> = to contain, <u>oponer</u> = to oppose, <u>atraer</u> = to attract. All of these compound verbs share the irregular characteristics of the base verb.

Gramática Apasionada
Reminiscences of a Love Affair with the Spanish Language

They are, of course, regular throughout the rest of the present tense conjugation.

Let us now sum up what we have covered to this point.

1. The vast majority of verbs in Spanish are regular verbs. In the present tense they are conjugated by adding the appropriate endings to the stem of the infinitive.

2. There are three ways that a verb may be irregular in the present tense. First, the verb may have a stem change; second, the verb may be irregular in the first person singular. The third way is about to be revealed.

And Weirder

The last group of verbs that are irregular in the present are the irregular irregular verbs - verbs that do not adhere to one of the two patterns of irregularity outlined above. They are few.

Haber translates 'to have' but it is not 'to have' in the sense of 'to possess,' that verb is tener. This is the helping verb 'to have.' It is used principally to help form the perfect tenses,[9] the Spanish equivalents of, for example, I *have* studied, they *had* eaten, she would *have* gone. The present indicative of haber is:

He	Hemos
Has	Han
Ha	Han

Then we have:

Ser (to be)		Estar (to be)[10]	
Soy	Somos	Estoy	Estamos
Eres	Son	Estás	Están
Es	Son	Está	Están

At first glance, estar may appear to be a candidate for the previous category of irregular verbs, verbs that are irregular only in the first person singular. What makes it totally irregular is the fact that it violates the accent pattern of the present tense.

One of the few statements about the present tense that was deemed important enough to be highlighted by italics was this: *in the present tense the stressed syllable is always the next-to-the-last syllable of the verb form.* Estar is totally irregular because the accent falls on the last syllable in every form except nosotros.

---

[9] See Chapter 12.
[10] The difference between ser and estar is discussed in Chapter 3.

Es-STOY, es-TAS, es-TA, es-TA-mos, es-TAN, es-TAN.

I have stumbled upon only one other verb where this is the case - prever, (to foresee).

Ir (to go) is unique in that it has no stem - take away the infinitive ending -ir and there is nothing left. So 'v-' will serve as well as anything for a stem. Except that now, when we add the endings for -er,-ir verbs we are stepping rather hard on the toes of ver (to see). For that reason we will use the -ar endings and throw in an irregular yo form just to make it interesting. Thus we end up with:

Voy	Vamos
Vas	Van
Va	Van

Why didn't they just call the verb var and be done with it?

If oír (to hear) were to be conjugated as a regular verb it would sound quite a bit like one of our primate cousins in heat: oo, oes, oe, oímos, oen, oen! That would not do - so some adjustments were made. Thus we have:

Oigo	Oímos
Oyes	Oyen
Oye	Oyen

That's better?

Consideration of one more small group of verbs will conclude (concluir) our study of the present indicative. There are perhaps twelve or fifteen infinitives that end –uir,[11] for example, influir, construir, distribuir, to name a few. All of these verbs insert a 'y' between the final 'u' of the stem and the ending (except in the nosostros form) to lubricate, or make more fluid, the transition from that 'u' to the vowel of the ending. They are all conjugated as in this model:

Instruir (to instruct)

Instruyo	Instruimos
Instruyes	Instruyen
Instruye	Instruyen

As we come to the end of this discussion of the conjugation of the present tense my lawyers have insisted upon this brief disclaimer: You will from time to time, if you pursue your study of Spanish, come upon an oddball verb not covered here. I hope that your

---

[11] We must exclude (excluir) from this group infinitives that end –guir and –quir. The 'u' does not sound after 'g' and 'q' so there is no need for the 'y.'

interest in Spanish will take you that deeply into the language. For if you reach that point, the discovery of a hitherto unknown irregularity will cause, not a groan of despair, but a chirp of delight. It is like noticing, for the first time, a slightly crooked tooth in a loved one's smile. It makes that smile even more endearing.

The last page of this chapter is a verb chart that summarizes in very compact form all the significant aspects of the conjugation of the present indicative. It encapsulates just about everything (please note disclaimer) you need to know about this most complicated, as regards conjugation, of the tenses in the Spanish language.

A Long Post Script

This lesson on the conjugation of the present indicative has been focused on conjugation as an oral exercise – the spoken language. Special emphasis has been placed on the importance of putting the stress upon the proper syllable. In the long run getting the accent to fall where it is supposed to will be your biggest challenge, not verb endings or irregularities.

But there is one more phenomenon that occurs in present tense verb conjugation in its written form. These are spelling changes—as opposed to *stem* changes—that show up when writing some verb forms. And that is the point! They *show up*. It is not your ear but your eye that tells you they are there. That is their purpose. Spelling changes are made so that you will not hear any change in the pronunciation of the core of the verb–the stem, or root— which contains the meaning of the verb.

This phenomenon occurs much more frequently in the subjunctive and imperative modes of the present tense than in the indicative. It is also a significant element in the conjugation of the preterit tense. It is dealt with in detail in the chapter on preterit conjugation, Chapter 6. But by way of illustrating what I am talking about let us look at one example of a spelling change in the present indicative.

Escoger (to choose) is a regular second conjugation (-ER) verb. But if you write out the present indicative forms of this verb you will have to make an adjustment in the spelling of the first person singular (yo) form of the verb. This is because the stem of the infintive (escog-) ends with the letter 'g.'

In Spanish the letter 'g' has two values. It is pronounced like the hard 'g' of the English words 'get' and 'gold' if the vowel following the 'g' is 'a,' 'o,' or 'u.' But if the vowel following the 'g' is 'e' or 'i' then that 'g' is aspirated – it sounds like the English letter 'h.'

In its infinitive form an 'e' follows the 'g.' Therefore escoger is pronounced [es-co-HAIR]. The aspirated 'g' is part of the characteristic pronunciation of the verb. That characteristic sound must be maintained as we speak and use the verb in its different conjugated forms. If I wish to say "I choose" in Spanish it will come out correctly sounding [es-COH-**hoe**]. But if I want to write "I choose" in Spanish I must substitute the letter 'j' for the 'g' – <u>escojo</u>. The first person singular ending (–<u>o</u>) attached to the 'g' of the stem (<u>escog</u>-) would then call for the hard 'g' [es-COH-**go**]. If we lose the aspirated 'g' we lose the characteristic sound of the verb – in other words, we lose the meaning of the verb. As all the other endings of the present indicative begin with the letter 'e' the aspirated 'g' happens automatically. There is no need to make any additional spelling changes.

As was mentioned, spelling changes are discussed in detail in the chapter on the conjugation of the preterit tense. The letter combinations that call for spelling changes are the same regardless of verb tense. So if you would like a complete picture of present tense spelling changes consult Chapter 6.

Gramática Apasionada
Reminiscences of a Love Affair with the Spanish Language

Indicative Mode of the Present Tense

REGULAR VERBS

-AR verbs			-ER, -IR verbs		
Stem of the +	-o	-amos	Stem of the +	-o	-emos or -imos
Infinitive	-as	-an	Infinitve	-es	-en
	-a	-an		-e	-en

STEM CHANGING VERBS

o → ue   e → ie   e → i

yo	nosotros
tú	ustedes
él, ella, usted	ellos

o → ue = poder, recordar, dormir, etc.
e → ie = querer, entender, pensar, etc.
e → i = pedir, seguir, repetir, etc.
u → ue = jugar (only)

IRREGULAR FIRST PERSON SINGULAR

-go		-zco	
tener	venir	conocer	ver (veo)
poner	traer	traducir	dar (doy)
decir	caer	----ucir	saber (sé)
hacer	oír	merecer	caber (quepo)
salir	valer	----ecer	
		nacer	

IRREGULAR VERBS

Ir		Ser		Estar	
voy	vamos	soy	somos	estoy	estamos
vas	van	eres	son	estás	están
va	van	es	son	está	están

Haber		Oír		Incluir (-uir)	
he	hemos	oigo	oímos	incluyo	incluimos
has	han	oyes	oyen	incluyes	incluyen
ha	han	oye	oyen	incluye	incluyen

Chapter Three

Shakespeare Didn't Get It

A funny thing happened to the Latin verb <u>esse</u> (to be) on its way to becoming the Spanish verb <u>ser</u>. It got mugged by its fellow Latin verb <u>sedere</u> (to sit).

The results of this 'verbal assault' are still being felt across the millennia. These consequences have particularly complicated life for twentieth century speakers of English who wish to learn Spanish. Even if one has only a sketchy knowledge of Ancient History it is obvious that blame for the resulting linguistic difficulties must be placed in the blood-stained hands of Brutus. For without the authoritative leadership of Julius Caesar your everyday Roman-in-the-street began getting sloppy about his personal speech habits. The beautifully crafted and rational Latin of classical times started becoming rather - how else can I say it? - vulgar.

In this specific case here's what happened. Instead of using <u>esse</u>, people began to use the verb <u>sedere</u> to locate things. They might have said, for example, "the goblet **sits** on the table," instead of saying, "the goblet **is** on the table." This is a seemingly innocuous substitution. But centuries later it would still be causing confusion and consternation across the breadth of a distant continent, from Connecticut to California.

As this usage became commonplace it precipitated a more general breakdown of the boundaries between the two verbs. Perhaps one might then have said for example, "the centurion **sits** ill," instead of, "the centurion **is** ill." In any case, <u>esse</u> and <u>sedere</u> were getting their wires seriously crossed. This encroachment upon its territory should have alarmed <u>esse</u> but it was in the middle of multiple identity crises (on its way to becoming <u>ser</u>, <u>essere</u> in Italian, etc.) and paid no attention. <u>Sedere</u>, meanwhile, which was by nature quite sedentary, got a lot of unaccustomed exercise during its raids on <u>esse</u>'s territory and slimmed down to <u>estar</u>.[12]

This process went on for many years. The result was that eventually Spanish (though not its French cousin) ended up with two verbs meaning 'to be.' This has proven to be a most vexatious problem for students of Spanish as a second language. So, listen up, Mr. Shakespeare, "to be or not to be" is *not* the question. To be (<u>ser</u>) or to be <u>(estar)</u>, *that* is the question!

---

[12]Robert K. Spaulding. *How Spanish Grew*, University of California Press, Berkeley, Los Angeles, London, 1971.

These two verbs (ser and estar) that translate 'to be' are not interchangeable, nor is their use haphazard. They serve distinct purposes. English speakers may initially be confused by this, but turn the case around and look at it from the other side. The Spanish verb esperar translates 'to wait,' 'to hope,' and 'to expect.' When the English-speaking student of Spanish learns this he or she frequently responds, "But those are such different things, how can they be lumped together into one verb?" And because English has created three separate compartments, i.e. verbs, we do see them as distinct activities. But give this a little thought. These are three very inter-related activities. Hoping and expecting both involve waiting, the difference being in the mental outlook of the 'waiter.' Spanish ignores this distinction and calls both kinds of waiting 'waiting.'

Likewise, when the Spanish-speaker who wants to learn English discovers that we have only one verb for ser and estar he might just as fairly ask, "But there are so many different kinds of being, how can you lump them all together into one verb?"

What Will Be 'Be' Will Be 'Be'

In order to get a sense of the different kinds of being expressed by ser and estar it might be helpful to list the nouns that share their root or stem with ser and some of the nouns that have a common root with estar.

There are only two common nouns in Spanish that come from the same root as ser. One is esencia or 'essence' - this is more obvious when you remember that ser comes from the Latin esse - and the other is ser itself. When used as a noun ser means 'being,' as in ser humano, 'human being.' So the verb ser relates to essence and being or existence.

There are a number of nouns related to estar. Here are four: estado, estación, estancia, and bienestar.

Estado means 'state.' It can be either a geographical state like el Estado de Nuevo México or un estado emocional o físico, 'an emotional or physical state or condition.' Estación is 'station' (among other things) as in train station, a place to get the train. Estancia means 'stay,' as in 'being there,' e.g. we had a pleasant stay in Madrid. (In the Americas an estancia may also be a cattle ranch). Bienestar is 'welfare' which refers to one's condition. The verb estar has to do with place or location and condition.

Many students who have come to me with a limited exposure to Spanish, perhaps a year or two in high school or college, have arrived at my door with the firmly imbedded belief that ser is for permanent things and estar is for the temporary. So let's deal with that misconception right now.

First, as a rule of thumb for making necessarily quick choices when you are out on the street actually speaking Spanish, this permanent/temporary guideline will make you right far more often than wrong. But it totally misses the point of ser and estar. Ser and estar are about two kinds of being, essence and condition. The essence of something may be temporary and a condition can be quite permanent.

Question: how do say, "He is young," in Spanish? Perhaps you, dear reader, know, as I do, that youth is a fleeting thing. It is temporary. So do we use estar? No. Age is one of the most essential characteristics of a person. El es joven. Age, the difference between being five, fifteen, and fifty years old, defines the essence of a person as much as being male or female, kind or cruel.

Question: how would you say, "Paul is very sick," in Spanish? Sickness is temporary. We get sick, we get better. Pablo está muy enfermo. Correct. The permanent/temporary rule worked! But what if Paul's illness is a mysterious viral infection that has defied diagnosis and various attempts at treatment for ten years? How would you say, "Paul has been sick for ten years?" This appears to be permanent. There is no cure. Do we now switch to ser? No. We are still talking about his physical condition, not his nature as a person. Hace diez años que Pablo está enfermo. But, Pablo es muy valiente. In his long struggle with illness Paul has remained cheerful, optimistic, involved with and caring about the problems of others besides himself. Now we are talking about Paul's character, his nature, the essence of him as a person.

Other words relating to the use of the verb ser are characteristics of, the nature of, the very existence of a person or thing. "Yo cogito por eso soy." "I think therefore I am."

Ser identifies and classifies. Soy Jaime. Soy hombre. Soy aficionado de las Medias Rojas de Boston. 'I am Jim.' 'I am a man.' 'I am a Boston Red Sox fan.'

It is common knowledge that time is of the essence. Therefore, not surprisingly, all references to time are with the verb ser. It is summer - Today is Friday - It is 5 o'clock - all ser. If Snoopy ever finishes his novel, and if he gets it published in Spanish as well as English, that magnificent opening line will use ser – "Era una noche oscura y tormentosa…"

Ser is also used for possession and origin. La chaqueta negra es suya. Es de cuero. Su dueño es un Angel del Infierno. 'The black jacket is his.' 'It is (made) of leather' (it has its origin in leather). 'Its owner is a Hell's Angel.'

Equations are expressed with ser. Dos y dos son cuatro. 'Two and two are four.' El precio de esta olla es 45 pesos. 'The price of this pot is 45 pesos.' In other words, the value of this piece of ceramic is equal to 45 pesos in money. You may want this pot but you may wish to pay less than 45 pesos. You bargain with the vendor. The price changes several times. But you continue to use ser for the price because you are still stating equations. Of course value is really an expression of essence, the inherent quality of something, its nature. So you would use ser for that reason as well.

But not all equations are expressed with numbers. For example, the statement, "I am a teacher," could also be written as follows: "I = teacher;" therefore in Spanish, "yo soy profesor." Most students accept this line of reasoning without too many misgivings. But the student who is still clinging to the neater and simpler permanent/temporary explanation of ser and estar will usually balk at the statement, "yo soy turista." "But you might be a tourist for just a weekend or even for one afternoon. How can you use ser for that?" Elementary, my dear Hijo de Wat - yo = turista - it is an equation

Finally, we use ser with impersonal statements. Phrases like: it is necessary, it is possible, it is difficult or easy, it is probable, all use ser because phrases such as these define the nature of a situation or a certain set of circumstances. **Es necesario que ellos estudien**. 'It is necessary that they study.' **Es fácil aprender el español**. 'It is easy to learn Spanish.'

Estar is used to locate people and things.

La Torre Sears **está** en Chicago. That is about as permanent as things get, but because we are locating the Sears Tower we use the verb estar.

"El rey **estaba** en la casa del tesoro…" "The king was in his counting house…"

Toledo **está** al sur de Madrid. Toledo is south of Madrid.

Yo **estoy** en Nuevo México pero **soy** de Massachusetts. 'I am in New Mexico' (that is my location) 'but I am from Massachusetts' (that is my origin).

There is one (what I find) curious exception to the use of estar to locate. Estar locates people and things but ser is used to locate events.

La reunión **será** en la oficina del jefe. 'The meeting will be in the boss' office.' Perhaps this is because the statement identifies the site of the event.

El juego **es** en la sala. 'The game is in the living room,' (is being played there). By way of contrast: el juego **está** en la sala, conveys the information that the game board and all the little wooden squares with letters on them are in the living room.

Estar is used to describe conditions.

That is a reasonably straight-forward statement. The problem for the English-speaker arises because our language has lumped all kinds of being into one verb. English does not force us to make distinctions among different states of being. We use the same verb to say: "the door is rather narrow" and to say "the door is closed." Everyday speech does not require that we identify what is characteristic and what is a condition.

When speaking Spanish you must give more thought to such things. These are philosophical issues. I once worked with a young man who had been a philosophy major in college. As we were discussing the difference between ser and estar it suddenly occurred to him that ser must express the Platonic and estar the Aristotelian mode of being. I lack the knowledge to confirm or to challenge his theory. I can testify that this young man was learning Spanish very quickly.

Another time during a class discussion of this topic a man suggested that ser expresses the masculine values and estar is for the feminine outlook. I do not endorse this theory.

But you must give more thought to such things. Once you establish the habit of making these distinctions, you will soon become quite good at making them. Before long you will be correctly choosing between ser and estar almost as automatically as native speakers do.

Go back to that rather narrow, closed door that was mentioned a few paragraphs above. Narrowness or wide-ness is characteristic of any particular door, just as sturdiness or flimsiness is.

Ser is used to speak of these characteristics of the door. This is the nature of the door. La puerta es bastante estrecha pero es muy sólida. 'The door is rather narrow but it is very sturdy.'

'Closed-ness or 'open-ness' results when something happens to the door - someone closes or opens it - the resulting condition of being closed or open is described with estar. La puerta está cerrada. La puerta está abierta. It is not the nature of the door that it be open or closed. You could take the door off its hinges and set it up on two sawhorses in order to paint or repair it. It would still be a door. It would still be narrow or wide. It would still be a sturdy or flimsy door. These are the characteristics of this door, its nature. But it would be neither open nor closed. It would just be a door sitting up on blocks.

By way of further example, here are a few other common conditions with estar contrasted with more or less parallel uses of ser.

Estamos cansados. 'We are tired' (a physical condition). But, nuestro trabajo es muy cansador, 'our work or job is very tiring.' To speak of a job as tiring is to refer to the nature of the work (ser). It is not easy work. It is physically and/or mentally demanding work.

María está muy alegre esta noche. 'Mary is very happy this evening.' (She has had a couple of glasses of wine, she is laughing and dancing, she is enjoying the party). Pero todos sabemos que María es una persona melancólica. 'But we all know that Mary is a very melancholy person.' (Now we are talking about her nature - not her condition at this moment.)

El muchacho está triste. 'The boy is sad.' (He just found out that the ballgame his father was going to take him to has been rained out). Es una situación muy triste. 'It is a very sad situation.' (The boy's enthusiastic expectations have been dashed). This will be but a brief episode in the boy's life, but for however long it lasts this is the nature of this situation - it *is* a sad situation.

When you ask the question, "¿Cómo **está** Juan?," you wish to know his condition. Is he sick or well? Does he have the Monday morning blahs? Etc. If you ask the question, "¿Cómo es Juan?" you are asking for characteristics. **Es alto**. **Es simpático**. **Es inteligente**. You want to know what kind of a person he is.

Here is an example that might require some extra thought. How would you say, 'he is rich,' in Spanish? We live in an 'easy come, easy go' world. Many people go through a cycle or two of relative wealth and poverty in their lifetime. Is wealth a characteristic or a condition?

Many Americans might view wealth as an economic circumstance of the moment, a condition. But the distinctions governing the use of ser and estar are not determined by the lifestyles of the rich and frequently infamous denizens of southern California and Dallas in the last years of the twentieth century. These distinctions were made in medieval Spain. The Royal Academy does not have its finger on the pulse of trans-Atlantic folkways in its efforts to keep the language up to date. El es rico. In medieval Spain one was rich or one was poor. And more than that, to be rich told other things besides economic condition. It spoke of education and status. The statement really speaks as much about class distinctions as economics. One finds a similar class distinction reflected in the two meanings of caballero. The word originally meant 'horseman,' (caballo is 'horse'). But the assumption that one who was wealthy enough to own and ride a horse would have the good breeding of the upper class led to the second meaning of caballero, 'gentleman.'

If your friend tells you that he is going to go over Niagara Falls in a barrel in order to win a $25 bet you would probably say to him, "¡**Estás loco**!" If he tells you that he is going to go over Niagara Falls in a barrel because an odd little man who lives inside his head has been urging him for years to do this you would say sadly to your friend, "**Eres loco**."

Making these choices is so ingrained in the minds of native Spanish speakers that it seems automatic to the outsider. Rarely does one find native speakers in disagreement about which verb to use. I recall just such a situation only one time.

I was with a Venezuelan couple the first time that they encountered snow. After a few minutes of enjoying with them their contagious delight in experiencing this wondrous new thing, I noticed that one of them was using ser and the other estar to talk about this very un-tropical miracle of the natural world.

When questioned about this discrepancy in usage they stood in the cold and generated some heat discussing which verb was correct. Both made a persuasive case.

And the verdict? A hung jury.

James K. Gavin

Watch Out! Here Comes a Spot Quiz!

This is the first of several installments of the story of an impassioned love affair plagued by poor grammar. It is titled "The Stair-Crossed Lovers." In the numbered blank spaces of the story below indicate whether <u>ser</u> or <u>estar</u> would be used if the story were in Spanish.

The year (1) is _ser_ 1956. Ramon Montaglioni, who lives in a fifth floor walk-up apartment in Queens, (2) is _estar_ in love, but in vain. To get away from it all he rents a cabin for two weeks in southern Arizona. The first day in the cabin he pours himself a beer and goes out to sit on the porch. The beer (3) is _estar_ cold. He looks at his surroundings and says to himself, "My goodness, the desert (4) is _ser_ dry!" Time passes. He notices that his glass (5) is _estar_ empty. He goes inside to get another beer. A sudden rainstorm soaks the whole area. Ramon goes back outside, looks around, and says to himself, "My goodness, the desert (6) is _estar_ wet!" He goes inside to answer the telephone. It (7) is _ser_ Julie Capuletski who lives in the apartment below him, his forbidden love. He comes from a long line of Yankee fans. Her family roots for the Dodgers. They pass on the stairs going up and down to the street but their love can never (8) be _ser_! She asks him about the desert. He tells her that the desert (9) is _ser_ very dry. He hangs up and goes back out to the porch. The sun has come back out. A hot wind blows gently. He looks around and says, "My goodness, the desert (10) is _ser_ dry!"

 ✓ 1. <u>ser</u> - reference to time
 ✓ 2. <u>estar</u> - emotional state or condition
 ✓ 3. <u>estar</u> - the temperature is a condition of the beer
 ✓ 4. <u>ser</u> - the nature of the desert
 ✓ 5. <u>estar</u> - being full or empty is something that happens to the glass, a condition
 ✓ 6. <u>estar</u> - the condition of the desert at that moment
 ✓ 7. <u>ser</u> - identity or equation
 ✓ 8. <u>ser</u> - existence
 ✓ 9. <u>ser</u> - Julie wants to know the nature of the desert
 ✗ 10. <u>estar</u> - the reference here is to the condition of the desert, it was wet, now it is dry.

This was a practice quiz. Your score will not be recorded. There will be a final exam after we finish discussing <u>ser</u> and <u>estar</u>. We are not done yet.

The Hive Continues to Fill with Be's

There is an interesting use of <u>estar</u> in situations that would normally require <u>ser</u>. This happens when there is an unexpected change or a 'deviation from a norm' as it is sometimes expressed.

For example, the Poet Laureate is going to give a lecture open to the public at the local college. This seems an interesting opportunity to learn something so you decide to attend. You know nothing about this person. You do, however, have an image of a Poet Laureate as a white-haired old man with a pipe in an ill-fitting tweed jacket with elbow patches. The speaker is introduced. Out strolls a neat, trim figure who looks more like he might be the president of the student body of the college than Poet Laureate. You turn to the stranger sitting next to you and blurt out, "¡**Está muy joven**!"

After the lecture, at home, your significant other asks you about the speaker. "**Es muy joven**," you reply. He is what he is. You have adjusted to the reality of the case. You state this essential fact about his nature using ser.

One more example of this phenomenon. I am happy to report to you that our "stair-crossed" lovers, Ramon and Julie, were finally able to get together. In 1958 the Brooklyn baseball franchise was moved to Los Angeles. The reason for the long-standing enmity between the two families ceased to exist. Julie is quite beautiful. Ramon uses the verb ser in reference to this characteristic, beauty, when he tells people, "Julie **es** muy linda." Finally it is arranged that Ramon go to the Capuletski's apartment to meet her family. Julie takes extra care in dressing and fixing her hair on this important occasion. Ramon walks down one flight and knocks on the door. Julie opens it. "¡Qué linda **estás**!" he exclaims. Julie **es** muy linda, but tonight she has exceeded even Ramon's heady expectations.

This seems a good place to mention that ser combines with the adjective bueno (good) which describes inherent quality or a characteristic of something, e.g. es un buen libro (it is a good book). Estar is used with the adverb bien (well) which refers to condition, e.g. yo estoy bien (I am well) or modifies a verb, e.g. ella toca el piano bien, (she plays the piano well). These two combinations are mutually exclusive. Bien does not go with ser because ser is not used to talk of conditions. Bueno is not used with estar because estar does not express inherent quality. The one exception to this mutual exclusivity is the case of a deviation from the usual or the expected. For example: la comida **está** muy buena esta noche, meaning, 'the food is really good' - it is even better than usual.

Our Busy Be's Work Overtime

To complete the survey of ser and estar we must move away from consideration of differing states of being. Each verb has one grammatical use that has nothing to do with the question of essence versus condition. These are two grammatical 'jobs' that someone had to do. Each verb was assigned one of these tasks.

Estar is used as the helping verb to combine with the present participle of the main verb (the '-ing' form of the verb) to make up the progressive tenses. (For more about the progressive tenses see Chapter Twelve).

    Examples of this form are: I am writing.   Yo **estoy** escribiendo.
                                   She was thinking.   Ella **estaba** pensando.
                                   They are eating.   Ellos **están** comiendo.

Ser got the job of helping to form the passive voice.

Here are some examples of the **active** voice:

1. The boy throws the ball.
   El muchacho tira la pelota.

2. Gabriel Garcia Marquez wrote One Hundred Years of Solitude.
   Gabriel García Márquez escribió *Cien Años de Soledad*.

3. Rock music ruined his hearing.
   La música *rock* arruinó su oído.

In each sentence there is action stated directly. Now each of these events will be expressed in the **passive** voice.

1. The ball is thrown by the boy.
   La pelota **es** tirada por el muchacho.

2. One Hundred Years of Solitude was written by Gabriel Garcia Marquez.
   Cien Años de Soledad **fue** escrito por Gabriel García Márquez.

3. His hearing was ruined by rock music.
   Su oído **fue** arruinado por la música *rock*.

Exactly the same information is conveyed by the second set of sentences, nothing more, nothing less. But the active voice, 'the boy throws the ball,' evokes an image in your mind of a boy throwing a ball, i.e. action. The passive voice evokes no such image, it states the action passively.

Choice of the active or passive voice is left to the speaker (or writer). It is a question of style, not of right or wrong. But not every active statement can be expressed in the passive voice. The sentence, "The boy throws with great accuracy," cannot be changed to the passive voice. The sentence must have a direct object in order to be convertible to the passive voice.

Especially if you are a beginner level student this may be as much as you want to know about the passive voice. If so, catapult yourself over to the recapitulation, review it, and then take your final exam.

But many of the ser/estar choices that have to be made come down to deciding whether some form of 'to be' with a past participle refers to an event (in this case ser) or describes the condition that resulted from an event (in which case estar). So it behooves the intermediate level student to give a bit more thought to how to distinguish the true passive voice from its many imitators.

If you are still with me go back to example sentence number one. In the active voice 'the boy' is the subject of the verb, the doer of the action. 'Throws' is the verb, the action word, the word that tells what is happening. 'The ball' is the direct object, it is the object acted upon by the verb, it gets thrown. In the passive voice, the direct object from the active voice sentence, in this case 'the ball,' becomes the subject. The verb 'to be' combines with the past participle of the active verb (throw) to give us 'is thrown.' Finally the subject from the active voice statement, 'the boy,' becomes the object of the preposition 'by,' thus the prepositional phrase 'by the boy' states the agent *by means of whom* the action got carried out. 'The ball is thrown by the boy.'

	subject	**verb**	**direct object**
active:	The boy	throws	the ball.
passive:	The ball	is thrown	by the boy.
	subject	**verb**	**agent**

In Spanish the passive voice is formed exactly the same way. The direct object of the active voice becomes the subject of the passive voice statement; the verb 'to be' (ser) combines with the past participle of the verb from the active sentence; and the active voice subject becomes the object of the preposition por (which means 'by' among other things) to identify the agent *by means of whom* the action gets done.

There is one extra step involved in forming the passive voice in Spanish. The past participle of the action verb serves as an adjective modifying the subject in combination with ser. Therefore it must agree in gender and number with the subject. In the example sentence number one, La pelota es tirada por el muchacho, la pelota is feminine singular. Therefore the past participle of tirar, which is tirado, must be changed to the feminine singular tirad**a**.

In both English and Spanish the agent by means of whom the action was able to occur may be omitted if that information is not deemed necessary in the context of the conversation. But there is an agent understood and it could be named upon request. For example, two old fogies are talking about rock music. One asks what happened to the Billy Smith's hearing. The other answers, "It was ruined." (By rock music) is understood and does not have to be stated in this context. "Fue arruinado," (por la música *rock*). Ser is required as this is the passive voice.

The existence of this agent (in the above case 'rock music'), even if unspoken, matters in Spanish. Its existence is the test for the true passive voice, and therefore for the use of ser. Otherwise estar is called for. If someone asks the Smiths how Billy's hearing is they would answer, "Está arruinado." Now they are talking about the condition of his hearing.

James K. Gavin

Don't Capitulate, Recapitulate!

In summary, here is what has been said about ser and estar.

SER	ESTAR
essence:	condition
characteristics/the nature of	
classifies and identifies	
equations	
location of events	location of people and things
origin	
time	
possession	
the passive voice	the progressive tenses
	deviations from the usual state of things

Final Exam Time

In the spaces provided indicate which verb, ser or estar, would be used to make the following statements in Spanish.

1. He **was** poor until he won the lottery. 1. fue

2. I think it **is** true, but I **am** not sure. 2a. es   2b. estoy

3. The child's clothes **are** filthy. 3. están

4. That **is** a filthy joke. 4. es

5. It **is** impossible to use ser and estar correctly. 5. es

6. The red shoes **are** Dorothy's. 6. son

7. It **was** two o'clock when he arrived. 7. fueron

8. It **was** sold for $100. (passive voice & equation) 8. fueron

9. He **is** always thinking of her. 9. está

10. The window **was** open when I went by. 10. estaba

11. That window **is** always open, it cannot **be** closed. 11a. está   11b. ser

12. The soup **is** hot. (jalapeño soup) 12. es

Gramática Apasionada
Reminiscences of a Love Affair with the Spanish Language

13. It **is** a small room. 13. es

14. Tomorrow she **will be** Queen for a Day. 14. (estará) Será (Equation)

15. "**To be** or not **to be**, that **is** the question." 15a. Ser 15b. Ser 15c. es

16. The room **is** empty. 16. está

17. The soup **is** hot. (temperature) 17. está

18. His watch **is** slow. 18. está

19. It **is** a Swiss watch. 19. es

20. They **were** young when they learned Spanish. 20. fueron

21. Ice **is** cold. 21. es

The answers are on the next page.

1. ser - economic status was not viewed as a condition in medieval Spain.
2a. ser - truth is essence, the nature of something.
2b. estar - describing mental state or condition.
3. estar - the condition of the clothing, it can be washed and made clean.
4. ser - the nature of the joke.
5. ser - the nature of the challenge.
6. ser - possession.
7. ser - reference to time.
8. ser - passive voice, it was sold by somebody (there is an agent implied).
9. estar - the helping verb to form progressive tense.
10. estar - the condition of the window.
11a. estar - it is still the condition of the window.
11b. ser - this is passive voice again, it cannot be closed (by anybody). Permit yourself a small smile of satisfaction if you got that one!
12. ser - the nature of the soup.
13. ser - characteristic or the nature of the room.
14. ser - equation, she = Queen for a Day.
15a. ser - Hamlet was talking about existence.
15b. ser - existence.
15c. ser - states an equation, also it identifies what the question is.
16. estar - the condition of the room.
17. estar - temperature is a condition of the soup.
18. estar - a condition of the watch, it can be adjusted.
19. ser - the origin of the watch.
20. ser - age is one of the essential things about people.
21. ser - this is the nature of ice, if it were not cold it would not be ice, it would be water.

Now please tally your score. There are a possible 25 points. Then refer to the scale that follows for a personalized comment about your performance on this test.

Score
24-25   Good job! You obviously did not need to buy this book. Sorry - no refunds!
20-23   You have done quite well. One additional *careful* reading of this chapter will take care of all your remaining shortcomings.
15-19   Your score falls into the "neither fish nor fowl" range. The only thing that I can think of to say to you is, "Thank you for buying this book."
9-14   As there are only two choices this is the coin-flipping range. Re-take the test. Try using a different coin.
4-8   Perhaps some other book explains ser and estar better. Sorry - no refunds!
0-3   Use ser when you think estar is called for and estar when you think that ser is required. You will do fine.

Paciencia y persistencia.

Gramática Apasionada
Reminiscences of a Love Affair with the Spanish Language

Chapter Four

Re: Dictionaries

In 1962 the Peace Corps sent me off to Venezuela to help stem the rising tide of Imperialist Communism in Latin America. I arrived clutching what I thought would be my two most necessary weapons in the struggle ahead - malaria pills and an English-Spanish dictionary.

My first two months of service were spent in rugged, beautiful mountains to the west of the capital - mountains that are, in fact, the last dramatic gasping for air of the Andes before they plunge into the sea after their spectacular 4,000 mile run north. The YMCA of Venezuela had a summer camp out there for boys from the poorest barrios of Caracas.

Conditions were primitive and living was made even more difficult by the fact that there was no level ground anywhere in those mountains except that which people before me had created with picks and shovels. When I left at the end of the summer to take up my permanent duties, the pills and my dictionary had disappeared. I do not now recall whether they were victims of rapid tropical decomposition or were washed off down to the Caribbean Sea in one of the violent downpours that from time to time turned the whole camp into a rough precursor of the aqua slides that are now so popular in stateside amusement parks.

In either case, I showed up at my permanent post without the pills or the dictionary, having caught a little Spanish and no malaria while in the mountains. By this time I had come to the conclusion that there were advantages to not having a dictionary. As one trying to learn Spanish I had found that there was more to be gained by asking the people about me what some unknown word meant. The alternative was to stop all discourse for seemingly endless momentitos while looking up the word. The one word acquired (and frequently soon forgotten) was of much less value than the several minutes of lively conversation that usually accompanied attempts at explanation and definition. This experience turned into a policy that is still strictly enforced in my classes today - *no se permite usar el diccionario durante la clase sin el permiso del profesor.*

Of course not having an English-Spanish dictionary did prove inconvenient from time to time.

I remember standing on a street corner at the end of a day talking with a friend about the project we were working on together. There was a problema. But problems always seemed more manageable at sunset than during the blazing tropical day. Down near the equator twilight is a lovely interlude between the harsh light and heat of the day and the dark,

James K. Gavin

sometimes suffocating night. There is often a light breeze off the ocean and the soft crepuscular glow lingers much longer than in northern latitudes. It is a good time for conversation - even about <u>problemas</u>.

Suddenly all our attention was focused on the word <u>ajeno</u>. It was obviously very important to my friend José, <u>el trigueño</u>,[13] that I understand this word. It was relatively early on in my Peace Corps career and I was operating linguistically at the level of perhaps a five-year old. He tried to explain the word in several different ways. Then he enlisted the help of an acquaintance who was passing by. Soon a crowd formed around us – every person present took a turn at me. It seemed to have become an imperative municipal duty that I be made to understand the meaning of this word. But I just did not get it. Eventually the hopelessness of their task sank in on them all. They stood in a silent circle around me, like a team of surgeons who had done their utmost and could now only stand by helplessly and watch the patient die.

More than three decades later I clearly remember the last desperate attempt by <u>el trigueño</u> to make me understand. Everyone else had backed off. He put his face up to mine, our noses almost touching. He said very softly but with a pleading intensity (as if the strength of his desire could supply the voltage necessary to jump the spark of knowledge across the gap between our noses and into my brain), "<u>¡Ajeno, Jeem, ajeno!</u>" Then he too gave up.

President Kennedy's splendid vision of America's youth scattered across the face of the planet helping the less fortunate pull themselves up by their own bootstraps had come down to this, one terminally dense gringo being waked by the very <u>tercermundistas</u>[14] he had come to save.

Having no dictionary some time passed before I finally learned the meaning of <u>ajeno</u>. But the scene just described stuck vividly in my mind. When I did discover what it meant I understood why there had been so much urgency and drama on that long ago tropical evening. <u>Ajeno</u> means 'alien; of others; not having to do with me.' José, who valued my high opinion of him, wanted me to know that the cause of our problem was <u>ajeno</u>, it was not of his doing.

In spite of the occasional frustration created by my policy of no dictionary I stood, and stand, by it for the reasons already stated. Besides, in unwary hands a dictionary can be a very treacherous companion.

Near the end of my two year stay in Puerto Cabello I did resort to an English-Spanish dictionary for a key word needed to convey some important information to my supervisors. There was a Peace Corps Director in Caracas but I answered to the <u>junta directiva</u> of our

---

[13] In common usage 'the brown-skinned guy,' but literally (and more poetically) 'the guy who is the color of wheat.'
[14] <u>Tercermundista</u> makes a neat <u>rompecabezas</u> for intermediate students (see Chapter 14).

project, a group of local businessmen and civic leaders. Only one of these men had a useful knowledge of English and he seldom attended our monthly meetings.

There had been concerns about how the project could go on if the Peace Corps did not send additional volunteers to carry on in our stead. That evening, I went to our board meeting armed with the Spanish word that some dictionary listed for 'replacement,' repuesto. I stood up and announced (so I thought) to the board that the project would get another two years of Peace Corps support because Washington had decided to send our much needed replacements, i.e. Peace Corps Volunteers. What I actually told them was that the project would get continued assistance because we were going to receive our urgently needed spare parts - and this at a time when organ transplant was a miracle being talked of only at a few 'cutting edge' medical facilities!

This somewhat astonishing declaration was received with courteous composure by the board. I have wondered since what their private reactions must have been - hilarity at my linguistic bumbling or wonder at the marvels of medical technology being wrought by el Coloso del Norte.

But I am not the only person to have decreed death to discourse by dictionary. An old friend who spent three years with the Peace Corps in Panama brought me a little gift he had picked up in Panama City. It was a box of matches, one of thousands put out around the country by an American firm. It had the company's logo and name - it was obviously intended for advertising and good will. Right under the scratch pad where an English matchbook would say "Strike Here," it said in bold letters, "HUELGA AQUI."[15]. Some yanqui businessman cum linguist, who should not have been allowed to use an English-Spanish dictionary except under close supervision, was inadvertently inciting labor unrest among the company's employees.

Here is one more classic example of the perils of naive reliance on an English-Spanish dictionary.

Former Speaker of the House, Newt Gingrich, was campaigning on behalf of a political ally in south Texas. In an attempt to show his sensitivity to the large Hispanic population in the region his office put out a press release in Spanish. It was signed, "Newt Gingrich, Hablador de la Casa." That title actually translates, "the person who talks your ear off at home." Perhaps he is that, but his position in the federal government was Presidente de la Cámara de Representantes. This misguided dictionary-derived translation is humorous but it also displays an insincere tokenism *vis-à-vis* the Hispanic community.

Anyway, here are some suggested guidelines for the use of an English-Spanish dictionary.

---

[15] Huelga means 'strike' in the sense of 'a work stoppage.'

James K. Gavin

Suggestion number one: Do not use the dictionary. People are a much better resource. If there are Spanish-speakers around consult them. They can tell you about multiple meanings and nuances far better than the dictionary can. And this, after all, is the primary purpose of language, people face to face - not lists of words in books.

Suggestion number two: If you must use the dictionary treat it as if it were James Bond's briefcase. There were all sorts of wondrous things in it like the fountain pen that could knock an ICBM out of the sky. But just as often as not it seemed that some agent of evil had booby-trapped the briefcase to explode upon opening. So, open in a cautious frame of mind.

Suggestion number three: Cross reference the words that you do look up. If that businessman/'linguistic genius' down in Panama City (there is a cultural arrogance in instances such as this) had cross-referenced the word he would have saved himself considerable embarrassment. He looked up 'strike' and found the word <u>huelga</u>. If he had then looked up <u>huelga</u> in the Spanish section of that same dictionary he would have discovered the true meaning of the word.

Suggestion number four: As you progress into intermediate level proficiency buy yourself a Spanish dictionary. Then put your English-Spanish dictionary in an inconvenient place that will discourage you from consulting it. Your new dictionary will tell you what words actually mean, as opposed to giving you what are sometimes only rough English equivalents. And, as you study the definition(s) of the unknown word, you will almost always learn something else that you did not know besides the meaning of the word that sent you to the dictionary in the first place.

Gramática Apasionada
Reminiscences of a Love Affair with the Spanish Language

Chapter Five

A Tale of Two Tenses

The on-again off-again romance of Ramon Montaglione and Julie Capuletski, whom you first meet in Chapter 3, is, unfortunately, off again. This is the result of a lack of sensitivity on Ramon's part - not insensitivity towards Julie, to whom he is totally devoted, rather an insensitivity to the difference between the preterit and imperfect past tenses.

This is their sad story.

When Julie was but ten years old she inherited from her dearly beloved abuelita a cameo with a gold filigree border and the profile of that fine lady carved into creamy ivory. Ramon had admired the piece many times pinned on the tender bosom of his own heart's desire. One calamitous day the treasured brooch disappeared, lost or stolen the heart-broken Julie knew not.

Ramon promised that if the cameo ever turned up he would pay what ever was asked to recover it. Time passed. Then one day Ramon came to Julie and told her that he had seen the brooch in a pawnshop in mid-town Manhattan. "Costaba $299," he said.

It was then that Julie burst into tears, and ran off, vowing never to speak to Ramon again.

Onward to the Past

Before we can proceed any further with this drama of young love gone awry, it will be necessary to take time to look at the two past tenses in the Spanish language. These tenses give the speaker two contrasting ways to make reference to past time. In English we do have ways to convey the same ideas but we do not have these methods neatly packaged in two fully developed and chronologically coordinated tenses.

The names of the two tenses, the preterit and imperfect, offer clues as to their distinct duties. 'Preterit' is defined as 'by-gone, past, without reference to duration.' 'Imperfect,' when used in relation to verbs and tenses, is defined as 'incomplete, in continuance.' This is how the two tenses are usually presented. The preterit tells completed actions and states of being or conditions in the past. The imperfect relates on-going action or condition in the past. This is fine as far as it goes, but I prefer a presentation of the difference between these two tenses that is put forth in a text called *Spanish for Communication*, written by Bull, Briscoe, Lamadrid, Dellaccio and Brown, published by Houghton Mifflin.

One finds the on-going vs. completed action concept schematized in various ways. For example:

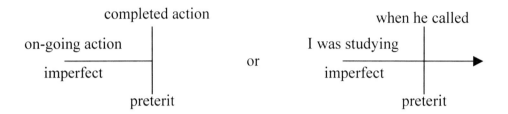

But Bull and his buddies added one feature to this more usual presentation of the uses of the preterit and imperfect tenses. To the concept of on-going action or condition and completed actions and states of being they added the beginnings of these actions and states. This addition gives a symmetry and wholeness to consideration of the preterit vs. imperfect problem that is both intellectually satisfying and reality based.

Their theory goes as follows. <u>Every event</u> (closing a door, spending a month in Seville, talking to the mailman, etc.) <u>or state of being or condition</u> (tiredness, happiness, heat wave, etc.) <u>that has occurred had three</u> aspects to it. It began, there was a point in time when it started happening. It had a duration of a certain amount of time, this may have been the fraction of a second that the action of blinking an eye takes or the twenty-seven years that Nelson Mandella spent in prison. And it ended, there was a point in time when the action or state of being came to its conclusion.

These three aspects of past events are connected to each other and to the ever lengthening series of happenings stretching out behind each of us. A person's past is not a murky ocean called Before Now in which all the past occurrences of our lives drift about and intermingle aimlessly like so much plankton. The past is an orderly continuum, a sequence of identifiable moments divided into years, months, days, minutes, seconds. All past occurrences are locked into that sequence and are permanently attached to specific years, months, days, minutes and seconds. Every time we use a past tense in English or in Spanish there is a specific place in the past or a definable period of time being referred to. Sometimes we believe it is important to specify the time – "Last Tuesday at 3:17 pm the girl of my dreams walked into my life!" — sometimes we do not — "I went to Disneyland once and vowed never to return to that supreme monument to profligate consumerism." Whether specified or not, every reference to the past occupies a specific place along the time line. So we (both speaker and listener) are not simply being tossed overboard into the vast Before Now each time the speaker uses a past tense. Rather we are being taken to a specific place along a calibrated continuum. This is so whether that place in time is specified by the speaker or not.

Now Bull and friends come along and tell us that within that specific place along the time line the speaker must make one of three choices. Does he wish to take the listener back to the beginning, to specify the first moment of the event. Does he want to focus on the point in time at which it was completed or reached its conclusion. Or does he wish to take his listener back to a time in between the beginning and end of the event, the time during which it was going on.

The person who wishes to speak of some past event or state of being must make this choice. He may make reference to the beginning aspect of that event or state of being,[16] he may reference its middle aspect (at any point in time along its duration excluding the moments of beginning and end), or he may refer to the end aspect, the moment when it ended or was completed. If he is speaking Spanish he will use the preterit tense if the reference is to the beginning or end aspect. The imperfect tense is used to make reference to the middle aspect of an event or s. o. b.

The double duty, beginning and end aspects, being done by the preterit will not be a source of confusion. (The alternative would be to create a third past tense to deal exclusively with beginning aspects of past events and s.o.b.'s - we do not want that, trust me!). In fact the great majority of the uses of the preterit is end aspect, they focus on completion or conclusion. The diagrams shown above would probably cover 90-95% of the uses of the preterit tense. But the recognition of the existence of a beginning aspect to past events and s.o.b.'s (they do, after all, have to start), gives us a framework for a more comprehensive way to look at the past.

We might diagram it thus:

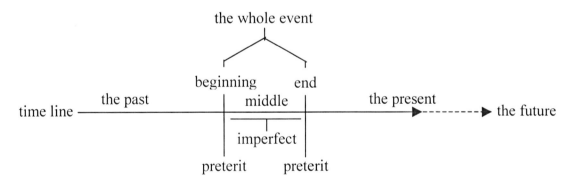

It is important to note that if reference is made to the middle aspect of the event that does not mean that the event has not ended - the speaker is simply ignoring the end or outcome. For example, if I were to say to you, "Yesterday I drove to Albuquerque," you would assume that I got there because the statement focuses on the end aspect, the completion of the event. If I were to say, "Yesterday I was driving to Albuquerque..." you would not know at this point whether I got there or not because I have taken us back to the middle aspect of the event, ignoring outcome - "was driving" is somewhere between leaving for and

---

[16]Footnote: For clarity and completeness the somewhat cumbersome phrases 'event or state of being' and 'action or state of being' will reoccur a number of times in this chapter; henceforth 'state of being' will be abbreviated as 's.o.b.'

arriving at Albuquerque. If the sentences goes on to say, "…when my car broke down," you might assume that I did not get there. If the sentences ends "…when I saw a golden eagle circling over the Rio Grande," you might assume that I got to Albuquerque. But, in either case, if you want to know for certain whether or not I got there you will have to employ an end aspect verb form and ask, "Did you ever get to Albuquerque?"

Bull, et al, suggest the following sort of exercise in English to accustom yourself to thinking about the past in this way. Analyze each of the numbered verbs in the following paragraph. In each case ask yourself if the verb is referencing the beginning, middle, or end aspect of the event or s.o.b. Indicate your choice of beginning, middle, or end aspect by writing 'b,' 'm,' or 'e' in the space provided after each verb. Answers and a brief explanation of each item will follow.

The alarm (1) rang ___ at 6:00 am. I (2) got up ___ and (3) shut off ___ the @#*#*#@ thing. I (4) was ___ in a foul mood. Right away I (5) made ___ coffee. The first sip (6) scalded ___ my mouth and throat. It (7) was ___ much too hot. I (8) dumped ___ it in the sink and (9) got ___ myself a glass of orange juice. The juice (10) was ___ too cold and (11) made ___ me cough. Outside, birds (12) were singing ___ and everything (13) glowed ___ in the soft morning light. "This is not," I (14) said ___ to no one in particular, "going to be my day!"

If the speaker had been telling us about the start of his day in Spanish he would have had to switch back and forth between the preterit and imperfect tenses several times.

Let us now check your answers.

1. - B. Clearly the reference is to the beginning aspect of ringing - it started ringing. This is the critical information, not how long it rang or when it stopped.

2. and 3. - E. End aspect - the speaker is reporting two things he did, the focus is on the completed acts.

4. - M. The speaker is on his feet starting the day. He tells us how he was feeling as he went about the early morning routine - when he started or stopped being in a foul mood is not germane to the story at this point - this is how he was feeling at the time - middle aspect.

5. - E. Again the speaker reports something he did, completed action.

6. - B. The scalding or burning sensation probably went on for some time. The speaker makes reference to the beginning aspect of that experience. The fact that the scalding started (not how long it went on or when it ended) motivated his next actions.

7. - M. The coffee *was being* too hot when he drank it - when it started or stopped being too hot is irrelevant.

8. and 9. - E. The focus again is on completion. The speaker reports that he did these two things.

10. - M. The important information here is the temperature of the juice when he drank it, when it started or stopped being too cold has no bearing on the story.

11. - E. The focus is on end aspect here. This is what happened, he was made to cough (it is understood that he did cough).

12. and 13. - M. How was the world around him as these events transpired? We are told with the imperfect tense, i.e. middle aspect. The beginning and end of the singing and glowing are not of concern to the flow of the narrative.

14. - E. He reports this completed action - he did say that.

A Clash of Titans: The Preterit vs. the Imperfect

From the English- (but not the Spanish-) speaker's point of view a few verbs actually take on a different meaning when used in the preterit and imperfect tenses. In trying to grasp this concept of beginning, middle, or end aspect of some event or s.o.b. in the past it might be instructive to look at how the meaning of some verbs changes as we shift the verb from middle to beginning aspect or from middle to end aspect.

In the following three pairs of sentences we will analyze the significant change of meaning (from the English-speaker's point of view) that occurs when we shift from the imperfect to preterit tense. It should be noted that these are select cases. Most verbs do not undergo such a pronounced change of meaning when used in the two past tenses.

1. <u>Fui a la fiesta pero no conocía a nadie.</u>
   I went to the party but I didn't know anybody.

2. <u>Fui a la fiesta pero no conocí a nadie.</u>
   I went to the party but I didn't 'know' anybody.

<u>Conocer</u> means 'to know' in the sense of 'to be acquainted with.' When <u>conocer</u> is used in the imperfect tense, i.e. in the middle aspect of 'knowing,' as in sentence #1 the meaning conveyed is that "I went to the party but I did not know anybody who was there." When <u>conocer</u> is used in the preterit it marks the beginning aspect of acquaintance, in other words, the moment when acquaintance began. Therefore, sentence #2 means, "I went to the party but I did not meet (make the acquaintance of) anybody new."

3. <u>José sabía eso cuando ella nos lo dijo.</u>
   José knew that when she told us about it.

4. <u>José supo eso cuando ella nos lo dijo.</u>

José 'knew' that when she told us about it.

Saber means 'to know' information, factual information, e.g. how to change a flat tire, or the year that Millard Fillmore became president of the United States. Sentence #3 informs us that José 'was knowing that' or already knew that when she told us about it, the middle aspect of knowing. When saber is used in the preterit it takes us to the beginning aspect of knowing, the moment when the information was acquired. Therefore sentence #4 translates, "José **found out** (he began knowing) about that when she told us about it."

5. El niño no quería ir al dentista.
The child did not want to go to the dentist.

6. El niño no quiso ir al dentista.
The child 'did not want' to go to the dentist.

Sentence #5 tells us how the boy was feeling about going to the dentist. He was not wanting to go, but as this is middle aspect we do not know what the outcome was. Sentence #6 tells us what happened. The preterit in this case is end aspect, it gives us conclusion. The boy did not want to go and he didn't go. This sentence would best translate, "the boy **refused** to go to the dentist."

The first three pairs of sentences gave us examples of an apparent change in the meaning of the verb in its preterit and imperfect uses. In the following paired examples the meaning of the verb does not change but the information conveyed is none-the-less very different.

7. La mujer que vivía al lado tenía gemelos.
The woman next door had twins.

8. La mujer que vivía al lado tuvo gemelos.
The woman next door had twins.

The first sentence, #7, uses the imperfect tense, middle aspect. It tells that there were twins among those people living next door. Sentence #8 informs us that twins were born to the family next door. The preterit here is end aspect, conclusion. Something happened. The woman next door gave birth to twins.

9. Ella podía repararlo.   She was able to (could) fix it.

10. Ella pudo repararlo.   She was able to (could) fix it.

The use of the imperfect in sentence #9 ignores the beginning or end, it is describing her ability. "She was capable of repairing it." Sentence #10 is preterit, end aspect. "She was able to repair it (and she did)."

11. Me gustaba el *sushi*.   I liked *sushi*.

12. Me gustó el *sushi*.   I liked *sushi*.

The imperfect, 'I was liking,' without a beginning or end to the liking, tells you that I used to eat and enjoy *sushi*. The second sentence, by using the preterit, implies a conclusion. I tried *sushi* once and I was pleased by it, I liked it.

13. John no hablaba español la primera vez que fue a México.
    John didn't speak Spanish the first time he went to Mexico.

14. Bill no habló español la primera vez que fue a México.
    Bill didn't speak Spanish the first time he went to Mexico.

The English translation of sentences #13 and #14 can mean two very different things. The change of tenses in Spanish eliminates the ambiguity of the English. Sentence #13, the imperfect, ignoring beginning and end, tells us that John was not a Spanish-speaker, 'he was not speaking Spanish' the first time he went to Mexico. #14 uses the preterit to tell of the outcome of Bill's first trip to Mexico. Bill could speak Spanish but 'he did not get to use his Spanish.' Everybody he dealt with spoke English.

15. Mi hermano tenía suerte. My brother had luck.

16. Mi hermano tuvo suerte. My brother had luck.

The first sentence of this pair uses the imperfect, ignoring the beginning or end of my brother's having luck. The message conveyed is, "my brother was a lucky person." The second sentence uses the preterit. This indicates conclusion. On a particular occasion "my brother had luck" - he bought a lottery ticket for one dollar and won thousands.

17. Martin Luther King tenía un sueño.
    Martin Luther King had a dream.

18. San José tuvo un sueño.
    Saint Joseph had a dream.

Martin Luther King crusaded about the country carrying in his head the image of an America in which the color of a person's skin made absolutely no difference. In the second sentence we are told that one night, soon after the birth of Jesus, Joseph had a dream in which an angel warned him of imminent danger to his infant son, precipitating the Flight into Egypt.

Finally, here are two questions I sometimes put to a student to try to illustrate the difference between a preterit and an impefect use of ser.

Quién **fue** el primer presidente de los Estados Unidos?

Who was the first president of the United States? (Conclusion – who was that person?)

<u>Quién **era** el presidente de los Estados Unidos cuando usted nació?</u>
Who was the president of the United States when you were born? (Who was being president when you were born?)

Ramon's Mistake

Perhaps now, thinking back to poor, forlorn Ramon (whose troubles we chronicled at the start of this chapter), you will see how he got into his predicament. In fact he had immediately, and with no misgivings at all, purchased the cameo for his beloved. Unfortunately he paid no attention to preterit/imperfect distinctions. The past was the past as far as he was concerned. What difference could it possibly make which past tense was chosen? Julie, on the other hand, completely understood the beginning, middle, and end aspect of events and s.o.b.'s in the past.

Ramon chose the imperfect to tell Julie that the cameo cost $299. She took that middle aspect to mean that the precious family heirloom was being offered at that price when he entered the pawnshop and was still being offered at that price when he left, in other words, he had not bought it. If he had said, "<u>Costó $299</u>," she would have known that it had been purchased at the cost of $299, the preterit would have informed Julie of conclusion. Much unhappiness would have been avoided.

Unfortunately we must again leave this unhappy couple in their separated and confused condition. We must press on with our study of the two past tenses in the hope that you, dear reader, will never inadvertently bring woe upon yourself for lack of understanding of this important and sometimes elusive concept. (I can tell you that we shall meet the distressed lovers anon on the slippery slope of the subjunctive).

On We Go "Borne Back Ceaselessly into the Past"

Within the context of the preterit/imperfect distinctions discussed above, there are some fairly common usages that are worth studying.

The first one we will look at is the situation represented in the two diagrams sketched earlier in this chapter. The diagrams are meant to show that one thing was happening or some condition or state was 'being' when something else happened:

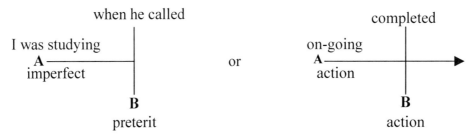

For example:

1. It <u>was</u> hot when the game <u>began</u>.
    A   **B**

2. Julie <u>was</u> still angry when she <u>got</u> the letter from Ramon.
        A   **B**

3. The baby <u>was born</u> while the taxi <u>was rushing</u> to the hospital.
            B   **A**

This is a 'formula sentence' which often occurs in everyday speech. The on-going action or s.o.b., expressed in the imperfect, is played against the preterit occurrence.

1. <u>Hacía calor cuando el juego comenzó</u>.
    A   **B**

2. <u>Julia estaba enojada todavía cuando ella recibió la carta de Ramón</u>.
        A   **B**

3. <u>El niño nació mientras el taxi corría para el hospital</u>.
      B   **A**

Another common usage is the reference to the past with the English phrase 'used to...' It is always expressed with the imperfect in Spanish.

1. The trolley used to go right by my grandmother's house.
   <u>El tranvía pasaba en frente de la casa de mi abuela</u>.

2. They used to play baseball almost everyday after school.
   <u>Jugaban al béisbol casi todos los días después de las clases</u>.

3. I used to go to the movies a lot when I was young.
   Or: I would[17] go to the movies a lot when I was young.
   <u>Yo iba al cine mucho cuando era joven</u>.

The imperfect is called for in all such cases by the nature of the phrase 'used to...' There is no beginning or end suggested. Rather we are told what was going on or how things were during some unspecified time in the past. 'Used to...' takes us back into an

---

[17]'Would' is the auxiliary word used to create the conditional tense in English, e.g. they **would** smile if there were something to smile about. It is, however, a common usage to substitute 'would' for 'used to...'. When 'would' is being used in the sense of 'used to...' the Spanish translation requires the imperfect past tense, not the conditional tense.

undefined continuation of time, and that is a good description of middle aspect, i.e. imperfect tense.

By way of contrast, let us look at that last model sentence, "I used to go to the movies a lot when I was young." I also kept a very detailed diary when I was young. Having just consulted it I can tell you that I went to the movies 83 times in 1957. In Spanish - <u>Yo fui al cine 83 veces en 1957</u>. The preterit is now necessary because I am making reference to specific concluded events (83 of them). When the focus is on conclusion we have end aspect, which is reported with the preterit tense.

From this last example we can make the following generalization: if you are going to state how many times or for how long something was done in the past you will use the preterit tense.

1. The Foreign Minister visited China seven times during the Allende administration.
<u>El Ministro del Exterior visitó China siete veces durante la presidencia de Salvador Allende</u>.

2. Last night our daughter did homework for almost eight and a half minutes.
<u>Anoche nuestra hija trabajó en su tarea por casi ocho minutos y medio</u>.

3. The Hundred Years War actually lasted 125 years.
<u>La Guerra de Cien Años duró 125 años en realidad</u>.

In order to be able to say how long the girl studied or how long the war lasted those events have to have concluded. Therefore the reference has to be to end aspect and that means preterit tense.

We could go on looking at different specific kinds of situations that call for the use of one tense or the other. But that seems to me the long way around. It is better that you learn to recognize which aspect, beginning, middle or end, of a past action or s.o.b. you are making reference to as you speak of the past. Then you will have no need to memorize which situations require the preterit and which would call for the imperfect. All situations are taken care of once you become accustomed to analyzing past occurrences in terms of beginning, middle and end aspect.

As with almost every other part of the language learning process this will take time and practice. So here and now you have an opportunity to practice. Read the following story and indicate in the space provided whether the numbered verbs are referencing beginning, middle or end aspect. Remember that the preterit is for beginning and end and the imperfect is used for the middle aspect of events and s.o.b.'s.

Gramática Apasionada
Reminiscences of a Love Affair with the Spanish Language

Just Another Night Out at the Movies

The riot started about halfway through the movie. The theater (1) was ___ packed. I was sitting somewhere in the middle of the theater. The movie (2) was ___ *One-eyed Jacks*, a western with Marlon Brando.

The evening had started badly. First they oversold the capacity of the theater by half. Then there was a delay long past the announced time of opening. The number of ticket-holders waiting outside in the street was getting bigger and more restless by the minute. Suddenly the doors (3) burst ___ open under pressure from the crowd. People poured in. There was a scramble for seats. On-lookers, recognizing an opportunity for a free movie, joined the rush. There was further delay while whoever was supposedly in charge tried to sort out who the legitimate ticket-holders were - an impossible task. Finally the show had begun.

The film (4) broke ___ right in the middle of a brutal scene. Brando, arms spread wide and tied at the wrists to the rail of a hitching post, looked like Christ crucified. One of the bad guys, with a sadistic smile of pleasure, (5) was slowly, deliciously breaking ___ Brando's thumbs so that he would not be able to use a pistol. Suddenly a fiery spot (6) appeared ___ in the middle of the projected image. In an instant it (7) spread ___ across the screen as the celluloid burned. Then the theater went dark. In the very next instant the riot erupted.

— Let us step out of the darkened theater into the slowly cooling Venezuelan night for just a moment to see how you are doing —

Here are my answers to the first seven examples with a brief explanation of why beginning, middle, or end aspect was chosen in each case.

1. Middle - The narrator is setting the stage, filling in the background against which upcoming events will take place. We are back in the middle of the time when the theater was packed.

2. Middle or End - Either the imperfect or preterit could be used here. The preterit simply identifies the movie for us, tells us what it was. The imperfect takes us more immediately into the story that is unfolding, the movie that I was watching was *One-eyed Jacks*.

3. End - That is what happened, the doors burst open, the completed event is being reported.

4. End - Conclusion of the event, the film did break.

5. Middle - He had already started but had not yet finished breaking Brando's thumbs when the film broke. Clearly he was in the middle of the event.

James K. Gavin

x 6. End - When something registers through our eye on our brain as having come into view it has appeared. We can go on seeing it, but the event of appearing has concluded.

✓7. Beginning or End - As soon as the fiery spot began to grow larger it can be reported that it has spread or begun to spread, beginning aspect of spreading. The additional information given in the text of the story, "it spread across the screen," suggests that it consumed the image projected on the screen, conclusion or end aspect. Either way the preterit is called for.

— Let's go back into the theater now – but keep your head down! —

People began tearing their seats apart. They (8) threw __e__ the pieces at the screen and against the walls. Others (9) ran __e__ for the exits. All the doors of the theater (10) swung __e__ inward so they could not be opened against the push of the panicky crowd.

The rioters (11) switched __m__ their anger to the crowds that were pushing futilely at the big metal doors. Under a barrage of chair parts those who were trying to escape from the theater (12) scattered __m__. Screaming people were running up and down the aisles in the dark. Heavy projectiles were banging off the masonry walls. As the screen itself (13) was __e__ simply a concrete block wall painted white, it was not damaged.

As if the only problem were a malfunctioning projector the movie suddenly started up again. The villain finished breaking Brando's thumbs. But the screaming, the clatter of broken chairs smashing against the walls, the ghostly figures running up and down the aisles, (14) did not stop __m__. I (15) stayed __e__ slumped low in my still intact seat and continued watching the movie. It (16) was __m__ not often that an American film came to our rather isolated and not very significant town. I wanted to see it. As it (17) was __m__ impossible to hear the actors I was reading the Spanish subtitles to follow the story.

As quickly as it had begun, the tumult suddenly ended. The theater (18) was __m__ on a corner so there were exits along one side of the hall as well as in the back. I (19) saw __b__ soldiers, menacing looking weapons drawn and aimed right at us, coming through all the doors. It was then that I (20) got scared __b__!

Here are the rest of my answers along with brief explanations of why beginning, middle or end aspect was chosen in each case.

✓ 8. End - What was the next thing the people did? We use the preterit (end aspect) to report what they did. They threw things.

e x9. Beginning - It is not necessary to wait until the runners get to their destination to say that they ran. As soon as they started running it can be reported that they ran. It is

48

Gramática Apasionada
Reminiscences of a Love Affair with the Spanish Language

the beginning aspect of running but that is the point. They 'started running' for the exits.

10. Middle - This is a description of what the doors could do or were capable of doing. The beginning or end of this capability is irrelevant to the story.

11. End - They made a decision, they changed their tactics. Conclusion is implied - end aspect.

12. Beginning - How did they react to the barrage of thrown objects? They started running in different directions - the beginning aspect of scattering.

13. Middle - The screen was there, in the middle of its existence.

14. End - If the statement had been, "It stopped," end aspect or conclusion would be obvious. The negative statement also focuses on conclusion but the opposite one - it did not stop.

15. End - I stayed put, I made the decision not to move. That is what I did - end aspect

16. Middle - This is how it used to be in that town. There is no reference to when it started or stopped being that way.

17. Middle - It 'was being' impossible to hear. That was one of the conditions prevailing or in progress at the time.

18. Middle - The theater was already on the corner as our story began and it was still on the corner (in spite of everything) when the story ended - so this is middle aspect of its being on the corner.

19. Beginning - As soon as the soldiers came into my view I saw or started seeing them. I went on seeing them for some time. But the critical information is the beginning point of seeing them - from then on I knew they were there.

20. Beginning - The focus again is on the beginning aspect of being scared. I went on being scared until the movie ended and I was able to walk out of range of those frightening looking weapons. But the story focuses on the moment when I started being scared.

You Will Have Two Pasts in Your Future

Reaching a point where he or she can make preterit/imperfect choices quickly and with a reasonably high degree of accuracy *and* then conjugate the verb correctly is one of the epoch-defining moments for a Spanish student. Like the child who has learned to ride a bicycle, the Spanish learner enters a new phase in his or her linguistic life - he or she is at a new level, more confident and much more convincing as a speaker. But unlike the child who struggles and falls and then in one magic moment rides away, mastery of the preterit and imperfect will come gradually without that sharply defined instant of triumph. But a realization will settle into the student's mind one day that he or she is using the past tenses comfortably. No longer is past speech a tiring series of high hurdles. The ground is being covered in fairly smooth strides.

Remember, paciencia y persistencia.

As was just mentioned, there are two steps involved in speaking in the past. First the student must choose the proper tense for the context, then the verb must be conjugated.

Having talked about the first part of the problem in the preceding pages let us move along to the second part of the process. The next chapter will present the conjugation of the preterit and imperfect past tenses.

Gramática Apasionada
Reminiscences of a Love Affair with the Spanish Language

Chapter Six

Achieving Conjugational Bliss

The conjugation of the two past tenses in Spanish, the preterit and the imperfect, offers an interesting contrast between the simple and the convoluted. It is as though the gods of the verb, having seen the misery caused by their preterit, have taken pity on us, poor mortals that we are. Their Olympian atonement takes the form of the imperfect tense.

The imperfect is about as near to a language student's dream of an ideal tense as is likely to be found in any language. Of course perfection would be No Irregular Verbs. The imperfect has three. Other than those three one simply learns the stem and the endings, no exceptions, no stem changes, no spelling changes, no spitballs, sinkers or curves.

The Imperfect Past Tense

```
        -AR Verbs                          -ER, -IR Verbs
Stem of the   +   -aba   -ábamos    Stem of the   +   -ía  -íamos
Infinitive        -abas  -aban      Infinitive        -ías -ían
                  -aba   -aban                        -ía  -ían

                    The three irregular verbs are:
       Ser                    Ir                      Ver
era      éramos        iba     íbamos         veía     veíamos
eras     eran          ibas    iban           veías    veían
era      eran          iba     iban           veía     veían
```

If there is one stumbling block to mastering these conjugations it would be getting the stress right, particularly in the first person plural. But this is simply the accent pattern of the imperfect tenses - you will encounter it again in the imperfect subjunctive. It is consistent, unvarying, throughout the tense. Practice this accent pattern by reading the following conjugations out loud. The syllable carrying the stress is highlighted by use of the upper case. *Pay special attention to the nosotros form.*

```
       Dar                              Estar
DA-ba    DA-ba-mos              es-TA-ba    es-TA-ba-mos
DA-bas   DA-ban                 es-TA-bas   es-TA-ban
DA-ba    DA-ban                 es-TA-ba    es-TA-ban
```

daba	dábamos	estaba	estábamos
dabas	daban	estabas	estaban
daba	daban	estaba	estaban

Caminar

ca-mi-NA-ba   ca-mi-NA-ba-mos
ca-mi-NA-bas   ca-mi-NA-ban
ca-mi-NA-ba   ca-mi-NA-ban

caminaba   caminábamos
caminabas   caminaban
caminaba   caminaban

Creer		Escribir	
cre-I-a	cre-I-a-mos	es-cri-BI-a	es-cri-BI-a-mos
cre-I-as	cre-I-an	es-cri-BI-as	es-cri-BI-an
cre-I-a	cre-I-an	es-cri-BI-a	es-cri-BI-an
creía	creíamos	escribía	escribíamos
creías	creían	escribías	escribían
creía	creían	escribía	escribían

Aprender

a-pren-DI-a   a-pren-DI-a-mos
a-pren-DI-as   a-pren-DI-an
a-pren-DI-a   a-pren-DI-an

aprendía   aprendíamos
aprendías   aprendían
aprendía   aprendían

Substitute other two and three syllable verbs and conjugate them using the patterns above to guide you. Four and five syllable verbs follow the same patterns. You just keep building the unstressed syllables out in front of everything, for example, <u>anochecer</u>: a-no-che-CI-a, a-no-che-CI-as, a-no-che-CI-a, etc.

The Preterit Tense

In contrast to the beautiful simplicity of the imperfect tense conjugations the preterit may at first glance seem a bewildering <u>trochemoche</u> (mishmash) of irregular shapes and forms, especially when spelling changes (which have no effect on the spoken language), stem changes (which minimally effect a small number of verbs), and a few other idiosyncrasies of the preterit tense are force fed to the student right along with the regular verb conjugations. The idea gets planted in the student's head that the preterit is a hopeless morass of irregularities, a conjugational swamp with no way out. That is a very unfortunate image to create in the learner's mind. If you want to assist a child to learn to crawl you do not put bricks and broken glass in her path, you clear the way as much as is possible. We shall now clear the way for the preterit tense. Probably 95 per cent (más o menos) of all the verbs in the Spanish language are regular verbs in the preterit tense. They are conjugated as follows:

REGULAR VERBS

-AR verbs			-ER,-IR verbs		
Stem of the	+ -é	-amos	Stem of the	+ -í	-imos
Infinitive	-aste	-aron	Infinitive	-iste	-ieron
	-ó	-aron		-ió	-ieron

As always, putting the stress on the right syllable is very important. Read the following conjugations out loud so as to hear and feel the accent pattern. Substitute other verbs and repeat the process.

Hablar		Trabajar	
ha-BLE	ha-BLA-mos	tra-ba-JE	tra-ba-JA-mos
ha-BLAS-te	ha-BLA-ron	tra-ba-JAS-te	tra-ba-JA-ron
ha-BLO	ha-BLA-ron	tra-ba-JO	tra-ba-JA-ron
hablé	hablamos	trabajé	trabajamos
hablaste	hablaron	trabajaste	trabajaron
habló	hablaron	trabajó	trabajaron

Facilitar
fa-ci-li-TE   fa-ci-li-TA-mos
fa-ci-li-TAS-te fa-ci-li-TA-ron
fa-ci-li-TO   fa-ci-li-TA-ron

facilité   facilitamos
facilitaste facilitaron
facilitó   facilitaron

Comer		Escribir	
co-MI	co-MI-mos	es-cri-BI	es-cri-BI-mos
co-MIS-te	co-miER-on	es-cri-BIS-te	es-cri-biER-on
co-miO	co-miER-on	es-cri-biO	es-cri-biER-on
comí	comimos	escribí	escribimos
comiste	comieron	escribiste	escribieron
comió	comieron	escribió	escribieron

Permanecer

per-ma-ne-CI	per-ma-ne-CI-mos
per-ma-ne-CIS-te	per-ma-ne-ciER-on
per-ma-ne-ciO	per-ma-ne-ciER-on
permanecí	permanecimos
permaneciste	permanecieron
permaneció	permanecieron

You may have observed that there appears to be no difference between the present indicative and the preterit of the <u>nosotros</u> form of the verb in the first (-AR) and third (-IR) conjugations. If you did, reach around (careful not to pull a muscle or pop your shoulder out) and give yourself a pat on the back. There is no difference.

The question then arises, how can one tell whether <u>hablamos</u> means 'we speak' or 'we spoke' or whether <u>vivimos</u> means 'we live' or 'we lived?' The answer, context, may not satisfy the struggling intermediate student. But context really is sufficient to make a clear distinction between the present and the past.

Two questions: Are there any verbs in English that are the same in both the present and the past? Can you name one? If you answered "no" to the first question, you are mistaken. If you said "no" to the second question it is because you have never noticed this sameness - there being no difference between the present and the past has caused you no confusion. Context has always made the time reference obvious. The sameness has been invisible to you.

There is a group of these verbs in English. I have my children to thank for expanding my list of them. As they were learning to talk they pointed several of them out to me. Playing in the yard, "Daddy, I hitted the ball!" And I would say, "That's great, sweetheart!" and be thinking, "Add 'hit' to the list of verbs that are the same in both the present and the past." (Just as the child created a past tense distinct from the present, many very good Spanish students have invented the preterit ending <u>-emos</u> to create a difference that their linguistic common sense insists ought to exist. <u>Hablamos</u>, 'we speak;' <u>hablemos</u>, 'we spoke.')

To finish the thought about English, all the verbs that I have stumbled upon that have no present/past distinction (except in the third person singular, of course) are one syllable verbs that end with 'd' or 't': to put, to set, to bid, to rid, to slit, to cost, etc. However, we cannot generalize from this. There are other one syllable verbs ending in 'd' or 't' that do have a separate past form, 'to get' and 'to find', just to illustrate the point.

Returning to the task of mastering the conjugation of the Spanish preterit tense, we have seen how almost all the verbs are conjugated. They are handled in two groups, as they are in most of the tenses in Spanish, -AR verbs one way, -ER and -IR verbs another way. To these two groups we must add a third group. Most of the grammar books that I have seen treat the verbs in this third group as though they were separate Acts of God, inflicted upon a trembling humankind like flood, fire, and famine. In reality, they share common characteristics and should be dealt with as one additional group. These are the verbs that have an irregular stem (which must be learned - we eschew the M-word, 'memorized') and share a common set of endings different from the regular endings shown above. Let us refer to this group of verbs as the 'regular' irregular verbs. Presently we will have to face up to the 'irregular' irregular verbs (three in all).

These regular irregulars form a small group of verbs, but because many of them are among the most basic verbs and are frequently used their prevalence is greatly magnified in the student's mind.

REGULAR IRREGULAR VERBS

Verb	Irregular Stem	+	Endings, -AR,-ER,-IR	
Tener	Tuv-		-e	-imos
Poner	Pus-		-iste	-ieron *(-eron)
Venir	Vin-		-o	-ieron *(-eron)
Hacer	Hic(z)-			
Estar	Estuv-			
Poder	Pud-			
Decir	Dij-*			
Querer	Quis-			
Saber	Sup-			
Traducir	Traduj-*			
Andar	Anduv-			
Haber	Hub-			
Traer	Traj-*			
Caber	Cup-			

There are a number of compound verbs created by adding prefixes to <u>tener</u>, <u>poner</u>, <u>traer</u>, and <u>decir</u>. All of these verbs share the irregular characteristics of the base verb. Also there are a few verbs ending <u>-ucir</u> which share the irregular characteristics of <u>traducir</u> (except, <u>lucir</u>).

Please note that the endings for the first and third persons singular in this group of verbs are unstressed. Read the following conjugations out loud to get the feel of this group of verbs.

<u>Tener</u>
TU-ve   tu-VI-mos
tu-VIS-te   tu-viER-on
TU-vo   tu-viER-on

<u>Venir</u>
VI-ne   vi-NI-mos
vi-NIS-te   vi-niER-on
VI-no   vi-niER-on

tuve	tuvimos	vine	viniste
tuviste	tuvieron	viniste	vinieron
tuvo	tuvieron	vino	vinieron

Decir		Estar	
DI-je	di-JI-mos	es-TU-ve	es-tu-VI-mos
di-JIS-te	di-JER-on	es-tu-VIS-te	es-tu-viER-on
DI-jo	di-JER-on	es-TU-vo	es-tu-viER-on
dije	dijimos	estuve	estuvimos
dijiste	dijeron	estuviste	estuvieron
dijo	dijeron	estuvo	estuvieron

The verbs that use the alternate ending (-eron) for the second and third persons plural all have an irregular stem that ends with the letter 'j.' The elimination of the 'i' in these cases demonstrates the practical nature of the human voice mechanism. Leave the 'i' in the ending and there would be a sequence of four aspirated sounds, three vowels and 'j' - (-ijie-) - which includes the stressed syllable demanding even more air. The form <u>dijieron</u> all but empties the lungs - the speaker must take a breath before continuing his sentence. Eliminating the 'i' of the ending greatly reduces the amount of air that must be pushed up out of the lungs to say the word - <u>dijeron</u> - the flow of speech goes on without any need to gasp for air.

With the three groups of verbs presented above — regular - AR verbs, regular -ER and -IR verbs, and the regular irregular -AR, -ER and -IR verbs — we have taken care of all but three verbs in the Spanish language. So now let us look at the irregular irregular verbs.

We will begin with some good news. You get two irregular irregular verbs for the price of one. <u>Ser</u> and <u>ir</u> share a conjugation in the preterit tense.

fui	fuimos
fuiste	fueron
fue	fueron

Again we have the question, how does one know whether <u>él fue</u> means 'he went' or 'he was'? Again the answer - context will make the meaning clear.

<u>El revolucionario mexicano, Emiliano Zapata, **fue** un gran líder y un verdadero hombre del pueblo. En abril, 1919, **fue** a la hacienda Chinameca para negociar bajo una bandera de tregua. Pero **fue** una trampa y lo fusilaron.</u>

The Mexican revolutionary, Emiliano Zapata, **was** a great leader and a true man of his people. In April, 1919, he **went** to the Chinameca hacienda to negotiate under a flag of truce. But it **was** a trap and he was gunned down.

One more sadness in the long, tragic history of a resilient and sometimes exuberant people.

We have one verb left to deal with, one more irregular irregular verb. <u>Dar</u> is an -AR verb but, for reasons known only to the Supreme Conjugator in the Sky, it borrows the endings for the -ER and -IR verbs in the preterit. Thus we get:

di	dimos
diste	dieron
dio	dieron

The chart below sums up what we know about the conjugation of the preterit tense

Conjugation of the Preterit Tense

REGULAR VERBS

-AR verbs			-ER,-IR verbs		
Stem of the Infinitive	+	-é -aste -ó	-amos -aron -aron	Stem of the Infinitive	+	-í -iste -ió	-imos -ieron -ieron

REGULAR IRREGULAR VERBS

Verb	Irregular Stem	+	Endings for -AR,-ER,-IR Verbs
Tener	Tuv-		-e -imos
Venir	Vin-		-iste -ieron (*-eron)
Poner	Pus-		-o -ieron (*-eron)
Decir	Dij-*		
Estar	Estuv-		
Poder	Pud-		
Hacer	Hic(z)-		
Traducir	Traduj-*		
Andar	Anduv-		
Querer	Quis-		
Saber	Sup-		
Traer	Traj-*		
Haber	Hub-		
Caber	Cup-		

IRREGULAR IRREGULAR VERBS

<u>Ser</u> and <u>Ir</u>		<u>Dar</u>
fui	fuimos	(Uses -ER,-IR endings)
fuiste	fueron	
fue	fueron	

James K. Gavin

If you are less than a strong intermediate level student I suggest that you stop here. This is all you really need to know about the conjugation of the preterit tense *for now*. Go back and spend some time studying the uses of ser and estar or, if it is a nice day, take a walk.

****

There are two more preterit phenomena that we must look at to complete our study of this conjugation. One, stem changes, affects the spoken language. The other, spelling changes, comes into play in reading or writing the language.

Stem Changes in the Preterit

When we looked at stem changing verbs in the present tense it was pointed out that there is no way for the student to tell whether or not a verb has a stem change simply by looking at the infinitive. It gives no clue. One learns them as they come along - but a book or a friend must identify them for you.

I have some good and some bad news for you. First the good news: verbs that have a stem change in the preterit are in one easily defined group. The bad news is that you must know the verb's present tense stem changing status to make that identification.

The verbs that make up the stem changing group in the preterit tense are the third conjugation (-IR) verbs that have a stem change in the present tense. From this group we must except venir and decir. They fit the definition but they are among the regular irregular verbs and are conjugated accordingly.

In the present there are three kinds of stem change (plus one maverick) and the change occurs in all the grammatical persons except nosotros. In the preterit there are just two types of stem change and they show up in the third person singular and the second and third persons plural.

One of the preterit stem changes is 'o' to 'u.' There are only two verbs in the language that have it. Thus:

Dormir		Morir	
dormí	dormimos	morí	morimos
dormiste	durmieron	moriste	murieron
durmió	durmieron	murió	murieron

The other stem change is 'e' to 'i.' There are a number of verbs where this happens. For example:

Pedir		Sentir	
pedí	pedimos	sentí	sentimos
pediste	pidieron	sentiste	sintieron
pidió	pidieron	sintió	sintieron

Some other verbs in this group are: seguir, repetir, sugerir, corregir, mentir, divertirse, medir.

Spelling Changes in the Preterit

Like the well-mannered children found in some 19th century British fiction (and few other places), spelling changes are seen and not heard. That is precisely their purpose. Spelling changes occur so that you will not hear a change in the sound of the root or stem of a verb. It is the stem of a verb that carries the meaning of the verb. The ending tells us time and person but it is the stem that tells us what the subject is doing. For example, in the verb form hablas (you speak), habl- tells us 'speak' and -as tells us that it is the second person singular speaking in the present tense; in hablaste (you spoke) habl- again tells us the action is 'speak' and the -aste indicates second person singular in the past. Therefore it is important that the sound of the root or stem remain constant so that meaning remains constant and clear. In the case of hablar that it not a problem, the stem habl- stays constant throughout its many conjugations.

But take by way of example the verb tocar (to touch or to play a musical instrument). If I wish to say, "He played the piano," there is no problem, él tocó el piano. But if I want to say, "I played the piano," (yo tocé) I do have a problem.

There is a problem because the Spanish letter 'c' has two values. It sounds [k] when followed by 'a,' 'o,' or 'u;' but it sounds [s] when followed by 'e' or 'i.' Therefore tocé is pronounced [toe-SAY]. The [k] sound, which is characteristic of the stem of the verb toc- [tohk-] and which carries the meaning of the verb, has been lost. This must not happen. So the spelling of this particular verb form is altered in order to preserve the sound [tohk-], yo toqué el piano. This same problem will occur in the preterit with any -AR verb whose stem ends with the letter 'c' (there will be no problem with -ER and -IR verbs because all the preterit endings for these verbs start with 'i' and the pronounciation of the 'c' is not challenged). So we may generalize and state our first preterit spelling change rule:

First conjugation (-AR) verbs whose infinitive stem ends with the letter 'c' will change that 'c' to 'qu' in the first person singular of the preterit tense.

Other examples: sacar, yo saqué; and buscar, yo busqué.

The Spanish 'g' also has two values. Like 'c' it pronounces one way when followed by 'a,' 'o,' or 'u' - in these instances it is the hard 'g' of English 'go' - and another way when followed by 'e' or 'i' - in these cases it sounds like English [h]. So we again run into a problem in the yo form of the preterit of -AR verbs. Llegar, for example, would be yo llegé which pronounces [yo yeh-HAY]. We lose the hard 'g' characteristic of the stem of the verb. We avoid this catastrophe by inserting a 'u' after the final 'g' of the stem. This 'u' does not sound. In a sense it is not a letter when used this way. Think of it rather as being a red flag being stuck onto the 'g' which warns us that in this particular case the 'g' must be pronounced as a hard 'g' even though the next letter is 'e' - thus we get llegué which is spoken [yeh-GAY] - hard 'g,' meaning of verb intact, day saved!

First conjugation verbs whose infinitive stem ends with the letter 'g' will take a silent 'u' after that final 'g' in the first person singular of the preterit tense.

Other examples: jugar, yo jugué; and pagar, yo pagué.

Incidentally, before proceeding, you might want to know that these spelling changes are not confined to the preterit tense. They occur extensively, and for exactly the same reasons, in the present subjunctive and imperative. Relatively rare, but not non-existent, are spelling changes in the present indicative. The imperfect past, bless it's heart, has none.

In Chapter 18 there is a discussion of the pronunciation of the Spanish 'z'. For reasons set forth in that chapter there is a spelling change required in -AR verbs whose infinitive stem ends with the letter 'z.'

First conjugation verbs whose infinitive stem ends with the letter 'z' will change that 'z' to 'c' in the first person singular of the preterit tense.

Examples: empezar, yo empecé; tropezar, yo tropecé.

Up to this point all the spelling changes have occurred exclusively in -AR verbs. This is because only the first conjugation set of preterit endings mixes vowels from the two groups (a, o, u) and (e, i) which govern changes in the pronunciation of the consonants 'c' and 'g.'.

But some second (-ER) and third (-IR) conjugation verbs also have spelling changes for a different linguistic reason.

Spanish does not like to present the speaker with the challenge of pronouncing three vowels in a row unless the middle vowel of that sequence is carrying the stress - creía or traía, for example. But if the stem of a second or third conjugation verb ends with a vowel we will be faced with a three vowel sequence in which the stress falls on the last of the three vowels when we need to use the preterit endings -ió and -ieron. For example: caer, infinitive stem ca-, would give us caió for the past 'he fell;' or, with oír, heaven help us!, oió for 'she heard.'

In instances such as these the human voice automatically evades this three-vowel difficulty by sliding toward 'y' when pronouncing the middle 'i' of the sequence. Spanish recognizes this natural tendency of the voice and has formalized it.

Second and third conjugation verbs whose infinitive stem ends with a vowel use the alternate ending -yó for the third person singular and -yeron for the second and third persons plural.[18]

<u>Caer</u>
caí   caímos
caíste   cayeron
cayó   cayeron

<u>Creer</u>
creí   creímos
creíste creyeron
creyó   creyeron

<u>Oír</u>
oí   oímos
oíste   oyeron
oyó   oyeron

In a linguistically similar vein there are a few second and third conjugation verbs whose infinitive stem ends with the letters <u>ll</u> or <u>ñ</u>. Because the last sound of these stems is [y] they combine awkwardly with the preterit endings -ió and -ieron. For this reason the 'i' of these endings is dropped. The verbs that fall into this category are not among the first one hundred verbs that the student will want to learn or is likely to run into. But to illustrate the point look at the conjugation of the verb <u>reñir</u>, (to scold, to quarrel) which also happens to have a stem change.

reñí   reñimos
reñiste   ri**ñeron**
riñó   ri**ñeron**

The initial vowels of the set of endings used for all the verbs in the regular irregular group are drawn from the two vowel groups (a,o,u) and (e,i). This creates the potential for the necessity of spelling changes. As it turns out only one verb in this group is so affected.

Refer back to conjugation of the regular irregular verbs. The preterit of <u>hacer</u> goes: <u>hice</u> [EE-say], <u>hiciste</u> [ee-SEES-tay], then comes the problem. If we write the third person singular <u>hico</u> which is pronounced [EE-koo] we lose the sound [ees] which is the sound of the irregular preterit stem of <u>hacer</u>; <u>hic-</u>, [ees]. So the spelling is altered, <u>hizo</u>, [EE-soo] thus maintaining the sound characteristic of the stem of <u>hacer</u> in the preterit.

hice   hicimos
hiciste hicieron
hizo   hicieron

Let's end with a pair of mavericks that I hope are or will be among the first one hundred verbs you need to know - <u>reír</u> (to laugh) and its silent partner <u>sonreír</u> (to smile). These are stem changing verbs in the present tense and, therefore, as -IR verbs they also have a preterit stem change. This would make the preterit conjugation: <u>reí, reíste, riió</u>! Double 'i' is about

---

[18]Please note that although <u>traer</u> fits the definition of verbs that use these alternative endings, it is one of the verbs listed among the regular irregular verbs and it is conjugated accordingly

James K. Gavin

as common a linguistic occurrence as double 'w' (quadruple 'u'?).[19] Linguistic common sense would suggest dropping one of the 'i's. That is exactly what was done.

reí	reímos	sonreí	sonreímos
reíste	rieron	sonreíste	sonrieron
rio	rieron	sonrió	sonrieron

---

[19]The biggest political party in Mexico, the oxymoronically named Partido de Revolución Institucional, is commonly referred to as el PRI. Its members and followers are called priistas creating a rare double 'i.'

Chapter Seven

All About Me, Thee, and Your Grace

"Doña...María, ...usted...sabe...que...yo...te...amo."

This declaration of love, spoken haltingly but with obvious sincerity, presents us with an apparent inconsistency. The speaker has begun the sentence referring to the object of his affection with the formal pronoun usted. Midway through the sentence he refers to the same person using the familiar te as the direct object pronoun. But do not jump to the same hasty conclusion that I did. The sentence turns out, in context, to be grammatically correct.

The speaker was a young man who had just completed a three-month Peace Corps training program. The woman who had captured his heart was a motherly, gray-haired Spanish teacher. In the market place of her Andean mountain home she would have been of unremarkable appearance. But mingling with a group of young Americans on this warm southern California evening she appeared distinctly short and stocky. I was present as el evaluador, having just spent two intense days conducting individual interviews in Spanish with about sixty volunteers-in-training for the purpose of determining their levels of language proficiency.

The three of us were chatting together at an end-of-program party. Soon the members of the group would be dispatched to locations scattered throughout Peru.

It was early in the evening. After two long, hard days of work I had not yet had time to shift from teaching mode into the fiesta spirit. I pointed out the flaw in the young man's otherwise beautifully crafted sentence.

"Oh no," he assured me, "there is no inconsistency in that sentence. As both you and doña María know, speaking Spanish is a real struggle for me. It took me so long to get that whole sentence out that by the time I got to the end of it I felt that I had known doña María long enough to switch to the tú form!"

In Spanish there are two pronouns meaning 'you' whereas in English we just have one. That volunteer's quick-witted and delightful response tells you the most basic fact you need to know about when to use the formal 'you,' usted, and when to use the familiar 'you,' tú.

The existence of these two pronouns where English has only one presents the Spanish student with what may seem like one more problem that he or she just did not need - when to use tú and when to use usted. However, the problem is not quite as foreign as it may at first appear. Even though English does not provide us with two distinct pronouns we

English-speakers do have to make similar distinctions between familiar and formal ways of addressing the people with whom we are in contact socially, professionally and casually. But the English-speaker has ways to evade the question of whether to use formal or familiar address. In Spanish it is all up front, built into the language. There is no place to hide. So it would be misleading to dismiss the whole issue with a breezy "hakuna matata."[20]

These are the basic guidelines for the use of tú and usted:

1. use the formal usted with other adults that you have just met or do not know well;

2. use the familiar tú with adults with whom you have an established relationship of some duration;

3. use the tú form with all children or when speaking to animals.

Those are the rules. To them I would add a fourth: whenever in doubt use usted. The rules raise many more questions than they answer. And the whole issue is further complicated by the fact that the choice of familiar or formal address is very much influenced as well by social class, status within the group, and individual personality.

English used to have this familiar/formal distinction. But we have long since all but totally abandoned the familiar 'thou' and its plural 'ye' ("Oh come, all ye faithful!") for the formal 'you.' In modern English the familiar form has been limited almost exclusively to poetic and religious uses. For example, the familiar 'thou' had passed from common usage centuries before Elizabeth Barrett Browning wrote, "How do I love **thee**? Let me count the ways." And among Christians the deity is addressed in the familiar in both English and Spanish. God is the Father. He is family. Perhaps the best-known prayer in Christendom begins, "Our Father who **art** in heaven, hallowed be **thy** name." In Spanish, "Padre Nuestro que **estás** en el cielo, santificado sea **tu** nombre." Likewise, the Father speaks to his children using the familiar form of address, "**Thou shalt** not kill!" Traditional Quaker communities continue to address each other as 'thou' to demonstrate the equality of all church members before God.

The English-speaker does have to make a similar choice when deciding whether to call the man standing before him or her "Mr. Brown" or "Robert" or even "Bob." And earlier in our Mr. Brown's life there was a time when people had to decide when to stop calling him "Bobby" and upgrade his maturing status to "Bob" or "Robert." However, when we find ourselves in that gray area of uncertainty, (do I call him Mr. Brown or Bob?), the English-speaker can usually finesse the potentially awkward choice by making eye contact and using the all-inclusive 'you.' Spanish offers no such refuge for the indecisive. Every relationship

---

[20]For the reader who may not have a child obsessed with the Disney film "The Lion King," the phrase means "be happy, don't worry." The author admits ignorance as to origin, the phrase may be authentic African speech or, perhaps, Disney-ese.

requires that a choice be made and declared. So it behooves us to pursue a fuller understanding of this topic.

The question of whether to use formal or familiar address is all but a none-issue if you are just going to be a tourist in Mexico or Spain for a week. It is unlikely, in that short time, that you would use anything but the formal usted in your dealings with hotel personnel, store clerks, or the friendly stranger with whom you might engage in casual conversation in a restaurant or while seated together on a bus.

On the other hand, if you do strike up a friendship with someone of approximately your age and sex (not approximately, exactly the same) you might take your cue from him or her. If this new friend switches over to the tú form it is appropriate for you to do the same. If your new friend is of the opposite sex, however, the guidelines are somewhat different. If this newfound friend starts using the tú form you might ask yourself the following question, do I wish to speed up or slow down this process of familiarization? You can still be perfectly friendly while continuing to use the formal usted, but you are sending the message that you do not want to get too familiar too fast. Questions about tú and usted definitely overlap into the area of relationships across the gender gap.

If you are in a situation where you will have long-term Spanish-speaking relationships there is really only one basic question. When (if ever) do I switch to the familiar form of address? There are many factors to consider.

In the camaraderie of young adulthood tú usually comes quickly, easily and naturally, sometimes without there ever having been an usted phase or one of very short duration. In the workplace the reign of formality is more established. The cultural newcomer is advised to observe carefully the use of tú and usted around him or her. When in Caracas do as the caraqueños do. Co-workers of similar rank and age might switch to the tú form more quickly among themselves than they would with a co-worker whom they saw as being of their parents' generation. The fact that the boss or a supervisor at some point starts addressing you as tú is not an automatic invitation for you to reciprocate. In this situation it might be wise to invoke the "when in doubt" addendum to the guidelines listed above.

In my interpersonal relationships I will switch from usted to tú more quickly with men than with woman, and also more quickly with people of my own age or younger than with those whom I view as my elders. This has, in a couple of instances, led a Spanish-speaking friend to say to me, "Jaime, vamos a tutear." (Jim, let's use the tú form.) To which I am happy to reply, "Yes, of course." As you will have observed, there is a verb, tutear, which means 'to use the familiar form of address.' So there is this potential backlash to the "when in doubt" addendum. If you go on using formal address too long you run the risk of beginning to seem aloof.

There is no verb ustedear. But I did just that anyway one time. I deliberately went on using the usted form to keep a colleague at arm's length. We had been put together to work on a project. Very soon it became apparent to me that there was a basic philosophical difference between us about our goals that would eventually lead to serious conflict. My co-worker was personable, a very likeable man. But to have used the tú form with him (as he did with me) would have been deceitful on my part. I knew that I had no intention of putting friendship ahead of purpose when the inevitable dispute finally came to pass.

When one is in any part of the Spanish-speaking world it is always interesting and instructive to observe who uses which form with whom (and how 'whom' responds). For a situation that is simply a matter of choosing A or choosing B there seem to be an astoundingly large number of possibilities and variations.

For a few years I was making frequent trips to Puerto Rico. It was business. I was always nicely dressed, not to be taken for some beach bum or hippie. Upon leaving the airport terminal to get a taxi the driver would almost invariably ask, "¿Adónde tú quieres ir?" And not just, "¿Adónde quieres ir?" omitting the pronoun but really throwing that tú right in my face. The tone of voice was neither hostile nor unfriendly, but a statement of some sort was certainly being made. I would always respond using usted - applying rule number one reinforced by the "when in doubt" addendum. So there we would be in a complete reversal of normal roles – I, the patrón, the man with the money, giving the orders, addressing his 'employee' as usted and the underling respectfully doing as he was told but tuteando the 'boss.'

My 15 cent socio-political explanation for this is that after a century, first as a territory and then as a commonwealth of the United States, democracy has crept into Puerto Rican Spanish. But this all took place in a very specific context. Please do not come to the false conclusion that Puerto Ricans have abandoned the use of usted. Such is not the case. This was sunny San Juan, not Jacobin Paris. During that most radical phase of the French Revolution it became politically incorrect to address anybody using the formal vouz. In that brave new world of fraternité, égalité, and liberté, everybody was tú.

There was one particularly memorable taxi ride through San Juan's overflowing streets. We honked and swerved and lurched along, contributing our fair portion of frenzy to the communal effort required to maintain the proper level of that quality in the city's traffic. The driver was openly drinking from a bottle of rum on the seat beside him.

But that was all right. He explained, "El jefe me dice que en este trabajo es muy importante ser amable. Por eso, cada día, yo tomo un litro de amabilidad."

Just following the boss' orders.

In another departure from the norm I have known married couples who addressed each other as usted. This use of the formal where one would certainly expect to find familiarity did not suggest coldness or distance. Quite the contrary, it seemed to say to the spouse and announce to the world at large, "I hold you in a special category, apart from all others." Perhaps these couples revert to tú in private moments together.

It is not out of the range of possibilities for one person to address another as both tú and usted. If you had a friend who was a teacher or a judge, for example, you might very well address him or her as usted in the classroom or courtroom and as tú when he or she came by the house for a beer.

Given that usted is formal and respectful address, is it then possible to use the tú form when there is deliberate intent to be disrespectful or insulting? The answer is yes. But it seems to be an option that is seldom exercised. Tú and usted are not just linguistic variants of 'you.' They symbolize a system of societal ranking and organization that is deeply imbedded in the psyche of the peoples of Latin America and Spain. Every individual knows which is his or her rung on the social ladder and that in turn plays a large part in determining who will be tú and who will be usted.

I worked for two years with young people in Venezuela. Imposing discipline was part of my job. I fell into disfavor with more than one youngster on more than one occasion. I was called some very unflattering things to my face. But never did a child or teenager call me tú. I was 'teacher.' I was 'usted.'

An anthropologist friend who has worked and traveled extensively in El Salvador told me that during that country's recent Civil War the infamous death squads always used the tú form when they sent threats and warnings to those that they considered their enemy. That added a chillingly special touch to a message whose mere receipt would have constituted a terrifying experience.

As was mentioned above, individual personality can play a big part in determining the use of tú and usted as well. There is a type of person (in my experience it has always been a man) who is ebullient and friendly and seems not to be aware that the usted form exists. He usually gets very familiar in the physical sense also. He slaps men on the back and drapes his arm on a woman's shoulder as he talks to her. The enthusiasm and extroversion are infectious. Rarely do people find this behavior offensive if it is genuine. At the other extreme there are people who present such a regal facade to the world that you would expect to be clapped into irons and thrown in a dungeon if you ever slipped up and sent a tú in their direction. (It would be interesting to observe a meeting between one of the former and one of the latter).

In a culture[21] that places such importance on these distinctions between formality and familiarity it should not be surprising to learn that there are other gradations of which we have not yet spoken. Costa Ricans have added a third level to the standard formal usted and familiar tú. The second person singular vos, which derives from the second person plural familiar vosotros, is used with the closest circle of family and friends. Vos even has a

---

[21]By virtue of its centuries-long ties to Spain and the Catholic Church there is a very broad commonality that can be called Latin American culture. But within that sweeping definition there is a marvelous diversity of ethnicity, language, history and culture. One of the great benefits of learning to speak Spanish is the access it gives to this fabulous richness of peoples.

separate present tense conjugation - vos hablás, vos comés, vos vivís - although it shares the conjugated forms of tú in all the other tenses. Much of Argentina and Uruguay also use vos, but I am told that vos has supplanted tú rather than adding another layer.

In general use throughout Latin America and Spain are the titles of respect don and doña, which are used in conjunction with a person's first name - don Miguel, doña Teresa. These titles, which are purely meritorious, can be conferred upon any person who deserves respect. They offer a very satisfactory choice in between 'Mr. Brown' and 'Bob.' Don Roberto allows one to move to a first name basis while retaining a certain level of formality. I especially like this form for addressing older people of whom I am fond but whom I would be uncomfortable addressing as tú. The English language would be enhanced by the addition of a similar title of respect.

****

These, then, are the possibilities for direct address in Spanish, all of which would translate as 'you' in English:

Singular	Plural
vos	vosotros
tú	ustedes
usted	

Vos, which is used only in a few specific regions, and tú, which is in use throughout the Spanish-speaking world, are singular and familiar. Usted is the formal 'you' (singular). Vosotros is the familiar 'you' (plural), but it is used only in Spain. The plural 'you' in all cases, both familiar and formal, in Spanish-speaking America is ustedes.

The formal pronoun usted is a reduction of the phrase vuestra merced which means 'your grace.' Spanish, which is not a language given to abbreviations and contractions, further reduces usted in its written form to ud. or Vd. and in the plural to uds. or Vds. The use of these abbreviations is optional. Please note the upper case 'V' if you choose that form.

Although it is common practice to omit the subject pronouns when speaking Spanish, such is not the case with usted. First, as usted is a courteous form its inclusion is a courtesy. Second, although in actual speech usted and ustedes are second person, i.e. the person or persons being spoken directly to, in all grammatical respects they are third person. That is to say that they call for the third person forms of the direct and indirect object pronouns, the third person reflexive pronoun, the third person possessive forms, *and* the usted and ustedes forms of the verb always are conjugated as third person singular and plural respectively - all verbs, all tenses. Therefore the likelihood of ambiguity or confusion is greatly reduced if the spoken subject usted or ustedes is included with its third person verb form.

This third person usage in direct address does have a parallel in English. It is not often heard because most of us do not know many people whom we address as 'your grace.' However, as chance would have it, Queen Elizabeth II dropped by my house unexpectedly

Gramática Apasionada
Reminiscences of a Love Affair with the Spanish Language

one day last year. I hastily switched off "Oprah," gathered up a week's worth of newspapers, shooed the cat off the best chair and invited Her Majesty to sit down. Hoping to put her at ease I asked, "Does Your Grace wish to have a spot of tea?" Then I turned to the man accompanying her, who was dressed just like the guy on the label of a bottle of Beefeater gin (he did leave his broadax or halberd or whatever it was at the door), and asked, "Do you want one too?"

Now, I am a linguistically perceptive person. While I was in the kitchen heating water and searching frantically for a teacup without a chip along its rim I had a startling revelation. It occurred to me that although I had been speaking directly to each of my unexpected guests I had changed the verb form when addressing Her Royal Highness. I did not ask, "**Do** Your Grace wish a spot of tea?" 'Do' is the second person form of the verb - I do, you **do**, he or she **does**. As inexperienced as I was at talking to a queen, I had *instinctively* used the third person form of the verb ('does') even though I was speaking directly to Her Grace. This extraordinary occurrence has led me to rethink the whole seemingly dead issue of the Divine Right of Kings.

It also led to two important realizations. First, American democrat though I be, I had resorted to grammatical léger-de-langue to diminish the audacity of an Oprah-watching slob like myself speaking directly to Her Imperial Majesty. This writer, a direct descendant of refugees from the Potato Famine, when speaking to the Queen of the persecutors of all of my great-grandparents had automatically used a third person verb form to deflect direct address thus sparing Her Highness the demeaning experience of seeming to be in communication with My Lowness. Not a proud moment for this great-grandson of the Old Sod - given another chance I would say, "Do Your Grace wish etc…?"

The second revelation has more relevance for this discussion of formal and familiar usages. I came to understand why usted and ustedes are always conjugated in the third person. It is a grammatical way of deflecting the presumption of familiarity. Just as a peasant might have kept his eyes downcast, avoiding eye contact, when speaking to the lord of the manor, the grammar itself deflects the directness of address by using third person forms.

Understanding the role of the familiar and formal modes of address is an integral part of learning to speak Spanish. But if the cultural newcomer mistakenly uses the tú form where the formal usted was called for or the other way around, it does not necessarily mean that banishment from genteel society must automatically follow. There is an international language whose major components are a smile, a courteous and respectful manner, and tolerance of other ways of seeing the world, that is 'spoken' and understood everywhere. When in use it overrides most linguistic deficiencies at a very basic level of human communication. And it nicely fills the vacuum created by the stranger's cultural ignorance. It is my belief that it is more important to speak this language well than either English or Spanish.

Chapter Eight

Jiffylex

The problem of building vocabulary is greatly simplified for the English-speaking person learning Spanish by the existence of a large numbers of cognate words. Cognate words are equivalent words in English and Spanish which evolved from a common root word in a parent language, e.g. 'theater' and teatro from the Latin theātrum. Said another way, an English word and its Spanish equivalent will often look alike (although they may sound quite different) because they both originated from the same parent word. And Latin is the primary source for English-Spanish cognates with Greek a distant second. The problem of learning these cognates is made even easier by the fact that there are large groups of words sharing some common characteristic that can be transposed from English to Spanish in a predictable way. Because large percentages of the vocabulary of both English and Spanish evolved from the same Latin root words there are established lexical relationships between certain English and Spanish words that can be learned and subsequently used to generate 'new' vocabulary. Absolutely no knowledge of Latin is required to do this.

To illustrate this process let us start with a large group of English nouns that end with the suffix '-ty'. Words like 'activity,' 'university,' and 'ability' can be turned into Spanish simply by replacing the English noun suffix '-ty' with the Spanish suffix -dad. Thus we get actividad, universidad, and habilidad. (Note the silent Spanish 'h' which plays no part in the English equivalent but which reappears in the related English word 'rehabilitation'). To demonstrate the rich vein of raw material lying right under your feet waiting to be mined there follows a list of 50 examples of this instant vocabulary. Read it over, study it, add to it.

austeridad	dificultad	identidad	personalidad	sobriedad
autoridad	dignidad	inmensidad	piedad	sociedad
babaridad	electricidad	integridad	posibilidad	solemnidad
brutalidad	eternidad	libertad	prosperidad	solidaridad
capacidad	facultad	majestad	publicidad	superioridad
caridad	familiaridad	moralidad	realidad	tranquilidad
comunidad	generalidad	nacionalidad	serenidad	unidad
complicidad	generosidad	necesidad	severidad	utilidad
curiosidad	hospitalidad	oportunidad	simplicidad	vanidad
densidad	humanidad	originalidad	sinceridad	variedad

All these words are nouns. They must have a gender designation in Spanish. Fortunately it is not necessary to learn them individually. All these -dad words are feminine. We may generalize even more - all Spanish nouns ending with the letter 'd' are feminine, e.g. la pared and la sed. There is a meager handful of exceptions to this rule, but none is an everyday word - perhaps the most common would be el ataúd, 'the coffin.' Huésped, 'guest,' will be masculine or feminine in accordance with the gender of the person visiting you.

As regards pronunciation it is important to remember that the letter combination 'dad' when spoken in Spanish bears little resemblance to the familiar way of addressing one's father in English. The Spanish is a much softer [dthahdth]. This sound is achieved by pushing the tongue forward against the back of the upper front teeth instead of hitting the roof of the mouth with the tongue as is done to make the English 'd.' With a bit of practice this 'unsoundly' Gringo speech trait can be eliminated. As -dad is the stressed syllable in all of these words it sounds particularly harsh to the Spanish ear if mispronounced.

A word of caution: from time to time this '-ty' to -dad connection will fail you. For example, 'majority' and 'minority' are mayoría and minoría, and 'rapidity' and 'timidity' are rapidez and timidez. 'Beauty' and 'purity' are belleza and pureza. It is always advisable to ask for confirmation of a word that you have invented if you are talking to someone or to check a dictionary. But you are playing very good odds when you make these transpositions.

You probably noticed as you read over this list that a few of the words ended -tad not -dad. Perhaps you made the additional observation that with each use of -tad the letter immediately preceding the suffix was a consonant rather than a vowel.

There are also a few predictable spelling changes that will occur as you transpose English words into Spanish. You may have already spotted some of them.

1. Double letters are much less frequent in Spanish than in English ('ll' and 'rr' are each an individual letter of the Spanish alphabet). When double letters do occur in Spanish they are both pronounced, as in leer, acción, and cooperación. But most double letters from English reduce to a single letter in the Spanish cognates. Thus you get comunidad, posibilidad, oportunidad, etc.

2. The combination 'th' which is so common in English does not exist in Spanish. When an English candidate for cognate-hood has a 'th' simply drop the 'h' from the Spanish equivalent. Thus 'authority' becomes autoridad, and, as noted above, 'theater' becomes teatro; also, católico, tres, método, auténtico, etc.

3. English 'ph' becomes 'f' in Spanish, e.g. elefante, frase, gráfico, fenómeno, and many more.

4. Spanish words do not begin with 's' and a consonant. In forming cognates of words that start 's'/consonant an 'e' is placed before the initial 's' of the English word: 'Spanish' becomes español, 'student' becomes estudiante, 'special' especial, 'structure' estructura, and so on. (A Spanish-speaker starting out to learn English

may have a difficult time pronouncing words like 'speak' and 'snow'; he will by the habit of a lifetime say, "espeak" and "esnow").

5. Although 'ch' is itself a letter of the Spanish alphabet, 'ch' as it occurs in English words usually reduces to just 'c' in the Spanish cognate. Thus 'charity,' from the list above, became caridad. Other examples are rico, carácter, eco, mecánico, caos, técnico and época. One notable exception, mucho.

6. The English 'ti' when it sounds [sh] will become 'ci' in the Spanish cognate, not just in the '-tion' words (as will be seen below) but in other cases like 'impartial' imparcial, 'essential' esencial, 'initiate' iniciar.

7. The Spanish letter 'y' has both a vowel and a consonant value. However, it will not stand alone between two consonants in Spanish acting as a vowel. Therefore 'mystery' is misterio in Spanish, 'symbol' is símbolo, 'myth' mito, 'synthetic' sintético, 'rhythm' ritmo, etc.

8. I am going to go out on a limb and declare that there are no Spanish words with the letter sequence 'ou' ('uo' yes, but not 'ou'). When transposing an English word with the 'ou' combination into Spanish one of the two vowels has to go. Which one disappears? That depends. 'To pronounce' is pronunciar, 'foundation' becomes fundación, 'group' grupo; but 'soup' is sopa, 'sound' son or sonido, and 'double' is doble.

9. When transposing the English consonant combinations 'ct' and 'nct,' the 'c' usually disappears. 'Sanctuary' becomes santuario, 'district' turns into distrito, the verb 'to respect' is respetar and the Spanish noun is respeto as it means 'esteem' or 'honor.' 'Respect' can also mean 'concerning' as in the phrase 'with respect to,' in this case the 'c' is not dropped in the Spanish - con respecto a.

Let us, then, look at another group of cognates. English words that end '-ant' and '-ent' require merely the addition of the letter 'e' to create the Spanish equivalent or equivalente. We must except from this group words that end '-ment.' These require the addition of 'o' instead of 'e.'

-ant = -ante	-ent = -ente	-ment = -mento
abundante	accidente	armamento
consonante	agente	documento
constante	cliente	experimento
dominante	conveniente	fragmento
elegante	diferente	implemento
elefante	evidente	linimento
ignorante	excelente	monumento
importante	incidente	sacramento
instante	inteligente	suplemento

radiante	permanente	temperamento
restaurante	presidente	testamento
significante	urgente	
tolerante	valiente	

As was said before, confirmation of your creations is recommended when possible. Occasionally you may miss the mark, although not by much in this family of words. 'Fragrant' is <u>fragante</u>. 'Dependent' and 'independent' are <u>dependiente</u> and <u>independiente</u>. Consulting spelling change rule number six 'patient' and 'impatient' become <u>paciente</u> and <u>impaciente</u>. 'Violent' chooses not to cooperate at all and is <u>violento</u> in Spanish. Nevertheless, there is a high degree of reliability in this family of words. And there are many more. All of the -<u>mento</u> words are nouns. The -<u>ante</u> and -<u>ente</u> words are either adjective or noun. Their English usage will indicate their Spanish function as well.

This is a good place to insert a group of nouns that are easily changed to become Spanish nouns. English words ending '-ance' and '-ence' become useful Spanish vocabulary by substituting -<u>ancia</u> and -<u>encia</u> respectively. For example, 'elegance' becomes <u>elegancia</u>, and 'difference' becomes <u>diferencia</u>. Many of these nouns pair nicely with adjectives from the preceding list. The adjective <u>abundante</u> becomes the noun <u>abundancia</u>, for example. The adjective <u>excelente</u> becomes the noun <u>excelencia</u>, and so on.

arrogancia	ignorancia	repugnancia
circunstancia	importancia	su(b)stancia
distancia	instancia	tolerancia
fragancia	predominancia	vigilancia
adolescencia	independencia	presencia
benevolencia	indiferencia	providencia
coincidencia	influencia	prudencia
consecuencia	inocencia	referencia
decadencia	insistencia	residencia
dependencia	inteligencia	resistencia
diferencia	jurisprudencia	silencio (whoops!)
existencia	negligencia	violencia
experiencia	obediencia	

Of course, it is very useful to be able to generate large groups of words this way. We will look at several more of these families of words. It can also be instructive and fun to be alert for stray cognates wandering about in unexpected places. For example, 'arm' and its Spanish equivalent <u>brazo</u> are not cognate words. They obviously share no common root. But the English verb 'to embrace' means 'to take into one's arms' and is a cognate of <u>brazo</u>. 'Hand' and <u>mano</u> are not cognates but to do something manually is to do it by hand. 'To eat' and the Spanish <u>comer</u> have nothing but meaning in common - are you familiar with the English word 'comestible?' It means 'fit to be eaten.' We English speakers would not have to face 'death' if we had no Germanic linguistic roots, but the Spanish <u>muerte</u> as well as

James K. Gavin

English words like 'mortal', and 'mortuary' can be traced back to the Latin <u>mors</u> and <u>mortis</u> meaning 'death.' Be on the lookout for more of these, what we might call, 'tangential' cognates. There are many. It is always rewarding suddenly to spot another one.

Let us now return to the task of learning more of those big groups of words.

If you have been wearing out <u>bueno</u> and <u>malo</u> for lack of any other more descriptive words, here is a group of adjectives that will add color and expression to your vocabulary. These words are genuine 'ready-mades,' they are the same in both languages. English words ending '-ble' are, with the exception of predictable spelling changes, the same or close to the same in both languages. The real challenge with these words is to pronounce them correctly. Sometimes their very similarity makes it more difficult to break free from the shackles of English habits of speech. Read the list, check for small differences from the English. Reading these words out loud is an excellent idea, but I suggest that you do it in the presence of a teacher or Spanish-speaking friend. Unless you are very confident of your pronunciation you may unwittingly be forming bad habits that will then have to be un-learned later. The accent falls on the next-to-the-last syllable in all of these words: a-bo-mi-NA-ble, ad-mi-RA-ble, etc.

abominable	formidable	inevitable	irreparable	posible
admirable	horrible	inexplicable	irresistible	preferible
comparable	imperceptible	infalible	lamentable	probable
considerable	imposible	inseparable	memorable	susceptible
deplorable	incomparable	interminable	miserable	terrible
durable	incompatible	intolerable	noble	variable
favorable	incurable	invariable	notable	visible

Another very large group of ready-made adjectives is found in the English words that end '-al.' With the exception of predictable spelling changes most of these words are identical in both languages. That is to say they are written the same, pronunciation is another matter. Cognates can be a real challenge to good pronunciation. Just maintain those pure Spanish vowel sounds and stress the last syllable.

artificial	espiritual	inicial	natural	radical
brutal	excepcional	intelectual	naval	rural
casual	experimental	judicial	normal	sentimental
central	federal	legal	original	superficial
colonial	fatal	local	parcial	tradicional
comercial	final	manual	personal	universal
cordial	formal	mental	principal	usual
cultural	gradual	monumental	profesional	verbal
esencial	habitual	municipal	provincial	vertical
especial	horizontal	nacional	provisional	vital

There are also a few '-al' words that are nouns. In most cases these nouns also act as adjectives. Although common in English it is a relatively rare occurrence in Spanish that the same word be both an adjective and a noun. While retaining the root of the noun Spanish usually gives the adjective a different form.

For example, escuela is the noun 'school' but in the phrase 'school year' in which 'school' is an adjective the Spanish is año escolar. The noun 'world' is mundo, but every October we baseball fans watch la Serie Mundial. 'College' or 'university' is universidad, but a 'college student' is an estudiante universitario. Here are a few Spanish words that deserve overtime pay for doing double duty.

animal	general	mineral
capital	ideal	oficial
criminal	material	rival

Do not be afraid to take chances generating needed vocabulary as you are speaking. Even though you are 'wrong' it is quite possible that you will be understood; which is, after all, your primary objective. For example, guided by the rules about English words that end '-al', you might create the adjective financial. In fact the Spanish is financiero. But if you have pronounced your non-existent financial well I'd bet twenty reflexive verbs against one indefinite article that you would be understood. If you doubt this, try the reverse case. If a Latin American learning English were to make the logical but erroneous transposition of humorístico (humorous) to 'humoristic,' would you understand him?

There will be pitfalls. So continue to ask friends for confirmation or check a dictionary. (I prefer the former. See: Chapter 4) 'Interval' is intervalo, 'influential' is influyente, 'mutual' is mutuo. 'Industrial,' which is only an adjective in English, does double duty in Spanish, as a noun it means 'industrialist.' 'Individual' is both a noun and an adjective in English, in Spanish it is an adjective only, the noun is individuo.

Watch out for English adjectives that end '-ical.' They may belong to the previous '-al' family (e.g. tropical and musical) or they may follow the pattern of the next group that we will study, adjectives that end '-ic' in English. There is some ambiguity in English here. Would you say 'magic powers' or 'magical powers,' for example? Would you say 'electric appliance' or 'electrical appliance?' 'Historic' and 'historical' actually mean different things. The little known Civil War Battle of Glorieta which took place in New Mexico in 1862, was a historic event (it helped to shape history). Its outcome determined that The West would remain under Union control. The re-enactment of the battle 125 years later was a historical event (it related to history). I suspect that most of the '-ical' adjectives (practical, classical, typical, etc.) fall into the next group, but if in doubt consult a friend or, if necessary, a dictionary.

Anyway, the next group of adjectives we will look at are the English adjectives that end '-ic.' These are converted to Spanish by adding an 'o' to them. Make the predictable spelling changes, pronounce the vowels with care, and stress the third-to-the-last syllable;

e.g. au-TEN-ti-co, CLA-si-co, e-co-NO-mi-co. An (n) indicates that the adjective also can be a noun.

apostólico	eléctrico	pacífico
aristocrático	exótico	pánico (n) only
artístico	fantástico	patético
atlético	frenético	plástico (n)
automático	gótico	público (n)
católico (n)	gráfico	romántico
característico (n) fem.	heroico	rústico
científico (n)	histórico	sintético
democrático	mágico	sistemático
diplomático (n)	magnético	trágico
dramático	metálico	sintético
elástico		

'Gigantic' is, of course, gigantesco. El músico is 'the musician,' la música is 'the music,' the adjective 'musical' is musical. Other English adjectives ending '-ical' that join this group become, in Spanish, físico, idéntico, lógico, místico, óptico, práctico, and típico. El físico is 'the physicist,' la física is 'physics.' 'Magnificent' was not listed with the '-ent' words because it is magnífico.

A question: why is there no written accent in heroico? Go to the head of the class if you can answer that one. Otherwise, see Chapter 17.

Another group of adjectives easily converted to Spanish is the '-ive' words. Simply change the final 'e' to 'o.'

activo	expresivo	negativo
afirmativo	festivo	objetivo
agresivo	fugitivo (n)	ofensivo
atractivo	imaginativo	pasivo
consecutivo	imperativo	positivo
decisivo	intensivo	primitivo
destructivo	instintivo	progresivo
excesivo	nativo (n)	relativo

None of these lexical relationships offers 100% assurance so consultation with Spanish-speaking friends or a dictionary is, as always, advised. 'Attentive' is atento, for example, 'impressive' is impresionante. Also there are some '-ive' nouns but they may go 'e' to 'o' or 'e' to 'a.' 'Motive' is motivo but 'iniciative' and 'perspective' are iniciativa and perspectiva. The organization known as a cooperative is a cooperativa. The adjective cooperativo carries the meaning 'collective' while 'cooperative' meaning 'helpful' is cooperador.

Gramática Apasionada
Reminiscences of a Love Affair with the Spanish Language

Many times linguistically alert students of mine have come up with the adjective serioso. They are building new vocabulary on the basis of knowing that 'famous' is famoso, 'curious' is curioso, and 'delicious' delicioso. But this promising connection that suggests that adjectives ending '-ous' in English can be converted to Spanish by substituting -oso often does not work. For example, Spanish for 'serious' is serio. Before looking at all the other things that can happen to '-ous' words going off to Spain, let us list a few more of the rather common words that create this sometimes misleading lexical association; ambicioso, fabuloso, furioso, generoso, glorioso, and precioso. But, like their buddy 'serious,' 'obvious,' 'erroneous,' 'ridiculous,' 'previous' and 'ficticious' become obvio, erróneo, ridículo, previo and ficticio. 'Various,' plural by nature, stays plural in Spanish, varios. 'Atrocious,' 'ferocious,' and 'precocious' are atroz, feroz, and precoz. 'Audacious' (do you prefer the Anglo-Saxon 'bold' or 'daring'? –see next chapter), 'efficacious,' 'loquacious,' 'rapacious' and 'tenacious' turn into audaz, eficaz, locuaz, rapaz, and tenaz. 'Humorous,' as referred to above, is humorístico. 'Illustrious' is ilustre, 'enormous' is enorme. So, although there are many valid adjectives to be created by the -ous/-oso connection beware that you are on thin ice when doing so, and that can be dangeroso - whoops! make that peligroso.

One can have fun playing with the Spanish suffix -ista. Like its English counterpart '-ist,' it means 'one who does…' or 'one who professes…,' 'a follower of…,' or 'pertaining to….'

An artist is one who does art. A Marxist is one who professes the ideas of Karl Marx. English has lots of '-ists.' We have the violinist, illusionist, tourist, Capitalist, dentist (one who does teeth, Spanish dientes), the Methodist. Spanish has all of these and then some. In the Spanish-speaking world the suffix is particularly frequently used in the realm of politics although it has many other applications. There has been a recent resurgence of the zapatista movement in southern Mexico. Zapata's contemporary, Pancho Villa, bandit or revolutionary (depending on one's point of view), was a genuine folk hero either way. I am sure there are still villistas roaming the deserts of northern Mexico. There are izquierdistas, centristas, and derechistas of every degree stretching form horizon to horizon. Adherents of the Cuban revolution are fidelistas. Use of Castro's first name to create the adjective may just be a folksy touch or it may have been done to avoid an unpleasant association with the verb castrar. Peace Corps volunteers in Latin America are called piscoristas.

Please note that the suffix -ista is both masculine and feminine. The man who drives the taxi is el taxista, if a woman is driving you around she is la taxista.

A baseball player is a jugador de béisbol or a beisbolista. There are also basquetbolistas, futbolistas, and tenistas. There are a number of students who have come back, year after year, to continue studying Spanish with me. I think of this select group of discriminating people as jaimistas (in Spanish my name is Jaime). Given the importance that I place on learning the verbs one might say that I take a verbista approach to teaching Spanish. My wife's love of chocolate makes her a chocolatista. (Chocolate is another exception to Predictable Spelling Changes #5).

Although it is fun to play with the -ista suffix, there is not a close correspondence between where the two suffixes are used in the two languages. A case in point, -ista will not get you the Spanish word for any of the scientists; psychologists, biologists, geologists, etc.

Getting back to a more reliable source of instant vocabulary, let us look at the English words ending '-ion.' These '-ion' words can be turned into Spanish simply by putting an accent mark over the final 'o', applying any predictable spelling changes and pronouncing the result properly, e.g., 'vision' becomes, in Spanish, visión. Pay special attention to Predictable Spelling Change #6. All the English words ending '-tion' will end '-ción' in their Spanish equivalent.

ambición	expresión	perfección
atención	fracción	profesión
comprensión	función	rebelión
condición	institución	región
constitución	instrucción	religión
corrupción	intención	restricción
decisión	intervención	revolución
descripción	interrupción	selección
discusión	introducción	sesión
emoción	misión	solución
excepción	nación	superstición
expansión	opinión	tradición
explosión	opresión	union

So, how do you say 'onion' in Spanish? You got it! Cebolla. It's easy once you know how.

All of these –ión words are nouns. They are all feminine. There are a few -ión words that are masculine but none can be formed directly from an English '-ion' cognate. Most commonly in use are el avión, 'the airplane,' and el camión, which means 'the truck' and in some parts of Latin America 'the bus.'

Learning to track down linguistic roots and build vocabulary is a very useful skill to acquire. It can also be a fascinating entertainment in itself. We have been looking at only the top layer of this process, i.e., the relationship between present-day English and Spanish based upon their common roots in Latin.

But Latin did not spring fully formed from the heads of Classical grammarians in 555 B.C. Nor did Old German (the source of much English vocabulary) come as a gift from the gods one cold afternoon during a mead-fired mid-winter volk festival. Both evolved out of earlier languages, or, as most linguist/scholars now believe, from a common source, the true Mother Tongue. And these scholars are hot on the trail of this very elusive prey. There is no direct physical evidence of the existence of this 'Adam and Eve' language. However, the accumulated body of linguistic knowledge strongly suggests its existence.

English 'night' and Spanish noche would seem to have little in common except the initial letter. If we take them back to the Germanic nacht and Latin nox the two may still not seem very much alike to the layman. But, linguistically, these two words are very similar - the initial 'n,' then a vowel, and ending with a guttural sound (made with the tongue against the soft palate, i.e., back where the hard roof of the mouth turns spongy).

Given the astronomically large number of possible combinations of sounds that can be used to make any word, this similarity defies coincidence. One could suggest that the Romans borrowed the word from a Germanic source or vice versa. There is ample historical record of Roman contact with the Teutonic tribes along the northern border of its Empire. But it strains the limits of linguistic logic to suggest that any language group would have to go to its neighbor to borrow a word for something as basic to all human experience as the night. It is much more plausible that nacht and nox evolved from the same word that belonged to an earlier original common language. What is more, there are many other 'coincidences' of this sort. As a matter of fact, linguists are painstakingly reconstructing this first language. They have given it a technically descriptive but colorless and clinical name, Proto-Indo-European. (I would have preferred a name with which the layman could more easily identify - Ice Age-ese or Cave Rap).

They believe that all the languages now spoken in a broad continuous belt from India through the Near East to Europe came out of this common parent language. The only European language that seems not to have its deepest roots in Proto-Indo-European is Euskadi, the language spoken by the Basques in northern Spain.

There is, of course, much borrowing of words among languages. But most borrowings accompany an innovation of some sort. When one culture adopts an invention or aspect of another culture it also frequently takes on the vocabulary that the innovators have created for this new thing. The Mexican cowboy perfected the art of riding herd in Alta California a century before the American West even existed. His American counterpart still uses a vocabulary learned from these first cowboys. The lasso (from lazo, Spanish for noose or slip knot), the lariat (from la reata, the rope), rodeo (from the verb rodear, to round up), chaps (Spanish chaparreras), buckaroo (vaquero, Spanish for cowboy), ranch from rancho, vamoose from vamos, savvy from sabe (he knows). And a corruption of juzgado, Spanish for 'tribunal' (from the verb juzgar, to judge) which suggests the peremptory nature of justice in the Wild West; because going before the juzgado became synonymous with going to jail, the hoosegow.

This kind of word borrowing led to an interesting item on the menu of a small restaurant in Costa Rica. Liberia, the capital of Guanacaste Province, was a very small city of unpaved streets and one-storied adobe buildings when I lived there for a year back in the early seventies. The Inter-American highway ran by the western edge of town and there was a restaurant out there by the roadside. From time to time an English-speaking traveler would stop in, so some thoughtful person who knew little English had used an English-Spanish dictionary to translate the menu.

James K. Gavin

Pie is a product of northern European cookery. The Spaniards took no such thing with them when they went off to colonize the New World. But just as Anglo-America has taken the tortilla, name and all, into its kitchen, so has much of Latin America recently discovered the delights of apple, cherry, and lemon meringue pie. The pie has been happily adopted and its name right along with it. The approximate sound equivalent of 'pie' written phonetically in Spanish would be pay. But although Costa Ricans (and Mexicans) pronounce the word pay, they continue to use the English spelling. So when the well-meaning menu translator looked up pie de manzana he came up with 'apple foot.' (I wonder how many turistas, passing through wild, exotic Guanacaste, request that particular dessert?).

And, on the subject of menus, one time, in a rather more elegant setting, while perusing the lista de cocteles, I came upon a 'Bloody Merry.' I believe that this is a real improvement upon the original name and this is how I have thought of the drink ever since.

But what sorts of words might the Romans and their Germanic neighbors have traded? My guess would be that if there was word-swapping, much of it would have been vocabulary relating to innovations in military weapons and tactics. The clean-shaven soldiers of Rome called the bearded invaders from the north 'Barbarians' (from Latin barba, 'beard'). Given the meanings of 'barbarity,'[22] 'barbarous' and 'barbaric' one can surmise that Caesar's centurions did not think kind thoughts about their adversaries. We should, however, be sure to exempt one group of individuals from the opprobrium associated with these 'barb-' words. The neighborhood barber is almost always an upright citizen and a friendly fellow.

Back on the trail of cognate groups, there are a number of English words ending '-ary' and '-ory' that are easily transposed into Spanish. Switching to -ario and -orio will usually 'do the trick,' or, if you prefer the more high-toned Romance English, 'accomplish this purpose.'

Some are adjectives:

arbitrario	judiciario	primario
contrario	literario	satisfactorio
hereditario	necesario	secundario
imaginario	obligatorio	solitario
involuntario	parlamentario	suplementario

A few will do double duty as both adjective and noun: revolucionario and voluntario.

---

[22]The Spanish barbaridad has a second less ferocious meaning as when it is used in the common expression "¡Qué barbaridad!". Readers of the comic strip "Peanuts" en español know that this exclamation is the translation of Charlie Brown's frequent cry of frustration and/or disappointment and/or disbelief, "Good grief!"

And there are some nouns, but watch for the occasional noun that takes the feminine instead of the masculine form.

   adversario   dormitorio   salario
   aniversario   la gloria   territorio
   Calvario   la historia   la teoría
   comentario   laboratorio   la victoria
   diccionario   la memoria   vocabulario

In their designation as noun, adjective, or both these Spanish words closely parallel English usage. As always you will get skunked every once in a while, e.g. 'temporary' is temporal.

Do not get the idea that you have to look for large groups of words with a common characteristic in order to take advantage of the cognate bonanza. Check out this small group of ready-mades.

   anterior   interior   ulterior
   exterior   posterior   superior
   inferior

These are useful words. Some of the meanings are obvious. But it would be instructive to check out these words in your Spanish dictionary. Some of the meanings might surprise you. For example, how does one say 'at the top,' or 'bottom, of the page?' En la parte superior, o la parte inferior de la página.

Every once in a while you will run into false cognates, a Spanish-English pair of words with a common root whose meanings have drifted apart over the centuries. One of the most famous examples is embarazada, it means 'pregnant.' Look up 'embarrassed' in an English/Spanish dictionary and it will say apenado or avergonzado. But there is a cultural difference here that the dictionary does not make clear. The Spanish words convey a deeper sense of shame. These words are not used by Spanish-speakers as casually as we tend to use the word 'embarrassed' in our culture. "Oh, I'm so embarrassed! I forgot the name of my brother's new girl-friend."

'Relations' is another. Easy transposed to Spanish it is correctly used in phrases like relaciones diplomáticas or relaciones públicas. However, your uncles and aunts, cousins and in-laws, etc. are your parientes. If parientes means 'relatives,' the logical next question might be, how do you say 'parents' in Spanish? The logical answer, given the predominance of the masculine in Spanish grammar, is that when you wish to refer to your padre and your madre collectively you call them your padres. (A student of mine was corresponding with a family in Mexico. He would write to them in Spanish. They, in turn, would practice their English when writing back. At one of our meetings he showed me the most recent letter he had received. It ended on a very happy note. "P.S. Great news! Pedro and María are going to be fathers!")

We use 'actually' to mean 'in reality' in English. "Actually (in reality) I'd rather have chocolate than vanilla." <u>Actualmente</u> means 'at the present time' in Spanish. Therefore, you should say <u>en realidad</u> when thinking 'actually.'

Another deceptive cognate is the verb <u>asistir</u>. It has a secondary meaning of 'to assist' or 'to help.' But it is used primarily meaning 'to attend' (a class or party or meeting). <u>Ayudar</u> is the more common verb meaning 'to help.'

There are others. However, the conclusion to be drawn here is not that it is risky to make these transpositions. Quite to the contrary, the odds are very much in your favor. It is advisable, as you seemingly pluck new words out of thin air, that you ask your listener for confirmation or consult a dictionary if you have doubts. But as they say, <u>El que no se aventura no pasa la mar</u>. "Nothing ventured, nothing gained."

Building vocabulary does not have to be a painful word by word process of memorization. Chasing down new words, discovering their origins, gaining new insights into our native tongue, is all part of the excitement of learning another language. The process can be fun as well as instructive.

This has not been an all-inclusive survey of the field of cognate words. The joy of discovering other word groups still awaits the eager student/reader of these pages. Nor are these lists complete. There are many additions to be made to the example groups. Furthermore, a careful study of the lists compiled herein will probably reveal a mistake or two. I make no claim to linguistic infallibility. The process of learning a language is life-long. But there is an important lesson here also. When you invent words as you are talking, the battle will be half-won simply by presenting your creations, *well pronounced*, in a firm confident voice which tells your listener that these words really do exist.

Chapter Nine

Uneeda Verb

One morning many years ago, I was deep in the bowels of the great market in the center of Guatemala City. By chance I overheard a very earnest looking man with a distinctly gringo accent and a limited supply of words to choose from say to a vendor, "<u>Yo no voy a poner arriba con esto</u>!" (Literally: "I am not going to put up with this!") This was a man, like many of his compatriots who speak Spanish as a second language, desperately in need of a verb. I did not linger to watch this scene play itself out. I knew how it would end. If one gets confrontational on foreign soil and in a second language the end result will be frustration and humiliation. The man-in-need-of-a-verb did not need an additional witness to his impending and almost certain mortification.

I do not fault the man-in-need-of-a-verb for his limited vocabulary. The natural laws of linguistics and mathematics dictate that a small vocabulary preceed a large vocabulary. As a matter of fact I give him credit for having used any verb at all. Many English-speakers learning Spanish put verbs in the same category as spiders and snakes – things they passionately wish to have nothing to do with. Verb avoidance is a psychological disorder of epidemic proportions among Anglo-Americans studying Spanish.

This conjugaphobia[23] is extremely unfortunate. The verb is the single most important element of any sentence. Margarita Madrigal, a writer of Spanish grammar books, makes this point very forcefully: "'Verb' is derived from the Latin '<u>verbum</u>,' which means 'word.' The verb is the master word, the king of words. It is the word that governs, dominates, and breathes life into a sentence." Omit or mishandle the verb at your peril.

To be a credible and convincing speaker of Spanish you have to conquer the verb, "the master word, the king of words." This dominance includes both conjugation (a subject addressed in other chapters of this book) and the building of a good-sized vocabulary of verbs.

Unfortunately it is not as easy for the English-speaker to generate verbs in quantity in the way that large numbers of Spanish nouns and adjectives can be created as was seen in Chapter Eight. There is, however, one large family of verbs readily available to you right now.

---

[23] Fear of verbs: not to be confused with conyugaphobia, fear of marriage. This latter topic will not be dealt with in these pages.

Here is an all but foolproof way to generate a slew of useful verbs on the spot. Start with any English noun that ends '-ation.' Then create the Spanish equivalent by substituting -ación for the '-ation.' Create the verb by putting -ar in place of -ación. For example, two verbs that were used already in this paragraph, 'generate' and 'create,' can be 'invented' in this way. From 'generation' we get generación and the verb generar; from 'creation' we get the noun creación and the verb crear. The following is a sampling of the verbs that can be generated in this fashion. There are many more.

English noun	Spanish noun	Spanish verb
admiration	admiración	admirar
celebration	celebración	celebrar
communication	comunicación	comunicar
cooperation	cooperación	cooperar
declaration	declaración	declarar
dedication	dedicación	dedicar
education	educación	educar
exageration	exageración	exagerar
examination	examinación	examinar
imagination	imaginación	imaginar
inspiration	inspiración	inspirar
installation	instalación	instalar
liberation	liberación	liberar
limitation	limitación	limitar
narration	narración	narrar
organization	organización	organizar
preparation	preparación	preparar
presentation	presentación	presentar
recommendation	recomendación	recomendar
separation	separación	separar

As you peruse the list of verbs just presented, and especially if you are a beginning or lower intermediate level student of Spanish, you may come to the conclusion that these are not the basic verbs that are most helpful to know at your linguistic level.

Please consider this: the English that we speak today has resulted from the mixing together in roughly equal parts of the Latin being spoken in the Britannia of the Roman Empire (modern day England and southern Scotland) and the Germanic languages spoken by northern European tribes that invaded the British Isles starting in the 5th century. Prominent among these peoples were the Saxons, the Jutes, and the Angles who eventually lent their name to the country, England, and to our language. Therefore, when we speak we are continually drawing from and choosing between that which has come from the Germanic and the Latin roots of our language.

Spanish, on the other hand, is a Romance language. It has evolved primarily out of Latin. Greek and Arabic have contributed a considerable amount of vocabulary but

Germanic tongues have had no significant influence on the development of the Spanish language. Latin is the common ground for the English- and Spanish-speakers.

My unscientific way of instantly turning you into a scholar of ancient languages is as follows: the Germanic words tend to be short, many of just one syllable with a predominance of consonants; our Latinate vocabulary is usually multi-syllabic with a relatively even distribution of vowels and consonants. Also, the letters 'K' and 'W' are not from the classical Latin alphabet. Chances are good that English words that contain either of these letters did not come to us from Latin.

Given the two-pronged taproot of our language we English-speakers can:

get a job - or - obtain employment; we can:
go to church - or - attend a religious service; we can:
drink beer, wine, and whiskey - or - imbibe alcoholic beverages; we can:
hit the deck - or - rapidly assume a prone position.

If things are going very well we may:

jump for joy - or - exuberantly express felicity;

but if things are going very badly we will:

try to stay cool - or - attempt to maintain equanimity.

We can:

learn lots of words - or - acquire an extensive vocabulary.

In short, we can:

"call a spade a spade" - or - call a spade a muscle operated implement with which to excavate terrestrial material.

The examples given above are meant to illustrate the fact that we English-speakers may express most any thought or idea with either a basically Germanic vocabulary or primarily in Latinate terminology. Of course the two are frequently intermingled as well. But the majority, and I would say a significant majority, of English-speaking Americans has a preference for, or a cultural bias toward, use of our Germanic vocabulary. People who prefer to draw more heavily from Latinate sources when speaking English are generally thought to be "putting on airs" or, in more Latinate terms, to be "intending to demonstrate a social or intellectual superiority."

No place is this bias more obvious than in our choice of verbs. There is a simple test for identifying many of the Teutonic usages. If the verb you are using is really a combination of a verb and a preposition or a verb and an adverb or, sometimes, a verb and an adverb and a preposition together; and, if the verb actually loses its intended meaning without the prepositional or adverbial add on, you are drawing from Germanic roots. We have many of these in English and we rely heavily upon them: for example, to put on, to put over on, to put off, to put up, to put up with, to put out, to put down, to put back, to put forth, to put through. The importance of being aware of and recognizing these combination verbs is that they cannot be translated directly into Spanish.

Do not confuse these 'verb-adverb-and/or-preposition' verbs with the simple verb 'to put.' "She put the book on the table," is the literal meaning of 'to put' – the preposition that follows it, 'on,' tells us where she put the book but does not change the meaning of the verb. This sentence can be translated directly - Ella puso el libro en la mesa. She could also have put the book **in** the refrigerator or **under** the twenty mattresses the princess was sleeping on. In these instances changing the accompanying preposition does not change the meaning of the verb which is 'to set or place.' However, the combination 'to put on' must be taken as an inalterable unit if the intended meaning is 'to tease or deceive:' "I thought she loved me, but she was putting me on."

Getting back to our man-in-need-of-a-verb - he made the mistake of going to the Teutonic well instead of the Romance Language pool to draw forth the words needed to express his displeasure. He translated all the words correctly but the resulting Spanish was gibberish – and verbal drivel will not create the desired effect as the first thrust in a duel of words. The verb in this instance, which in reality is a verb-adverb-preposition (to put up with), is from our Germanic linguistic roots. It will not translate directly to Spanish. What the English-speaker must do in this situation is to think of another English verb from our Latinate vocabulary that says the same thing as 'to put up with.' In this case, although certainly not in every case, the answer is right at hand. 'To put up with' is 'to tolerate.' And given that we have the word 'toleration' it is another quick two-step to the Spanish verb tolerar. "Yo no voy a tolerar esto."

The key point in all of this is that our linguistic bias toward the Germanic will almost inevitably lead us astray. When we try to translate English thoughts that are phrased in those stubby little Teutonic words into Spanish we end up in trouble. We must learn to recognize and utilize the vocabulary that has Latin roots. And this is particularly true of verbs.

Here is another group of 'verb-preposition-and/or-adverb' verbs that are simply dead-end streets if translated directly into Spanish. Many of them even have multiple meanings in English with the result that they would translate as several different verbs in Spanish:

to hold down = to maintain (a job), to suppress (blood pressure), to oppress (a group of people);
to hold up = to rob (a bank), to delay (the airplane's departure), to support (the roof), to display or offer (as a role model);
to hold over = to extend (the run of a movie), to threaten or coerce;

to hold out = to resist, to offer (the olive branch);
to hold back = to suppress (tears), to impede (someone's progress), to contain (flood waters);
to hold against = to resent.

How about: to give up, to give back, to give way, to give away, to give out, to give in, to give (oneself) over to.

Or: to take in, to take on, to take over, to take back, to take up, to take to (She **took to** skiing immediately - she enjoyed it from the first moment; or, she **took to** skiing everyday - she started going up to the slopes every day), and, to take out [Her husband took out (removed) the trash, the dentist took out (extracted) three teeth, the teenage boy took out (dated) the girl next door, the mobster took out (murdered) his rival].

And it will be left to the reader to make a list of the many possibilities with the verb 'to get.'

This discussion of the Germanic and Latin origins of English began after the demonstration of a process for generating Spanish verbs from English words ending '-ation.' The observation was then made that you might not think these verbs especially useful. The purpose of the last few paragraphs is to make the point that these are the verbs in Spanish!

You cannot 'speed up' in Spanish but you can accelerar. Conversely, you cannot 'slow down' but you can 'reduce speed.' Which raises the interesting and related question, how do you say 'speed' in Spanish? 'Speed' looks Germanic to me - one syllable, three consonants, a double vowel (not common in Latin) but only one vowel sound. Is there another English word that means exactly the same thing as 'speed' but which might come from Latin and therefore be more amenable to 'invention' by a clever Spanish student? Yes, and it is a '-ty' word. So what does one see along the roadsides of Mexico and Spain? Signs that say, "Reduzca la velocidad" or "Disminuya la velocidad."

You cannot 'get rid of' something but you can eliminar it. You cannot 'get in touch' with someone but you can comunicarse with him. Work cannot 'pile up' on your desk while you are away on vacation but it can acumular. And so it goes.

Therefore, I say unto thee, cast off thy aversion to the polysyllabic! Salvation, for the English-speaker who wishes to speak Spanish, will be found, more often than not, among the big words.

The dual origins of our language even have National Security applications. Our Pentagon people regularly slip into Latinate English to protect us. With great facility they can say, for example, things like "a person-powered fastener-driving impact device" thus assuring that any Russian or Chinese spies lurking in all those miles of corridor will not know that they are talking about a hammer.

James K. Gavin

Unfortunately there are no other tricks like the –ation/-ación/-ar connection by which you can be served up fifty-plus new verbs on a silver platter. But we do not have to abandon the hunt for verb cognates. And the process will go faster if, rather than learning new verbs one by one, we look for groups or clusters of verbs.

Here is a cluster of verbs worthy of your attention. It is those verbs whose infinitive ends –ecer. There is often a big clue to the meaning of the verb in the root word fragment preceding the final four letters. Establ-ecer is 'to establish.' Ofr-ecer is 'to offer.' We have obed-ecer, 'to obey,' (don't forget that the 'd' shows up in 'obedience'); and desobedecer. There are apar-ecer, 'to appear,' desaparecer, and reaparecer. (Please see Chapter Ten for an explanation of the significant difference in Spanish between aparecer and the very useful verb parecer, 'to seem'). Parecer aside, these are admittedly not among the first twenty five verbs the eager student needs to know. But these are verbs, as was mentioned before, that will enrich (enriquecer) and embellish (embellecer) your vocabulary. There are more – favor-ecer, 'to favor;' mer-ecer, 'to deserve or merit;' perman-ecer, 'to remain or stay;' perten-ecer, 'to pertain or belong to.'

In many cases the root containing the meaning will not present the English-speaker with a cognate clue, rather it will test his Spanish vocabulary, e.g. envej-ecer, 'to grow old' or 'to age' – the root -vej- should recall to mind viejo and vejez, 'old' and old age.' If, however, you have discovered The Fountain of Youth you can rejuvenecerse. Emblanquecer means 'to whiten,' enrojecer is 'to redden;' and 'to redden yourself,' enrojecerse, means 'to blush.' On a darker note, anochecer is 'to become night,' and obscurecer or oscurecer means 'to darken, or 'to get dark.'

As you begin using these verbs, as you get comfortable with the sometimes lengthy conjugated forms, you will find it gets easier and easier to add to your collection of –ecer verbs. Even verbs whose roots give no obvious clue, in English or Spanish, to their meaning will start creeping into your vocabulary – agradecer, 'to express gratitude;' carecer, 'to lack' or 'to be in need of;' padecer, 'to suffer;' to name a few.

You might also begin a collection of -ear verbs. I'll help you get it started: desear (often the first of this group of verbs people learn); batear (for fellow baseball fans); telefonear; deletrear, 'to spell' (literally 'to de-letter'); pelear, 'to fight'; - and –iar verbs; estudiar, cambiar, enviar, espiar, esquiar, enfriar, etc.

As is true in the case of the –ecer verbs, once you become comfortable conjugating any one of the –ear verbs (desear, for example), you have a model for conjugating any –ear verb. This makes it much more likely that other verbs of this group will begin to sneak into your speech. This is not true for the –iar verbs. There are two models for the accent pattern of their present tense conjugation. Chapters Two and Seventeen will tell you more about that.

Ignoring this slightly discordant note, we will continue searching out clusters of verbs.

The Spanish verb satisfacer (to satisfy) will serve to introduce us to another cluster of interesting verb vocabulary. The Latin facere means 'to make.' So the verb literally means 'to make sated.' A number of other verbs have this 'to make...' construction. It is not, however, as easy to recognize them because the –facere has evolved into –ficar, or, –izar (which sometimes combines with a Greek root word as well).

The Latin magnus, 'large' or 'great,' combines with 'make' to create the verb 'to make large,' magnificar, 'to magnify.' Latin rectus, 'straight,' and 'make' give us rectificar, 'to rectify' or 'to straighten out,' if you prefer the less toney Teutonic equivalent. Verificar, 'to verify,' comes from veritas, 'truth;' from amplus, 'ample,' we get amplificar; 'to make many,' multus-facere, became multiplicar, 'to multiply.' By the same process we have gotten justificar, significar, mortificar, diversificar and fortificar.

Turning to the –izar verbs, let us start with one of the most used (and misused) verbs in this group – realizar, 'to realize,' literally, 'to make real.' Spanish usage has stayed true to the literal meaning of the verb; e.g. he realized (made real) his dream of conquering the master word, the king of words – realizó su sueño.... In English we do use this verb in its literal and original sense. But much more often we use this verb with the meaning 'to become aware;' e.g. he suddenly realized (became aware) that nobody had understood a word he had said. The Spanish realizar is not used in this sense. The idiomatic expression, darse cuenta de..., literally, 'to give oneself account of...,' is used; de repente se dio cuenta de que nadie había entendido ni una palabra que él había dicho.

Organizar, 'to organize,' is another such verb. The Greek, organon, means 'tool.' So our organs - heart, kidneys, liver, etc, - are tools. They do work. They pump blood, filter the blood, they produce digestive juices, etc. 'To organize' literally means 'to make a tool.' Which is, in fact, what we are doing when we organize – we are making a tool. We make a tool to achieve some end like getting a candidate elected, or cleaning up the trash in the neighborhood, or getting better wages. When we say, "Let's get ourselves organized," we are saying, "Let's make ourselves into a tool."

The Greek, hypnos, 'sleep,' gave us the verb hipnotizar. Other verbs in this family are familiarizar, generalizar, finalizar, analizar, dramatizar, paralizar, and the very expressive polvorizar from the Latin pulvis, 'powder' or 'dust.' Therefore, 'to pulverize' is 'to make into powder,' or, 'to reduce to dust;' as, for example, "Yesterday the Red Sox pulverized the Yankees, 16-0!" Or, look at the interesting (even if not desperately needed in your vocabulary) verb, sincronizar. It comes from the Greek, syn-, (sometimes sym-), meaning 'together;' and chronos, 'time.' Thus we get 'together/time/make,' 'to synchronize.' Replace chronos with pathos, Greek for 'emotion.' Now we have formed the word 'together/emotion/make,' 'to sympathize,' simpatizar.[24] 'Life' in Greek is bios, so 'symbiosis' is 'together/life.'

---

[24]The Spanish verb compadecer, literally 'to suffer with,' is a better translation of 'to sympathize.' Simpatizar has come to mean 'to get on well with,' and its related adjective, simpático, means 'congenial' or 'nice.'

Once you start looking at words this way this process can go on indefinitely. Combine syn- with phonos, Greek for 'sound' and you have 'together/sound,' symphony, sinfonía in Spanish. Attach phonos to tele-, 'from a distance' in Greek, and you get 'from a distance/sound,' 'telephone,' Spanish teléfono. Tele- and the Greek word for 'writing,' graphia, give us 'telegraph,' Spanish telégrafo. Going back to bios and graphia, we get 'biography' in English and biografía in Spanish – in other words, 'life/writing.' The Greek word logos means 'word,' 'reason,' 'discourse.' Reasoned discussion was the way in which things were studied in the time of the great Greek philosophers, so biology is 'the study of life.' And Mexican students study biología.

'Philosopher' itself came to us from the Greek philos, (lover), and sophia, (wisdom). A Francophile is a lover of things French, a bibliophile loves books. A philanthropist loves anthrop, Greek for 'mankind.' A philanderer is one who loves, if not too much, too many. And when William Penn established a new city on the banks of the Delaware River he wanted to give it a name that would express his religious ideals as well as his hope for the new settlement. He decided to call it The City of Brotherly Love. Then, as he gave it more thought, he started worrying about all the ink, paper and time that would be wasted writing that long name on every municipal document. So he switched to a more concise Greek word that said the same thing – Philadelphia.

A sophomore is a 'wise/moron' or, more freely translated, 'one with a lot of knowledge that he does not know how to use.' Thinking back on my own college days, my friends and I were definitely bigger on the '-more' than the 'sopho-.'

As I said, one can go on and on. But we have wandered rather far from verb vocabulary.

Next you will see how the effort that was put into mastering the irregular verbs tener, poner and traer, can bring increased fruit many times over.

English verbs with a prefix in front of '-tain' keep the same (or a very similar) prefix in Spanish and attach themselves to -tener. For example: the verb 'to contain' is contener in Spanish; additionally we get:

detener, to detain; entretener, to entertain; mantener, to maintain; obtener, to obtain; and sostener, to sustain.

To conjugate these verbs you keep all the irregularities of the base verb and simply add the appropriate prefix.

Again you might ask, "Are these really verbs that I will use very much?". And the answer again is, "Yes, you will find these verbs very useful." As a matter of fact, if I had written the preceding paragraph in Spanish I might have used two of the -tener verbs. The Anglo-Saxon 'keep' (the letter 'k' gives it away) which was used twice above will not translate directly to Spanish. You have to find another English verb that says what you want to say. Therefore, "...**retain** the same (or a very similar) prefix..."; and, "To conjugate these verbs you **maintain** all the irregularities...".

The English verbs that end '-pose' can be made into Spanish verbs as follows: keep the prefix and substitute -poner for '-pose.' Thus we get:

componer, to compose; oponer, to oppose; suponer, to suppose; imponer, to impose; exponer, to expose; proponer, to propose; disponer, to dispose, (El hombre propone y Dios dispone); and descomponer, to decompose.

As always, be prepared for the occasional curveball. There is a verb reponer, but in this case it is the verb poner, (to put) with the prefix re-, which in Spanish as in English carries the meaning 'to do again.' So reponer means 'to replace.' 'To repose' is reposar.

"And how about 'decompose'?," you ask. "Now that is really an everyday word!"

Well, that depends on what kind of shape your car is in. But every time that old "bucket of bolts" of yours leaves you stranded somewhere, that is the Spanish verb you will use. 'To decompose' is 'to break down.' Mi carro se descompuso.

Two of these verbs can also be used by disgruntled husbands in a play on the well-known proverb cited above: el hombre propone y su mujer descompone. And in fairness to the other fifty percent of the population, an irate wife could certainly switch the subjects around.

For the student who works at building his vocabulary of verbs there is a bonus. And these -poner/-pose verbs offer a particularly good example of this bonus.

Frequently there is a noun or adjective (or both) associated with a verb. Keeping in mind that the past participle of poner is irregular (puesto) here is some of the bonus vocabulary you get from this verb cluster.

Puesto itself is a noun meaning 'post,' as in 'job.' Mi hermano tiene un puesto importante con el gobierno federal.

The sunset is la puesta del sol.

El opuesto is 'the opposite.'

Un impuesto is 'an impost,' something that is imposed on us, a tax.

Una propuesta is 'a proposal.'

The expression por supuesto (it is taken as supposed) means 'of course."

Supuestamente is 'supposedly.'

Presuponer means 'to presuppose,' so if a government or a company or a family sits down and presupposes its expenses for the up-coming year they are making un presupuesto, 'a budget.'

'To be willing to…' is estar dispuesto a…. She is willing (disposed) to help us.
Ella está dispuesta a ayudarnos.

And descompuesto, as mentioned above, means 'broken' in the sense of 'not working.'
El televisor está descompuesto.

This does not exhaust the possibilities for extracting vocabulary from these -poner/-pose verbs. But let us move along to the last of the three prefix/verb clusters mentioned above.

Finally, the verb traer plus prefix matches up nicely with the English '-tract' and prefix. Therefore:

Atraer, to attract; distraer, to distract; extraer, to extract; sus- or substraer, to subtract; contraer, to contract.

So, if some fine day while speaking Spanish you 'put your foot in your mouth,' you will not have to 'eat your words,' you can simply and graciously retraer them.

Adding matching prefixes to the Spanish –primir will get you the verbs 'to compress' (comprimir), 'to suppress' (suprimir), 'to oppress' (oprimir), 'to repress' (reprimir), to depress' (deprimir), 'to impress' (imprimir), and 'to express' (exprimir).

The 'press' in these verbs refers to 'pressure' and the prefix indicates the result of exerting pressure; for example, the prefix 'com-' means 'together,' which is what happens when you compress something, things get closer together. 'To impress' is 'to press into' so imprimir means 'to print.' Technology has wrought changes, but printing the page of a book originally involved exerting a lot of pressure on the paper (hence, the printing press). However, if your mastery of "the king of words" impresses your friends the verb will be impresionar. The prefix 'ex-' means 'away from,' so exprimir is the verb used when one applies pressure to get the juice away from the orange or the flavor out of the coffee bean (expresso!). If you want to express your feelings in Spanish the verb is expresar (some women might think exprimir a more appropriate verb in the case of husbands 'expressing' feelings!).

Here is a tidy little packet of six verbs:

    admitir   omitir   permitir   remitir   transmitir   emitir

Not too tidy, however; 'to vomit' is vomitar and 'to submit' is someter.

As we continue on our clusters get smaller. Perhaps two of anything cannot even be considered a cluster. But it does speed up (accelerate) the building of verb vocabulary if you learn verbs in related pairs, frequently, but not only, as paired opposites – to come and to go, to begin and to end, etc. Say them together repeatedly in your head or out loud. Create a strong association between them. Then, if one of the two is relatively easy to remember because it has an English cognate, the other will be easier to recall because of its close association with the first. A good example of this is dormir and despertar. Dormir (to sleep) is easy to learn because of the cognate words 'dormant' and 'dormitory.' Despertar (to awaken) has no such convenient English vocabulary to associate it with. However, if you have tied despertar to dormir in your mind, you will be able to produce it when needed because of its link to dormir.

Enseñar and aprender is another useful pair to link together. The first verb, 'to teach,' has no obvious connection to any related English word; but the second, 'to learn,' can be remembered because of the cognate 'apprentice' – an apprentice is one who is learning.

'To say' and 'to tell' might seem a logical pair of verbs to learn together. But if you learn one you have learned them both. They both translate decir. There are some interesting cognates connecting decir to English. The root dec- (dic- in some of its conjugated forms) shows up in 'predict' (to say before), 'verdict' (the true saying – what the jury says, at least in the legal sense, is the truth), 'dictator' (the one who tells you how things are going to be), and 'contradict' (to say against).

Leer (to read) and escribir (to write) go together like ham and eggs or grammar classes and drowsiness. In the root -scrib- we see writing related words 'scribble,' 'scribe,' and 'script.' If you happen to know that leer came from the Latin, legere, you might also recognize the common stem in the English words 'legible' and 'illegible.' Even without the Latin, however, you know the meaning of leer because of its association with escribir.

Two very useful verbs that students almost always have trouble filing away in a place where they are easily retrieved are salir (to leave) and llegar (to arrive). They are handy to know just for their basic meanings. But they are additionally useful because, by extension of their basic meanings, they have idiomatic uses - salir bien (o mal) (to turn out well or badly) and llegar a ser (to become) - to name two. Neither of these verbs, unfortunately, gives the English-speaker anything to hold onto, any way of making a useful association through some common root.

But do not give up on salir and llegar.

Learning verbs in pairs works well if diligently done – every time you use one verb of a pair, say, or at least think of, the other verb. And cognates are not the only tool available to help you remember them. There are other mnemonic tactics one can try. One student who struggled unsuccessfully to memorize these two verbs finally latched onto the root of salir, sal-. Sal also means 'salt.' Too much salt is not good for you, so when you encounter sal you leave. If that works for you, fine. If not, try this.

Salir also pairs up as the opposite of entrar (to enter). Entrar y salir. Salir y entrar. Remembering entrar is a slam dunk. So you get salir from its link to entrar and then llegar from its link to salir. ¡Pedazo de bizcocho!

Recordar seems to be one of the easier verbs to learn. To record something in your mind is to remember it. Its opposite, olvidar, is not as easy to remember. That may not really matter very much, because if you cannot remember how to say, "I forgot," you can always say, "I don't remember." But perhaps this will help you to remember olvidar. Even though the 'b' becomes a 'v' and the order of the consonants has been reversed, **olvi**dar probably shares the root of the English '**obli**vion.' The letters 'b' and 'v' did tend to flip back and forth as Latin drifted into Spanish and English – to have, haber; beverage, bebida; cavalry, caballería; tavern, taberna; fever, fiebre; government, gobierno, and more.

Having mentioned recordar it should be pointed out that this is not the verb to be used if you are talking about making a tape recording. That verb is grabar. And in another interesting example of a 'b' – 'v' flipover the Spanish grabar shares the stem of the English 'to engrave.' Spanish uses grabar because the first records were made by engraving the pattern of the vibrations of sound in a continuous groove on a wax disk. The record was then played by running a sensitive needle along in the groove. This recreated the vibrations and reproduced the sound. So those first records were truly engravings of sound. The technology for recording sound has advanced greatly, but in Spanish the end product is still called 'an engraving,' una grabación. (English also has its share of verbal anachronisms. Perhaps you or an elderly relative still refer to your refrigerator as an icebox – which is what it was back in the days before the invention of electric refrigeration, back in the days when "the ice man cameth").

Vocabulary building – verbs, nouns, whatever – will be facilitated if you will turn your mind loose to make these sorts of connections. Let your mind reach out and grab hold of less obvious possible associations. Dirigir (to direct) became cemented into my permanent vocabulary when it occurred to me that a dirigible was a lighter-than-air craft that was 'directable,' in other words, it could be steered. The first lighter-than-air craft, balloons, could only drift with the wind. Corregir (to correct) was easier to remember after I linked it to 'incorrigible,' 'uncorrectable,' e.g. an incorrigible liar. That in turn brought to mind the name of the island in Manila Bay where American troops made their last stand against the overwhelming force of the Japanese army when it invaded the Philippine Islands in the early days of World War II. Corregidor (The Corrector) Island was undoubtedly so named by the Spanish. It was a fortress island and prison – an ominous name if you were a convict being sent there. It would seem that the Spaniards were in a better mood the day that they named that chunk of rock in San Francisco Bay, Pelican Island, Alcatraz – a word, ironically, that in English has become synonymous with, not the graceful fisher bird, but 'prison.'

Verb vocabulary can also be increased by creating your own tailor-made verb for a specific situation. We do this in our native tongue without even realizing what we have done. Nouns easily become verbs in English. He **muscled** his way into the ticket line. They **school** people in the art of making friends. It is an idiosyncrasy of the English language that, at least in popular speech, we can even turn expressions into verbs. Simply insert the words-that-would-be-verb in the slot allocated for the verb in the sentence. He **deep sixed** the report because it contained unflattering references to him. Not long ago *The New Yorker* magazine had a cartoon in which the name of a television program was turned into a verb. In the drawing one couple is showing their recently purchased home to some friends. One of the proud new owners says, "Of course we are going to **This Old House** it." By making a few changes in the drawing the punch line could just as easily have been, "Of course we're **This Old House-ing** it;' or, "Of course we **This Old House-d** it." A person's name can be a verb. She **Scarlett O'hara-ed** her way through graduate school. Even initials can be used as a verb. "Did you **r.s.v.p.**?"

Verbs can also be created in Spanish. But Spanish requires that you first create an infinitive with its characteristic ending, -ar, -er, or –ir. Then you can use it as you would any other verb. (The verb ustedear was created in Chapter Seven of this book).

So in English nouns can be verbs. In Spanish, on the other hand, any verb can become a noun by placing the definite article el before the infinitive. El **vivir** bien es la mejor venganza. "Living well is the best revenge."

There are areas of the United States where Spanish is fighting a difficult battle to survive in the face of the dominance of English in government, business, education and entertainment. People with Hispanic roots but little contact with formal Spanish as spoken outside our borders are creating a rich new regional vocabulary of verbs. Taipiar (escribir a máquina), flirtear (coquetear), and imeiliar (enviar una carta electrónica) are examples of these Juanito-come-lately verbs.

Some people shudder at these neologisms. But it seems logical to me that if all the fruteros in the market in Caracas call that fleshy yellowish orange fruit with the big seed a melocotón, there is no sense going around asking where to buy a durazno. At least not if what you want is to eat a peach. By the same token, if you are having trouble getting your car to stop and el mecánico in the shop in Juarez only knows the word breques there is not much point in telling him that you have a problem with the frenos. *But,* ideally, one eventually learns when, where, and to whom to say pavo, to whom to say guajolote, and to whom to say torqui.

So you have my blessing if you wish to indulge in neologism-ism. I have invented quite a few verbs over the years (some of them intentionally). Just make sure that your linguistic jewel has an infinitive that ends –ar, or -er, or –ir; (-ar seems to be the preferred ending for new verbs). The crucial question, as with any invention, is, will anyone else want to use it? Two of my more durable inventions are cayaquear (to kayak) and nevepatear (to snowshoe). They were created so that students in conversational classes could talk about their favorite activities without resorting to expressions like "<u>fuimos</u> snowshoeing." It is far better, in my mind, that the students have an 'inflectable instrument' (Oh, the allure of alliteration! – I mean, 'verb,' of course) to deal with, for once created a verb must strictly adhere to the rules governing conjugation.

There is a fringe benefit that comes with verb invention. Learning a second language can seem a daunting task, a solemn formidable process in which the learner is more often wrong than right. Playing with the language takes the solemnity out of the process. Enjoy your creations. Laugh at your mistakes. Your confidence in your ability to learn and speak will soar.

But please, all you future Thomas Alva Edisons of the verb, heed these words of caution. Spanish has a large store of very serviceable verbs. Learn them. Use them!

Chapter Ten

Don't Go for the <u>Gusto</u>

"I am not able to like anybody but many people please me a lot," said the friendly Spaniard.

You may wonder what is meant by this opening sentence. Perhaps, given just this sentence with no context, you might make sense of it in psychological terms. "He's not emotionally capable of actively liking, but he can passively be pleased" or something of the kind.

But we are into grammar-babble here, not Freudian analysis. The intention of that sentence is to dramatize the important fact that THERE IS NO VERB IN SPANISH MEANING 'TO LIKE.' You can love and you can hate but you cannot like anything in Spanish. You cannot say, "I like Paris in the springtime," in Spanish. You must substitute the verb 'to please' for the verb 'to like.' "Paris in the springtime pleases me."

This matters because when you substitute the verb 'to please' for the verb 'to like,' as the English-speaker must do when speaking Spanish, the grammar of the sentence is radically altered. The subject of the English sentence, the doer of the liking, becomes the object of the Spanish sentence, the person to whom something is pleasing. The person or thing liked in the English sentence, i.e. the direct object, becomes the subject, the person or thing doing the pleasing, in the Spanish sentence. The student who thinks of <u>gustar</u> as a translation of 'to like' will continually generate confusion when trying to express liking or dislike in Spanish. Any time you begin a sentence, "<u>Yo gusto...</u>," you are in grammatical hot water.

THERE IS NO VERB 'TO LIKE' IN SPANISH. <u>Gustar</u> means 'to please.'

The first sentence of this essay cannot even be translated into Spanish. To do so you would have to use the verb <u>gustar</u> in both clauses, ending up with the second clause contradicting the first - <u>Nadie es capaz de gustarme pero muchas personas me gustan mucho</u>. (Nobody is capable of pleasing me but many people please me a lot).

THERE IS NO VERB MEANING 'TO LIKE' IN SPANISH!

Perhaps you have noticed by now that I am trying to emphasize this important point - i.e. THERE IS NO VERB MEANING 'TO LIKE' IN SPANISH, because if you will accept and internalize this truth you will be half way to victory in the battle to come. And it has been my experience that most students, when so informed, will reject, deny, or ignore this basic fact, *to wit*, THERE IS NO VERB IN SPANISH THAT MEANS 'TO LIKE.'

As THERE IS NO VERB MEANING 'TO LIKE' IN SPANISH you will substitute the verb <u>gustar</u>, 'to please,' when you wish to express liking or dislike. That also means that, before you jump into Spanish, you must first re-phrase the English thought *in English*.

Therefore, follow this easy two-step procedure. For example, how do you say, "We like to do the macarena," in Spanish?

Step Number One: re-phrase the sentence *in English* using the verb 'to please.'
It pleases us to do the macarena.

Step Number Two: translate the re-phrased sentence into Spanish.
<u>Nos gusta hacer la macarena</u>.

If you will follow this easy two-step procedure your success rate in achieving accurate communication of likes and dislikes in Spanish will soar. Unfortunately, what I have found over and over again is that students either will not be bothered with an easy two-step process (when it is so much easier to be wrong in one simple step!) or refuse to believe that THERE IS NO VERB MEANING 'TO LIKE' IN SPANISH. After more than three decades studying and speaking Spanish the use of <u>gustar</u> is reasonably automatic for me. Even so, I still occasionally revert to the use of this simple two-step process when confronting a particularly convoluted question of multiple likes and dislikes, for example: He does not like it when I am not pleased that he doesn't like what we like to do which is to please the boss who dislikes coffee breaks.

In the next section of this essay you will do an exercise to practice this two-step process. Before you do that let us review the basic structure of a sentence employing the verb <u>gustar</u>. Listed below are the components of a typical <u>gustar</u> sentence. The components in bold print are essential to the sentence. They cannot be omitted and their order is fixed and inviolable (see Chapter 13). The other elements are optional. They are typically placed as shown, but they may be moved about for poetic or dramatic effect or simply because of a stubborn resistance on your part to doing things the way everybody else does them.

prepositional phrase	**negative** (if needed)	**object of verb**	**verb**	subject

For example: John doesn't like to sing. Re-phrased: To John it is not pleasing to sing.

<u>A Juan</u>   **<u>no</u>**   **<u>le</u>**   **<u>gusta</u>**   <u>cantar</u>.

A few comments about the components of a <u>gustar</u> sentence as shown above:

The object of the verb - this essential element tells to whom something is pleasing or not pleasing. There are six possibilities:

<u>me</u> - to me
<u>te</u> - to you (singular familiar)
<u>le</u> - to you (singular formal)
    to her, to him, to it
<u>nos</u> - to us
<u>os</u> - to you (plural familiar - used only in Spain)
<u>les</u> - to you (plural - all cases, familiar and formal, in the Americas)
    to them

The verb - <u>Gustar</u> is a regular first conjugation verb. As is the case with any verb it must agree with its subject. With this verb the subject is usually third person singular or plural (some verb books do not even list any first or second person verb forms for <u>gustar</u>, but the verb is capable of full conjugation and that is occasionally required - see practice sentence #7 below).

The prepositional phrase - The preposition that begins this phrase is always <u>a</u> (to) because the phrase specifies **to whom** something is or is not pleasing. It is used principally to clarify the ambiguous object pronouns <u>le</u> and <u>les</u> as they have multiple meanings. Unless context has made very clear to whom <u>le</u> or <u>les</u> refers this clarifying phrase should be used to specify to whom the subject of the verb is pleasing. Its use may sometimes be redundant but it is never grammatically wrong to include it in the sentence. So if you are in doubt about the clarity of the <u>le</u> or <u>les</u> referent add the clarifier. Some sentences would make no sense without them.

For example: He liked it but she didn't.
    The sentence re-phrased: It pleased him but it did not please her.
        <u>Le gustó pero no le gustó</u>. Huh!?
        With the clarifying phrases: <u>A él le gustó pero a ella no le gusto.</u>

The prepositional phrase may also serve to add emphasis:
    <u>Me gustó</u>. I liked it
    (more emphatic) <u>A mí me gustó</u>. I really liked it.

In informal conversational situations the prepositional phrase may stand alone in place of a grammatically complete sentence with its required verb and object pronoun:
    <u>¿Les gustó la película?</u>
        <u>A mí, sí; a mi esposa, no</u>.

The Subject of the Verb - As is always the case in Spanish, the inclusion of a stated subject of the verb in the sentence is optional. The primary consideration is always clarity. If in the context of the conversation there is no ambiguity or doubt as to the subject there is no need to include it. It is never grammatically wrong to state the subject. Its inclusion may, at times, sound redundant, but far better redundancy than confusion. The subject may also, of course, be stated for other reasons - drama, contrast, emphasis, poetic effect, or needlessly, simply to irritate the person to whom you are speaking.

And Now, A Two Step Drill

THE FIRST STEP - To accustom yourself to this easy two-step process, let us practice Step Number One. Re-phrase the following sentences by substituting the verb 'to please' for 'to like.' You may find this a rather simple exercise. The point is to get into the habit of doing it. So do it, please! The answers will be found in the next section as the drill continues.

1. I don't like to talk on the telephone.

2. Mary likes sad songs.

3. He likes to walk, but she doesn,t.

4. Did you like the hot sauce?

5. We like Bach a lot but we like the Beatles even more.

6. I would like to paint that submarine yellow.

7. We like them but I don't know if they like us.

THE SECOND STEP - you will now translate the seven sentences that have been re-phrased, using the verb 'to please' of course.

1. It does not please me to talk on the phone.

2. Sad songs please Mary.

3. It pleases him to walk but it does not please her.

4. Did the hot sauce please you?

5. Bach pleases us a lot but the Beatles please us even more.

6. It would please me to paint that submarine yellow.

7. They please us but I don't know if we please them.

Now check your translations against these Royal Academy approved translations. There is some room for variations of word order. The non-negotiable and inviolable segments of each sentence are in bold print. Keep in mind that there is no 'it' as subject in Spanish.

1. **No me gusta** hablar por teléfono.
2. A María **le gustan** las canciones tristes.
3. A él **le gusta** caminar pero a ella **no le gusta**.
4. ?**Te gustó** la salsa picante?
5. **Nos gusta** mucho Bach pero **nos gustan** aun más los Beatles.
6. **Me gustaría** pintar de amarillo ese submarino.
7. **Nos gustan** ellos pero yo no sé si **les gustamos** nosotros.

Get some extra mileage out of *me, te le, nos* and *les*

There are other verbs in Spanish that are usually handled in the same way as gustar, i.e. the third person singular or plural of the verb in combination with one of the object pronouns. Four of the most common ones are parecer, importar, interesar, and doler. Unlike gustar, however, these verbs do not require any major re-phrasing of the English before they can be translated. Each does present its own small challenge.

The English-speaker may run afoul of parecer, (to seem), because we often use 'to seem' and 'to appear' synonymously in English. In fact, 'it seems to me…' and 'it appears to me… usually mean the same thing. The two phrases would not be interchangeable, for example, if the subject of the conversation were a ghost. "It appears to me only at midnight." The Spanish parecer and aparecer (to appear) are never synonymous. The Spanish aparecer makes reference to visual phenomena, apparitions like that of the ghost. When the English-speaker says "It appears to me…" meaning "It seems to me…" the Spanish is always me parece. Speaking of parecer it is worth noting that when used reflexively, parecerse, means 'to look like'. Mucha gente me dice que yo me parezco a Mel Gibson. (Really! See the photograph on the book cover).

Importar offers another small challenge of recognition of intent of meaning for the English-speaker. One of the meanings of importar is 'to import'. However, unless you are involved in international commerce you will not use it a lot in that sense. The verb also means 'to be important, to matter'. It is in this second sense that it can be a handy verb to keep around for most of us. It is in this second sense that it is used like gustar, i.e. in the third person with an object pronoun. If you want to say, "It doesn't matter to me" or "I don't care", importar is the verb for you. No me importa. (It is not important to me). "He doesn't care." No le importa a él. "We don't care." No nos importa. Or just plain, "it doesn't matter", no importa. The key to success is to recognize that 'matter' and 'care' sometimes mean 'to be important'.

'Care' is a word that should alert you to consider meaning any time you are translating English thoughts into Spanish. Consider these sentences: 1. "I don't care if he goes." 2. "I don't care for him to go." 3. "I won't care for him if he goes." 4. "I won't care for him even if he goes."

These four sentences require four different verbs to translate 'care' into Spanish.

1. <u>No me importa si él va</u>. (It doesn't matter to me if he goes).
2. <u>No quiero que él vaya</u>. (I don't want him to go).
3. <u>No voy a cuidarlo si él va</u>. (I'm not going to take care of him if he goes).
4. <u>No lo amaré aunque vaya</u>. (I will not love him even if he goes).

<u>Interesar</u> (to interest) is another verb that is usually found in the third person with an object pronoun. This sometimes requires the English-speaker to make a quick adjustment before translating. The English-speaker might say, "They are interested in Mexican history," or "Mexican history interests them". The second of the two goes more smoothly into Spanish. <u>A ellos les interesa la historia de México</u>. 'To get interested' or 'to become interested' is a different story. As is often the case, 'to get...' or 'to become...' translates to Spanish by use of the reflexive (see Chapter 13). "They got (or became) interested in Mexican history after they heard Carlos Fuentes speak." <u>Se interesaron en la historia de México después de escuchar la charla de Carlos Fuentes</u>.

Finally let us consider the verb <u>doler</u> (to ache or hurt). Here again we have to be aware from head to toe of how we phrase things in English. For example, we are more likely to say, "I have a headache," than, "My head is hurting me." But we would probably say, "My feet are killing me," rather than "I have aching feet." So we can and do refer to our aches and pains in two ways. We can have an aching body part, or that body part can be hurting us. The Spanish-speaker also has these two options. However, given the fact that he or she does not shy away from the <u>me gusta</u>, <u>te gusta</u>, <u>le gusta</u> format of verb and object pronoun (and, in fact, is rather comfortable with it), the Spanish-speaker is more likely to express aches and pains in this way. <u>Me duele la cabeza</u>, 'my head hurts me.' <u>Me duelen los pies</u>, 'my feet hurt me.' Please note that as both feet are causing discomfort the verb is conjugated in the third person plural.

And here are two additional cultural/linguistic observations thrown in at no extra cost.

1. We Americans live in a culture that places a very high value on (is obsessed with?) respect for private property. In our every day speech we constantly define possession in situations where possession is obvious. The Spanish-speaker has no such compulsion needlessly to make these my/your distinctions. He says, "*The* feet are hurting me." He or she assumes, correctly I am sure, that you, the interlocutor, understand that it is not your feet but his or her own feet that are causing the problem. Spanish does have possessive adjectives. If you are dancing together and *your* feet are hurting him or her, the Spanish-speaker will employ the possessive forms to make clear exactly whose feet are hurting whom.

Avoidance of unneeded declarations of ownership generally applies in Spanish: I washed *my* hands, me lavé *las* manos; he put on *his* hat and left, se puso *el* sombrero y se fue.

2. We Americans also love our new digital cameras and our titanium golf clubs. We adore cherry Garcia ice cream smothered in triple chocolate sauce. We love to ski Aspen and soak in a hot tub afterwards. But we should not use the verbs amar and adorar to express our enthusiasm for such things when speaking Spanish. Those two verbs take direct objects like hijos, amigo, patria, Dios. Inject all the passionate intensity you want into the statement but say, "Me gusta mucho...," or "Me gusta muchísimo...," when talking of your 'love' for things.

Now it would please me to summarize, reiterate and re-emphasize:

1. THERE IS NO VERB IN SPANISH MEANING 'TO LIKE;'
2. The English-speaker who wishes to express liking or dislike in Spanish must use the verb gustar (to please);
3. The English sentence must be rephrased substituting 'to please' for 'to like;'
4. This verb substitution changes the grammar of the sentence significantly;
5. The English-speaker then translates the altered sentence into Spanish.
6. As always, the student continues to be patient but persistent.

Chapter Eleven

An Alternative to Conjugation

My Peace Corps partner had an approach to speaking Spanish (and in particular to dealing with those pesky verbs) that remains, today, unique in my experience. After more than three decades of teaching Spanish as a second language and socializing in a world primarily of Spanish-speakers and other people who in greatly varying degrees have knowledge of the language, I believe that my judgment in this matter deserves the status of a pronunciamento.

A bit of background: with a guaranteed supply of highly motivated guinea pigs on whom to try out different teaching techniques, the Peace Corps rapidly developed effective language programs. But in its first year of operations, when my group started training, there was still much to be learned. Our language instructors were short on both training and experience. They were, I suspect, hired on the basis of being nice people and native speakers of Spanish.

Allen, my future work partner, and I both started our Peace Corps careers as zero-beginners in Spanish. I still clearly remember our first hour of instruction in the language. There were ten or twelve of us, beginners all. We were sitting in the glassed-in porch of a large house on a Vermont hillside under a gray New England sky. We spent the time repeating "buenos días," "buenas tardes," "buenas noches," individually and in ragged unison - not exactly cutting-edge methodology. Later we spent a month in Puerto Rico. During that time we had more hours of jungle survival training (which proved to be of little use in the cities of Venezuela) than Spanish class. Then we were sent out into the field and we were on our own. So we got a nudge to get us started but, basically, we had to teach ourselves to speak Spanish.

Many Americans who spend a great deal of time in Latin America and are self-taught speakers of Spanish develop a verb-less Spanish but manage to get along on a good-sized vocabulary. "Mi carro - problemas - motor malo." or "Mi amigo y yo - dos cervezas - frías por favor." For many people that level of communication is sufficient. Others take the process one step further by learning the infinitives of useful verbs and plugging them in where the verb ought to go but without subjecting themselves or the verb to the ordeal of conjugation. "Nosotros querer una habitación con baño privado."

My co-worker, Allen, went one step further - beyond what we might call the 'infinitivist' approach. He created his own personalized way of dealing with verbs and I have never encountered its like since.

He would pick one form of each verb and use it for all tenses and with all subjects. For example, from the verb <u>hacer</u> he took the past participle, <u>hecho</u>, and proceeded to use it in all situations that called for any form of that verb. <u>Yo hecho</u>, <u>tú hecho</u>, <u>él hecho</u>, etc. To create past tense he would add a word or two to establish context, e.g. <u>ayer yo hecho</u>. From <u>decir</u> he took <u>diga</u>; from <u>tener</u>, <u>tiene</u>; from <u>conocer</u> he got <u>conozca</u>. With a few of the most frequently used verbs he even made a singular/plural distinction. He said, "<u>yo va</u>" but "<u>nosotros van</u>," which made me wonder if he might one day burst forth in full-blown conjugations

There was no discernible pattern to the choices of a verb form that he made. They seemed so random that I eventually settled upon the "Theory of the Hatchling" to satisfy my need for an explanation.

There is a species of duck that takes for its mother the first living creature that it sees upon hatching. In the usual order of things it sees its actual mother. However, if it happens to see a cat or a cow first it will go through life believing that cat or that cow to be its mother (of course, if the first living creature it sees is a cat it will probably have a very brief and unhappy mother/child relationship). That may be the key to understanding Allen's way of handling verbs.

One of the most frustrating aspects of going off to work in another culture and language is the difficulty in understanding what others are saying to you. One learns to express oneself in limited fashion fairly quickly. But there is no controlling the vocabulary and manner of speaking of those around you. The daily intense concentration and effort spent trying to understand what others are saying to you wears you out. It may well be that the first time Allen understood a verb as it was being spoken to him, actually recognized it for what it was, at that sublime moment of recognition that particular form of the verb (whatever it might be) would imprint itself in his brain as the 'mother form,' the form with which he would identify forever after. Thus it became the form that he would use henceforth when he had need of that verb.

Whatever the reason, his was a colorful and truly unique way of managing those irksome verbs. He speech often caused amusement, sometimes amazement, but not ridicule. He was a much too highly valued member of the community for that. His linguistic inventiveness did not make him an ineffective volunteer. Quite to the contrary, his other strengths overcame his weakness in the area of accurate verbal communication. He was a trained social worker full of energy and enthusiasm, and he had a deep and genuine desire to be of service to the young people of our adopted Venezuelan city.

While I struggled to improve my pronunciation, to learn all the traps set by irregular verbs, and to acquire local vocabulary and expressions, Allen gaily bulldozed the elaborate and sometimes delicate structure of grammar and syntax that is humankind's greatest achievement, i.e. language, in the specific case, Spanish. He was never hesitant to speak, was never embarrassed by his repeated errors, and he seemed oblivious to the confusion he often created. He never seemed to learn from his mistakes, and, I suspect that he never even noticed or cared.

The goal of our project was to establish a recreational center and to design and run programs for the youth of the city. The U.S. government gave us a living allowance but any money for building facilities or buying equipment had to be raised by us locally. Our 'annual' campaña financiera never ended. We worked at raising money year round. Thank goodness for Allen! I knew how to kick a soccer ball and had a good jump shot but Allen brought to the task the organizational and administrative skills that were needed.

One of my most vivid memories of our version of peacecorping was a visit to the office of el comandante of a unit of the Venezuelan army that had its barracks guarding the only land access to the city. It was a time of considerable political agitation accompanied by internal terrorism.

Although most of the violence was concentrated in Caracas it was a nervous time. One did not trifle with the Venezuelan military.

Allen figured that if the commandant could be persuaded to order all of his men to make a small contribution to our center it would add up to a sizeable sum of money. Just getting an appointment to see him was a minor triumph of international diplomacy. But one morning we found ourselves waiting in the antechamber of this considerable personage. Our long wait accurately reflected the difference in social stature between him and us. El comandante did not even look up when we were finally ushered into his presence. He was studying some document on the desk before him. Allen walked right up to the desk with a cheery "Buenos días."[25]

Allen had in his hand a foldout pamphlet that described the purpose of our center and even included a photograph or two of smiling barrio children playing chess or shooting a basketball. He placed the pamphlet *on top of* the papers that el comandante was studying and launched into his sales pitch.

Even I, who was used to his Spanish and familiar with the English thoughts he was translating, could barely follow what he was saying. But there was no misunderstanding the enthusiasm and sincerity as he went on and on about los muchachos (that one he always got right!).

Meanwhile the stunned comandante simply stared in amazement, his mouth opening more and more as his jaw dropped further and further. A dissident army faction executing a coup d'etat would have shown more deference (even with weapons at the ready) upon

---

[25] In reality, he probably said, "Buenas días". He routinely said, el casa and el plaza, but when he came upon the occasional noun ending in 'a' that was actually masculine he would handle it as a feminine noun. I came to suspect during the almost two years that we worked together that his mangling of Spanish had less to do with a lack of aptitude than it did with some psychologically driven need not to speak it correctly.

entering his office than had this babbling Gringo. If he caught any of Allen's impassioned plea it can only have been the frequent repetitions of <u>los muchachos</u>. <u>Los muchachos</u> this, <u>los muchachos</u> that, and then yet again <u>los muchachos</u> something else.

When Allen's spirited speech finally came to an end I waited with considerable alarm for the reaction of <u>el comandante</u>. He could not court martial us, and civilians on the outside knew where we were going that morning so I did not think that he would 'disappear us' (although it was the Latin American military that turned 'disappear' into a transitive verb!). He could most certainly order us out of his office and off his base forever. What did happen was the thing I expected least - nothing. Allen's performance had rendered this most powerful man in the province speechless. When it dawned on me that <u>el comandante</u> was still too astonished to speak I stepped up to the desk. In my limited but intelligible Spanish I explained briefly what we were doing and how we hoped he might help us.

Our Laurel and Hardy 'strategy,' totally unplanned though it was, worked perfectly. A devastating one-two combination of punches. Allen, the picador, softened up the tough old bull with his dazzling incoherency. Then I, the matador, stepped in for the quick clean kill. The commandant not only agreed to our proposal but delivered on his promise in a very timely manner. Not long after our visit to the base a jeep pulled up in front of the weed-filled plot of land that we called our center. A soldier jumped out, handed us a check, and drove off. We never saw <u>el comandante</u> again.

A few additional observations

To speak Spanish well is a matter of constant attention to endless small details. *It is the sum of these correctly executed minutia that constitutes good speech.* And it seems to be an all or nothing business. Never have I met, for example, some one who had mastered conjugation but was careless about number/gender agreement or who could put all the object pronouns in their proper places but pronounced all the vowels as indistinguishable 'uhs' and 'ehs.' Painstaking care in some areas of language while ignoring others does not seem practical or even possible. One is careful about details or one is not. And the combined aggregate of the details of grammar, conjugation, pronunciation, vocabulary and fluency[26] add up to language proficiency.

Some years after my time in Venezuela I worked as a consultant to the Educational Testing Service. ETS had a contract with the Peace Corps to evaluate various language-teaching techniques and to track linguistic progress made by volunteers in the field after their training. These assessments were made on the basis of a ten or fifteen minute interview in Spanish with each volunteer. A number was then assigned to the volunteer that indicated language proficiency. These FSI scores went by half steps from 0 to 5 - five being Spanish comparable to that of an educated native speaker.

---

[26]Fluency here is used in a more restricted sense than the popular meaning of the word. Fluency is flow, smooth as opposed to halting speech. Allen, for example, was quite 'fluent' but he did not speak Spanish well.

On one occasion I was sent to Panama to track down and interview all one hundred or so volunteers working there. I recall one pair of back-to-back interviews during that trip because of the sharp contrast between the two speakers and something their dramatically differing styles demonstrated about speech.

The first of these interviews was with a young man who spoke a cautious and carefully crafted Spanish. He made very few mistakes within the limits of his knowledge and scored a solid 3. But talking to him I was reminded of a piano concert I had once attended. The program was all Beethoven, some of my favorite pieces, and the pianist never missed a note. While technically correct he played with no passion and the music felt flat and dead.

The next interviewee was a cowboy-type who handled the language roughly as though bulldogging a calf. He scored significantly lower on the FSI scale. But I am sure that working out in the field he communicated more effectively than the previous volunteer with the higher score and a diffident and distant way of talking. 'Cowboy' looked you in the eye. He smiled and laughed. Whether talking or listening he was engaged - it was you, not the language, that mattered to him. He was an excellent illustration of the fact that the true purpose of language, i.e. communication, is something more than the mastery of grammar, conjugation, pronunciation, etc. There is a human factor that the FSI scale cannot measure.

Later on as the cowboy and I were talking of our Peace Corps experiences he told me his philosophy about speaking Spanish. "Hell," he drawled, "it's their language not mine. I just dump it all out there in front of them and let 'em pick out what they need." I am a stickler for getting all the details right but I have not forgotten the cowboy's words or his engaging manner. There is something more to speaking Spanish than accurate verb conjugation - but it is something that is not measured by any test nor learned in any classroom.

An extreme example of this 'human factor' involves again my partner Allen. We did not spend a lot of our free time together. He had a girlfriend with whom he spent mucho tiempo. However, one evening I accompanied him to visit his novia. We sat on her porch in the warm tropical dark and talked in soft voices of sundry things. At some point I made a reference to the neighboring country of Colombia. An animated Allen started telling us about his days at Columbia University in New York where he had studied. Patti joined in with a liveliness equal to his speaking of the next-door country about which Venezuelans hold opinions somewhat akin to those that Vermont folks have about New Yorkers. I just listened in wonderment as they talked happily past each other. It was not a lengthy exchange. Before long the conversation headed off in a new direction without either of them having realized that they had been talking about different Columbia/Colombia's. The misunderstanding was total but communication went on undeterred.

Perhaps that is not a good example of the human factor in communication - it may have been more the 'raging hormones factor' at work. Nonetheless Allen does make an excellent example of this intangible element of successful speech. His defective Spanish was obvious, glaringly obvious, to all. Yet he worked very effectively. He was an excellent Peace Corps volunteer in my estimation. His linguistic shortcomings were like a wart on the tip of a friend's nose. One simply ceases to notice after a while. He got along quite well with his Spanish-on-crutches enhanced by gestures, warm smiles, and a general simpatiquismo.

This human factor is not an aspect of language that I emphasize as I try to drill correctly spoken Spanish into my students' heads. It seldom comes up unless someone under my tutelage is about to depart for Mexico or other Spanish-speaking parts. Then, feeling like the mother bird watching a fledgling leave the nest, I tell him/her that the precision and accuracy that we have been striving mightily to achieve are not really all that important. Courtesy and friendliness will more than compensate for an incorrectly conjugated verb or a misplaced direct object pronoun. And that is true up to a point.

For the tourist ordering meals, checking bus schedules, or shopping in the marketplace that is fine. But my Peace Corps partner really was limited when it came time to discuss philosophy, policy and planning with our local Board of Directors. He was not able to express coherently his ideas about how and why we should do things one way rather than another. In these circumstances a warm smile was of little value. Ultimately, careful attention to those endless details does matter.

And anyway, why not a friendly smile *along with* good grammar?

Chapter Twelve

Now You Too Can Speak Perfectly (and Imperfectly)

There are two special verb forms in both English and Spanish called participles, the present (or, perfect) participle and the past (or, imperfect) participle. Each of these participles is the nucleus around which clusters a group of tenses - the perfect tenses in the case of the past participle and the progressive tenses which employ the present participle.

These useful verb forms and the tenses generated around them deserve special attention.

First we will look at the perfect tenses. Here are some examples of the perfect tenses in English:

> I have spoken;
> she has studied;
> we would have gone;
> they had eaten.

The Spanish perfect tenses are really quite easy to master. They are much less conjugationally challenging than the other tenses in the Spanish language and their uses closely parallel English usage. So what's the problem?

There are two.

The first is simply recognizing what the perfect tenses are in English so that you will know when to use them when speaking Spanish.

The second problem is coming to understand why something called "the *present* perfect" refers to past events.

Before proceeding to look more closely at the perfect tenses let us talk about verbs in general.

A conjugated Spanish verb contains three bits of information. It tells us who, what and when. By way of example, take the verb form <u>comí</u>. The stem, <u>com</u>-, tells us the what, the action – eat, and the ending, -<u>í</u>, tells us who and when - in this case, first person singular and preterit past - in other words, 'I ate.' An English verb form gives us only two bits of information, the 'who' has to be stated separately. [Of course the 'who' that the Spanish verb ending tells us is the grammatical who - a subject noun or pronoun is frequently required to identify the specific person(s) or thing(s)].

Gramática Apasionada
Reminiscences of a Love Affair with the Spanish Language

But let us now look at the two special verb forms called participles. They are so named because, although they have certain characteristics of a verb, they may also participate in speech as nouns or adjectives. The present participle is always characterized in English by the verb ending '-ing,' and in Spanish by the endings -ando or -iendo. The past participle is characterized by the ending '-ed' in English (although English has many irregular past participles) and by the endings -ado or -ido in Spanish (with a handful of irregular forms).

When acting as a verb the Spanish past participle gives us only one and one-half of the three bits of information that other verb forms tell us. The past participle, comido, for example, gives us one and one-half bits of information - com-, the stem, tells us what or the action, 'eat,' and the ending -ido tells us that the action is completed but does not tell us when or who. To supply the missing one and one-half bits of information the participle needs help. It gets that help in the form of a verbal partner called 'the **helping** verb' – 'to have' in English, haber in Spanish. The helping verb supplies the missing information. For example, has comido: the helping verb, has, gives us the missing information. The subject is tú and it is present tense: therefore, 'you have eaten.' So the perfect tenses are formed by combining the past participle of a verb with the helping verb.

If the helping verb is in the present tense it creates the present perfect tense, if it is in the past it creates the past perfect or pluperfect tense. The helping verb may also be in the present or imperfect subjunctive, or the conditional or future tenses so there are six common perfect tenses. But no matter what you do to the helping verb, the past participle is a rock, as unchanging as Gibraltar. Neither a change of person (subject) nor of tense affects the form of the participle.

In English 'to have' does double duty as the verb meaning 'to possess' and as the helping verb of the perfect tenses. In Spanish 'to have,' meaning 'to possess' is tener, but Spanish has a separate verb, haber, whose all but exclusive function is to help the past participle.

It is this double function of the verb 'to have' in English that is the cause of the first problem mentioned above. It is the main problem that the English speaker has with the perfect tenses when speaking Spanish. 'To have,' meaning 'to possess,' is such a common verb, and it is used so much, that the English speaker hardly notices when he or she is using it as a helping verb. So the solution to this first problem is simply to engage in a forced campaign to heighten your awareness of your use of the perfect tenses when speaking English. For a few days assign one small clump of brain cells the job of watching for and announcing each time you use, hear or read a perfect tense. It is just a matter of awareness. Once you put yourself on alert for the perfect tenses it will become habitual. You can then reassign those brain cells to other more critical tasks. As was mentioned before, the use of these tenses in Spanish closely parallels their use in English, so awareness is half the battle.

(Please note that the helping verb always comes before the participle. Also note that although it is common usage in English to answer a question asked in a perfect tense using only the helping verb to respond, - e.g. Q. "Have you been to Scarborough Fair?" A. "Yes, I have." - this is *never* done in Spanish, you must include the past participle.

Turning to problem number two, let us see what purpose the perfect tenses actually serve. 'Perfect' when used in relation to verbs and tenses means 'completed.' The past participle (or 'perfect participle' as some call it) tells us that the action is completed. The helping verb gives us our point of reference in time. If the helping verb is in the present tense we know that the action is a completed action with reference to the present moment. "I have seen that movie." This statement does not tell you when I saw that movie, it only tells you that the action (of seeing the movie) was completed before the present moment. With the helping verb in the present tense ("I have…") we are using the present perfect tense - the present is our point of reference - but we are speaking of a completed or past action.

If you wish to know when I saw that movie you must use a different tense. "When did you see it?" you ask - this would be the preterit tense if we were doing this in Spanish. I will answer, also using the preterit, "I saw it last Friday." I cannot answer, "I have seen it last Friday." The present perfect tense cannot place an event at a specific point in the past. The present perfect can make reference only to the present moment.

The pluperfect operates the same way but we establish a temporal point of reference in the past. "Tom **had** studied Spanish for one year in college before he started taking classes with me." Our point of reference in time is now the moment when Tom began taking my class. The pluperfect tells us that the action ('study' in this case) was completed before that point in past time. Again, if I want to know exactly when Tom had studied Spanish I must switch to the preterit tense. "What year did you studied Spanish, Tom?"

The future perfect is used if we wish to establish a point in future time as the reference point for completion of the action. "She **will have** visited all fifty states before she turns thirty."

When the present perfect is used the point of temporal reference is always very specifically the present moment. In other perfect tenses the point of reference in time does not have to be as specific as it was made to be in the example sentences given above. "Tom had studied Spanish as a child." "Some day soon she will have visited all fifty states."

Gramática Apasionada
Reminiscences of a Love Affair with the Spanish Language

The Perfect Tenses

Haber		plus	The Past Participle	
(present)			-AR → -ado	
He	Hemos		-ER, -IR → -ido	
Has	Han			
Ha	Han		Irregular Past Participles	
			Hacer	Hecho
[past (pluperfect)]			Decir	Dicho
Había	Habíamos		Escribir	Escrito
Habías	Habían		Ver	Visto
Había	Habían		Abrir	Abierto
			Poner	Puesto
(conditional)			Volver	Vuelto
Habría	Habríamos		Morir	Muerto
Habrías	Habrían		Romper	Roto
Habría	Habrían		Cubrir	Cubierto

I have spoken – Yo he hablado — She has studied – Ella ha estudiado
We would have gone – Nosotros habríamos ido
They had eaten – Ellos habían comido

Remember that it was said that participles can participate in speech as nouns and adjectives as well as being verbs. This is not to say that all past participles are also nouns and adjectives. In English there is not a great number of nouns – 'thought' and 'given' are two examples - but there are many adjectives - a **closed** mind, a **complicated** story, a **dedicated** teacher, an **illustrated** manuscript, a **driven** personality, and many more.

Some Spanish past participles also serve as nouns or adjectives. As is the case in English there are many more of the later than the former. The name of our country gives an example of both, los Estados Unidos.

Estado is the past participle of estar and is also the noun 'state.' Unido is the past participle of the verb unir, 'to unite,' and also the adjective 'united,' thus: the United States. Please note that when a past participle is participating in speech as an adjective it behaves like an adjective. Estados is masculine plural so the modifying adjective (unido) must agree with it - Unidos.

In addition to the list of irregular Spanish past participles shown above there is a considerably larger group of verbs that have both a regular and an irregular past participle. The usual practice with these verbs is to employ the regular form in conjunction with the helping verb and to use the irregular form as the adjective. By way of example: bendecir, 'to bless;' <u>El obispo ha bendecido el agua, ahora es agua bendita</u>. Here are a few more of the more common verbs of this kind: <u>freír, freído, frito</u>; <u>despertar, despertado, despierto</u>; <u>fijar, fijado, fijo</u>; <u>salvar, salvado, salvo</u>.

The Progressive Tenses

Now let us look at the other participle and the cluster of tenses, the progressive tenses, built around it. Here are a few examples of progressive tenses in English:

> we are talking;
> he was thinking;
> I am writing;
> they will be working;
> you were eating.

As is the case with the past participle, the present participle (the –ing form of the verb) gives us only one and one-half of the three bits of information that a conjugated verb form does. So, like its buddy the past participle, the present participle needs help. The helping verb for progressive tenses in English is 'to be,' and in Spanish <u>estar</u>.

Look at the sentence fragment: "<u>Estabas comiendo</u>…" The present participle, <u>comiendo</u> in our example sentence, gives us one and one half bits of information. The stem, <u>com-</u>, announces the action – 'eat' - and the ending, <u>-iendo</u>, tells us one aspect of the action, that the action is in progress, that it is happening. But it does not specify whether the action **was** in progress, **is** in progress, or **will be** in progress at some future time. Nor does it say who. Again the helping verb comes to the rescue. It fills in these unknowns. <u>Estabas</u> tells us that the doer is <u>tú</u> and that the reference in time is past. "You were eating…," that action was in progress, "…when the tornado hit,"or "…when someone called urging you to change your long-distance telephone company."

The English present participle is a prodigious participator in speech as both a noun, e.g. - **swimming** is a low impact form of exercise, more low cost **housing** is urgently needed, the human **being** is an odd creature; and as an adjective - **flying** saucer, **burning** desire, **helping** verb, **weeping** willow, **depressing** circumstances, and so on. Its Spanish equivalent really does not deserves the name 'participle.' It participates in the language only as a verb.

Spanish does not use the present participle as a noun. The nouns <u>hacienda</u> (a self-sufficient ranch or estate - a place of much 'doing') and <u>vivienda</u> (housing) come close but <u>no cigarro</u>.

Nor does Spanish use the present participle as an adjective. However, there are a number of adjectives that combine the stem of the participle with other endings like <u>-dor</u>, and <u>-iente</u> to make adjectives equivalent to the English -ing forms: flying (<u>volando</u>) saucer, <u>platillo volador</u>; burning (<u>ardiendo</u>) desire, <u>deseo ardiente</u>; running (<u>corriendo</u>) water, <u>agua corriente</u> and so on.

Estar is the helping verb for the progressive tenses in Spanish. But the Spanish present participle can also be used in combination with the verb seguir (to follow). In these cases seguir translates 'to keep on' or 'to continue to' or 'to go on'.

He **goes on being** an optimist in spite of a series of setbacks.
Sigue siendo optimista a pesar de una serie de trastornos.

The Progressive Tenses

Estar	plus	The Present Participle
(present)		-AR→-ando
Estoy Estamos		-ER, -IR→-iendo
Estás Están		
Está Están		(Present participles with spelling changes are outlined below).
(past)		
Estaba Estábamos		
Estabas Estaban		
Estaba Estaban		
(conditional)		
Estaría Estaríamos		
Estarías Estarían		
Estaría Estarían		

We are talking – Nosotros estamos hablando —- He was thinking – El estaba pensando
I am writing – Yo estoy escribiendo
They will be working – Ellos estarán trabajando

An example of the conditional progressive: <u>Yo **estaría viviendo** felizmente en Río de Enero si el agente del FBI no me hubiera visto abordando el avión en Miami.</u> 'I **would be living** contentedly in Rio de Janeiro if the FBI agent had not seen me boarding the plane in Miami.'

There are two circumstances in which the creation of the present participle in Spanish varies slightly from the simple process shown above. Fortunately these circumstances can be defined quite clearly.

First: if the stem of the infinitive of a second (-er) or third (-ir) conjugation verb ends in a vowel the present participle ending (-iendo) changes to -yendo. This avoids the messy situation caused by three successive vowels: for example, traer, trayendo; oír, oyendo; leer, leyendo. (The verb ir presents a unique case. Drop the ending, -ir, and there is nothing left.

The present participle of <u>ir</u> is <u>yendo</u>. It should be noted here that Spanish *rarely* puts the verb <u>ir</u> in a progressive form).

Second: think back to the discussion of the conjugation of the preterit tense. Third conjugation verbs (-ir) that have a stem change in the preterit have that same stem change in the present participle; therefore, <u>dormir</u>, <u>durmiendo</u>; <u>pedir</u>, <u>pidiendo</u>; <u>seguir</u>, <u>siguiendo</u>; etc. Also the verbs <u>decir</u>, <u>poder</u>, and <u>venir</u> have a slightly altered present participles, <u>diciendo</u>, <u>pu</u>diendo, and <u>vi</u>niendo.

Note: the Spanish present participle is not used after a preposition as its English equivalent is (there are some exceptions allowed in the case of the preposition <u>en</u>). Spanish uses the infinitive in these situations. Examples: Castro talked for five hours **without stopping** - <u>Castro habló por cinco horas **sin cesar**</u>; Always read the fine print **before signing** any document - <u>Lea siempre la letra chica **antes de firmar** cualquier documento</u>.

Alert students frequently ask if there any difference between the imperfect past and the imperfect progressive tense, and if so, what is the difference? For example, the sentence, "I was sleeping when you called," could be translated either, "<u>Yo dormía...</u>," or "<u>Yo estaba durmiendo cuando me telefoneaste.</u>" Both are correct translations of the sentence. But the use of the progressive tense, requiring two words instead of one, calls a bit more attention to that action – sort of like, "Hey, I was sleeping!" Having noted this relatively subtle distinction, it can be said the imperfect and the imperfect progressive are often interchangeable. But do not forget that the imperfect form of the verb may carry the meaning 'used to…'. "<u>En su juventud él corría largas distancias.</u>" "In his youth he used to run long distances." The imperfect progressive cannot be substituted for the imperfect tense if the intended meaning is 'used to…'.

When speaking in the past progressive, the helping verb is almost always in the imperfect past form – <u>estaba</u>, <u>estabas</u>, etc. This is because the imperfect form suggests the on-going-ness of the action. Once in while, however, the speaker may wish to refer to an on-going action in the past but also want to place emphasis on the fact that it came to an end. In such cases the helping verb should be conjugated in the preterit tense; for example, <u>Los muchachos **estuvieron** fumando hasta que sus padres regresaron del cine</u>. 'The kids were smoking until their parents got home from the movies.'

An additional note of caution - Spanish remains more literally true to the purpose of the progressive tenses, i.e. to refer to actions that are *in progress*, than does English. In English we sometimes substitute the present progressive for what is in fact a future action; for example, if I were to say to you in October, "My sister **is coming** to Thanksgiving dinner," the Spanish would have to be, "<u>Mi hermana **va a venir** a la cena del Día de Acción de Gracias</u>." (She **is going to come**… unless, of course, my sister, who lives 2,000 miles away, has decided to come on foot and has already started walking to New Mexico as I speak to you in October).

The verb sentarse presents another instance in which the literal adherence of Spanish to the intent of the progressive tenses clashes with the more casual use of these tenses in English. Take the sentence: Julia Roberts **was sitting** beside me on a flight from New York to Los Angeles. If you translate the sentence: J. R. **estaba sentándose** al lado de mí durante etc...., the information that you would actually be conveying is that she took an awfully long time to lower her shapely posterior into the seat next to you. She probably sat down quickly and easily (especially since you were undoubtedly traveling in the roomy firstclass compartment). For the rest of the flight ella estaba **sentada** al lado de usted (she was **seated** beside you).

So let the participles participate. Just keep in mind that the rules for their participation in the two languages are not exactly the same in all cases.

Chapter Thirteen

The Killer Bees of Spanish Grammar

"Yo no...se te...me lo...le gustó...¡me!," sputtered the increasingly red-faced student just before slumping forward and commencing to strike at the crimson forehead of said visage with his fist.

Variations of this scene have played themselves out before my eyes many times over the years. Once again the frustration of trying to sort out all the object pronouns leads to aggression directed against self. It does sometimes seem that those little Spanish pronouns swarm about the verb like Africanized killer bees intent upon rendering any attempt at coherency D.O.A., (dead on articulation), and reducing the student/speaker to skull-banging humiliation

It does not have to be so. Let us break the problem down into its several components - word order, direct object, indirect object, and the reflexive object pronouns (with special attention paid to the seemingly ubiquitous 'se').

Word Order

It is natural that, having done something successfully a certain way all your life, your mind will resist doing it differently. But in several basic ways Spanish word order is different from English. Spanish is, after all, a different language. They have a right to do things differently.

You are quite happy and comfortable saying, for example, "He gave it to me." Spanish demands that you say, "He to me it gave." This disruption of the 'natural order' of things will initially cause confusion. But the rules are clear and constant. They can be learned in three minutes. Learning to apply them in speech will take more time. The secret is practice – repetition, repetition, repetition. Say, "He to me it gave, he to me it gave, he to me it gave...," fifty times and you will find it begins to sound natural. Then say it fifty times in Spanish. "Él me lo dio, él me lo dio, él me lo dio..." Before long él dio lo me will start to sound strange.

The speaker or writer of Spanish has a lot of freedom when composing a sentence. Many elements of a sentence may be moved from one position to another within the sentence for dramatic effect or stylistic reasons. But at the core of every sentence there is at least one conjugated verb. And related to that verb there is a prescribed sequence of grammatical elements that goes as follows:

negative/indirect object pronoun/direct object pronoun/verb.

Not every sentence will have all four of these elements. Most will not. The only element that every grammatically correct and complete sentence requires is a verb. But any of the other three elements will be set into the sentence as needed in the sequence shown above. This word order is inviolate. No other information, including the subject, that the speaker wishes to include in the sentence may interpose itself within this sequence.

Now let's see if we can begin to extract some of the honey that those bees have made for us.

The Direct Object

The direct object is that entity (person or thing) in a sentence that receives the action of the verb. Said another way, it is that entity that is directly acted upon by the verb.

Look at the sentence: the boy hits the ball. The boy is the subject of the sentence, he is the doer of the action. The action the boy does - hits - is the verb. The ball was on the receiving end of the action – it got hit. So the ball is the direct object, the object that was directly acted upon by the verb.

Consider the following sentences:

1. They snatched the cooling pie from the back porch.
2. They ate it up in less than three minutes.
3. They left the pie tin near the dog house.
4. They behaved angelically upon returning home later.

To find the direct object (who or what received the action of the verb) in each of these sentences ask the question:

Who or what got _____?

Fill in the blank space with the past participle of the verb whose direct object you are seeking. The answer to that question is the direct object of the verb.

1. Who or what got <u>snatched</u>? The pie got snatched.
2. Who or what got <u>eaten</u>? It (the pie) got eaten.
3. Who or what got <u>left</u>? The pie tin got left
4. Who or what got <u>behaved</u>? Nothing and nobody. There is no direct object. 'They' did the behaving but nothing in the sentence received the action of the verb - nobody and nothing 'got behaved'. In fact, 'to behave' is an intransitive verb, that is to say, it cannot take a direct object.

James K. Gavin

In sentence #1 the direct object 'pie' is a noun and must be placed outside the boundaries of the inviolate Spanish grammatical sequence of negative/indirect object pronoun/direct object pronoun/verb shown above. In English a direct object noun is placed after the verb. This is also generally true in Spanish but Spanish does allow more flexibility than English.

In sentence #2 the direct object is still the pie. But the noun 'pie' has been replaced by the pronoun 'it.' Now we have a direct object pronoun. Its placement in the Spanish sentence would be dictated strictly according to the rules for word order outlined above.

In sentence #3 the direct object is again a noun, 'pie tin.' It goes outside the prescribed word order.

Sentence #4 has no direct object.

The example sentences demonstrated only one direct object pronoun, 'it' in sentence #2. Here are the other possibilities in English covering the six grammatical persons.

    First person singular: Lightning struck **me**.
    Second person singular: Lightning struck **you**.
    Third person singular: Lightning struck **him**, **her**, or **it**.
    First person plural: Lightning struck **us**.
    Second person plural: Lightning struck **you**.
    Third person plural: Lightning struck **them**.

In Spanish the direct object pronouns are:

	singular	plural
first person	**me**	**nos**
second person	**te**	**los, las**[27]
third person	**lo, la**	**los, las**

These, then, are the pronouns that may occupy the slot labeled 'direct object pronoun' in the diagram of word order shown above.

Before reviewing the indirect object pronouns this might be a good place to mention a phenomenon of Spanish grammar relating to direct object nouns, the personal '<u>a</u>.' English has no corresponding entity because there is no need for it. In the sentence: - John sees Mary - there is no question who is seeing whom. English word order dictates that the subject come before the verb and the direct object (noun or pronoun) be placed after the verb. Spanish does dictate the position of a direct object pronoun but it leaves more flexible

---

[27]Please keep in mind that <u>usted</u> and <u>ustedes</u> are second person in fact, i.e. the person or persons being spoken to; but in all aspects of Spanish grammar they are treated as third person. In the Americas the familiar second person plural, <u>vosotros</u> is not used. Therefore, the direct object pronouns that refer to <u>ustedes</u> have been inserted in the chart instead of <u>os</u> in the position of second person plural.

the position of the subject and a direct object noun. Therefore the sentence: - Juan ve María - leaves some doubt as far as who is doing the seeing and who is being seen.

Normal Spanish usage would suggest that John sees Mary; but to eliminate any doubt or possible confusion Spanish grammar employs the personal 'a.' 'A' personal is a flag placed in front of a noun that refers to a person or persons (Juan, mis hermanos, la estudiante, etc.) if that noun is the direct object of the verb.

Juan ve **a** María leaves no doubt who sees whom. **A** Juan ve María says just the opposite - now Juan is the direct object and María is the subject, the one doing the seeing. If we change the sentence to: Juan ve las montañas - there is no need to specifically label the subject and the direct object because mountains cannot see, there is no ambiguity. Even if we make the sentence: Juan ve el toro - there is no uncertainty who sees whom. Of course bulls can see, but if Juan, a person, were the direct object, the one being seen, instead of the subject, the personal 'a' would be required - **A** Juan ve el toro. 'A' *person*al means what it says. It is for persons only.

There is no doubt who sees whom in the sentence: - Juan y Pedro ven María. The plural verb form ven makes it clear that Juan and Pablo are the subject of the sentence and Maria is the direct object. But Spanish has taken the specific cases where there could be confusion, for which the personal 'a' was presumably created, and generalized the rule to include all references to people as direct objects. Therefore, one must say, Juan y Pedro ven **a** María.

'A' personal is required only if the reference is to specific people. A generic reference to a kind of person or persons does not call for the 'a.'

Buscamos enfermeras para trabajar en la noche.
We are looking for nurses (any nurses) to work at night.

Buscamos **a** las enfermeras que trabajaron anoche.
We are looking for the nurses (specific people) that worked last night.

It is not frequently done but one can take poetic liberties with the personal 'a.' When I was living in Puerto Rico I saw many people wearing a T-shirt that said, "Tengo **a** Puerto Rico en mi corazón." Residents of the island were using a grammatical trick to personalize their homeland, to endow it with the quality of a living and much loved being.

Coincidentally, tener is exempted from using the personal 'a.' One does not say, "Tengo **a** dos hijas." 'Hijas' is the direct object of the verb and a reference to people. But, Tengo dos hijas, is correct.

Another verb, querer, has two meanings, 'to love' and "to want.' Use or omission of the personal 'a' makes that determination. Returning to the hospital:

Yo quiero la enfermera. (The bedpan needs emptying).

Yo quiero **a** la enfermera. (She is the woman for me).

The Indirect Object

The indirect object is that entity (usually, but not always, a person or persons) in a sentence that, although it is not acted upon directly by the verb, is indirectly involved in the action of the verb.

Example:

He gave his old pickup to his son.

First apply the direct object test.

    Q. Who or what got given?
    A. His old pickup truck got given.

That is the direct object. But the truck was given to his son. His son is not the direct object of the verb, but his son is indirectly involved in the giving as the truck was given to him. He (the son) is the indirect object of the verb.

In the example sentence both the direct object, the truck, and the indirect object, his son, are nouns. Continuing the story we might say:

He gave it to him on his sixteenth birthday.

Having established what we are talking about with the nouns, we may now substitute the direct object pronoun 'it' for the truck and the indirect object pronoun 'him' for his son.

The indirect object pronouns in English are the same set of pronouns that are used as direct object pronouns.

The Spanish indirect object pronouns differ in part from the direct object pronouns. They are:

	singular	plural
first person	**me**	**nos**
second person	**te**	**les**
third person	**le**	**les**

These, then, are the pronouns that go in the slots labeled 'indirect object pronoun' in the word order diagrams shown above.

The third person direct object pronouns <u>lo</u> and <u>la</u>, <u>los</u> and <u>las</u>, make a gender distinction. The corresponding indirect object pronouns do not. <u>Le</u> means 'to him' and 'to her,' also 'to

Gramática Apasionada
Reminiscences of a Love Affair with the Spanish Language

you' (a usted) in formal address; les means 'to them' or 'to you' (plural) whether the reference is to a masculine or a feminine entity.

Students often have trouble sorting out lo, la, le and their plural counterparts. As a mnemonic device. I have often suggested to students who have trouble remembering which is which, that direct objects are more important than indirect objects. This is not a position I would want to argue in formal debate. But does it not seem that something labeled 'direct' would be more important than something labeled 'indirect'? Because the direct object pronoun 'matters' more it gives you more information. Lo and la tell gender as well as number (singular, not plural). Le tells you only number, not gender.

Sorting out lo, la and le is further complicated by the fact that Spanish speakers are divided into two camps - not warring factions but distinct groups as regards a specific grammatical usage - loístas and leístas. Loístas always use lo, la, los and las as their third person direct object pronouns of choice; leístas do not.

There are a number of verbs that can have a direct object but not an indirect object - ver, conocer, and invitar, to name three. In combination with verbs such as these a leísta will use le and les as third person direct object pronouns as there is no possibility of needing le or les as an indirect object pronoun with that verb.

A loísta would say, "Yo lo conozco" (I know him) and "Yo la conozco" (I know her). A leísta would say, "Yo le conozco" for both. One is not clearer than the other, for in either case the speaker must first have established to whom lo, la, or le refers before substituting a pronoun for the noun.

But just as the Spanish student is beginning to think that he or she has gotten direct and indirect object pronouns straight in his or her mind, he or she[28] hears an educated native speaker of Spanish use le where he or she (the student) would have sworn that lo or la should have been used. This is a win-win situation, everybody is right. The speaker just happens to be a leísta.

Amongst leístas there are two groups. One uses le and les for both masculine and feminine, the other uses le and les only for the masculine and la and las for the feminine. I do not know which of these factions claims to represent mainstream leísmo.[29]

In neither English nor Spanish does one use both a direct object noun and its corresponding pronoun at the same time in conjunction with one verb. One does not say, "He was reading **it the newspaper** while driving in rush hour traffic." One establishes the

---

[28]English could use new forms that would do for 'he or she', 'him or her', 'his or her' what 'Ms.' has done for us in the case of 'Miss' and 'Mrs.'

[29]El Diccionario de la Lengua Española, the dictionary put out by the Royal Academy, refers to leísmo as a "vicio," a "bad habit." In my experience, many polished, educated native speakers are leístas.

antecedent by using a noun ('newspaper,' in this case) and then may substitute the pronoun 'it' with succeeding verbs as the story continues. "Going along at fifty miles per hour the wind suddenly blew **it** up against his face."

The same rules apply to the use of indirect object nouns and pronouns in English. One does not say, "He told a different story to **him the policeman**." But with indirect objects Spanish plays by a different set of rules.

If there is an indirect object in a Spanish sentence one of the indirect object pronouns (from the list above) must be used in conjunction with the verb in the slot labeled 'indirect object pronoun'. In addition, a prepositional phrase commencing with 'a' may be used to supply the indirect object noun(s) needed to clarify the reference made by the indirect object pronoun. So we would translate the previous example sentence: "El **le** dijo un cuentazo diferente **al policía**."

Given the ambiguous nature of le (to her, to him, to you [usted]) and les (to you [plural], to them) this doubling up of the indirect object noun and pronoun is a frequent occurrence.

This doubling up of the indirect object does serve other purposes besides necessary clarification. It may also be done for emphasis and/or contrast. There is nothing ambiguous about the indirect object pronoun in the statement:

Me gustó esa película. I liked that movie.

But:

A mí me gustó esa película, provides emphasis, (I really liked that movie), or, in a different context, contrast, (Maybe they didn't like that movie but I did).

Some Additional Observations about Word Order

At the beginning of this essay the word order for certain grammatical elements in a Spanish sentence was presented: negative/indirect object pronoun/direct object pronoun/verb. English also has rules about word order. But English tolerates tampering with the relationship between verbs and negatives in ways that would be inconceivable in Spanish. As an example, in a negative statement English, as a norm, also places a negative word before the main verb of the sentence. But Spanish would not have allowed Patrick Henry's dramatic exhortation to his fellow Virginians, "I know not what course others may take, but as for me, give me liberty or give me death!," or President Kennedy's inaugural appeal, "Ask not what your country can do for you…" On the other hand, the double (and triple) negative, a definite no-no in English (the hyphen here staves off bi-negativity), is quite proper in Spanish as long as only one negative is placed before the verb. Nunca me dan nada or no me dan nada nunca. "They never give me anything."

Gramática Apasionada
Reminiscences of a Love Affair with the Spanish Language

There are three exceptions to the Spanish sequence of negative, object pronouns and verb shown above.

The first is the case of affirmative commands. The word order in these instances is:

verb/indirect object pronoun/ direct object pronoun.

For example: Hágalo - Do it; Dámelo - Give it to me; Díganos - Tell us. The negative of the three examples given would revert to using the general rule for word order - No lo haga, no me lo des, and no nos diga. You will have observed that when the object pronouns come after the verb they are attached to it and constitute one word. This requires you to give extra thought to the possible need for a written accent mark (see Chapter 17).

The second exception is when there is an infinitive in the sentence. Again the word order is:

infinitive/indirect object pronoun/direct object pronouns

This word order is optional if, as is usually the case, the infinitive is in combination with a conjugated verb form. For example:

¿Quieres ir conmigo? Do you want to go with me?

Sí, quiero acompañarte. Yes, I want to accompany you. (Please note that the direct object pronoun, 'te,' is again attached to the verb because it comes after the verb).

Or the speaker could have chosen to respond:

Sí, **te** quiero acompañar.

The information conveyed is the same. However, isolating the direct object pronoun before the verb does allow the speaker to place a little more emphasis on the 'te' if desired. This might be done to load the response with subtle additional information – e.g. "It's really you I want to go with, not someone else."

If, on the other hand, the infinitive stands alone in a prepositional or infinitive phrase the posterior position of the object pronouns is not optional, it is required.

Al conocerla uno se enamora de ella. Upon meeting her one falls in love with her.

Decírnoslo no te costaría nada. To tell us about it would not cost you anything.

The third exception to the standard word order is when the sentence contains a present participle (the '-ing' form of the verb). Usually the present participle will be found in the company of its helpful friend <u>estar</u> forming a progressive tense, i.e. speaking of something that is, was, or will be in progress (see Chapter 12).

<u>Para crear la apariencia de normalidad el presidente **estaba jugando** al golf cuando las Fuerzas Aéreas iniciaron el asalto.</u>
To create the appearance of normalcy the president was playing golf when the Air Force launched its assault.

As was the case with the infinitive, the word order:

present participle/indirect object pronoun/direct object pronoun

is an optional alternative to the standard word order when the participle is in combination with the helping verb.

<u>Mi amigo estaba escribiéndo**me** una carta cuando la primera bomba explotó.</u>
or: <u>Mi amigo **me** estaba escribiendo una carta cuando la primera bomba explotó.</u>
My friend was writing to me when the first bomb exploded.

But, as with the infinitive, when standing alone the present participle receives object pronouns after and attached to it.

<u>Encontrándo**se** en gran peligro, mi amigo abandonó la carta y la casa inmediatamente.</u>
Finding himself in great danger, my friend abandoned the letter and the house immediately.

The Reflexive Pronouns

The attack of the killer bees culminates in the reflexive, led by the busy pronoun '<u>se</u>' that sometimes seems to be in five places at the same time.

The reflexive itself is not a difficult concept to grasp. We have such a thing in English, but the Spanish version is more frequently used and does seem to generate a <u>blitzkreig</u> of object pronouns around the verbs. There six different ways in which the pronoun <u>se</u> may be used.

1. A reflexive verb is a verb in which the action of the verb reflects right back on to the doer of the action. In other words, the subject and the direct object are the same person or persons.

"I scrubbed myself with tomato juice for 45 minutes after my encounter with the skunk."

I did the scrubbing. But, who or what got scrubbed? Me. I am both subject and direct object. This is what the reflexive is.

The English reflexive pronouns are: myself, yourself, himself, herself, oneself, itself, ourselves, yourselves, and themselves.

In Spanish they are:	singular	plural
first person	**me**	**nos**
second person	**te**	**se**
third person	**se**	**se**

The ambiguity of 'se,' which can mean 'himself,' 'herself,' 'yourself' (usted), 'oneself,' 'itself,' 'yourselves,' or 'themselves,' is not really a problem. By the nature of what the reflexive is the 'se' must agree with the subject of the verb - he/himself, she/herself, etc.

However, English does not use the true reflexive (I scrubbed myself) nearly as often as does Spanish. We say in other ways what Spanish expresses with the reflexive. For example, all of the following English expressions with the verb 'to get' would be stated as reflexive verbs in Spanish: to get sick or well, married or divorced, dirty or clean, dressed or undressed, wet or dry, lost, angry, happy, sad, confused, bored, and more.

Quite possibly the very first statement you learned to make in Spanish was, "Yo me llamo Roberto o Carolina o Fulano." "My name is Bob or Carol or whatever." Literally you were saying, "I **call myself** Bob or Carol or whatever."

Furthermore, we get up, sit down, lie down, fall asleep, wake up, go away, hide, take a shower or bath, take off our hats and shoes, put on gloves and neckties, and fall in love; all reflexive verbs in Spanish.

These are true reflexives in Spanish. In English one 'gets up,' in Spanish one literally 'lifts oneself'' - levantar means 'to lift,' levantarse means 'to lift oneself.' Yo me levanté, 'I lifted **myself**.' In English one 'takes a bath,' in Spanish one 'bathes oneself,' bañarse. Both of these Spanish verbs, as well as any other reflexive verb, have a non-reflexive application. If I lift a 200 pound weight to tone up my nicely sculpted deltoids, I am the subject of the verb, the doer; but the barbell is the direct object, it gets lifted, and it gets treated like any other direct object. Yo lo levanté 25 veces. 'I lifted **it** 25 times.' If mother bathes her infant child the verb is not reflexive, the subject and the direct object are not the same.

"How," you might ask, "can 'to get married' be a reflexive verb? One does not marry oneself."

Of course not. But look at the verb, casarse. Casa means 'house.' Marriage is about starting a new household. Jeff se casó con Susana. Jeff **housed himself** with Susan. Jeff married Susan.

2. There is also a reciprocal reflexive. With the reciprocal reflexive the verbs and pronouns are handled in exactly the same way as with the true reflexive but the meaning is different. People do not do things to themselves, they do things to each other. For example:

Hace muchos años que nos escribimos. We have been writing to each other for many years.

Los novios se miraban fijamente sin darse cuenta de que el tren se acercaba rápidamente. The lovers were staring intently at each other unaware that the train was rapidly approaching.

The second example sentence nicely illustrates the seemingly ubiquitous nature of 'se.' It shows up three times, first as the reciprocal 'each other,' and twice more as a true reflexive.

Darse cuenta literally means 'to give oneself account of,' in other words 'to notice' or 'to become aware of.' Acercarse means 'to near oneself to,' in other words 'to approach.'

If the speaker fears that his reciprocal meaning may be taken for a reflexive he may tack on the phrase 'el uno al otro' to make his intention clear.

Se odiaban. They hated themselves? No. Se odiaban el uno al otro. No. They hated each other.

3. The reflexive is also used with a limited number of verbs to intensify the action. Yo caí means 'I fell,' yo me caí might translate 'I fell down.' The information conveyed is really the same, but the reflexive makes for a more dramatic statement, an intensified action. Calla, niña is like, "Be quiet, child." ¡Cállate! means "Shut up!" Ella murió ayer and ella se murió ayer both tell me that she died yesterday, but the reflexive would suggest, "She dropped dead yesterday." A few other interesting uses in this vein are: él lo comió, 'he ate it;' él se lo comió, 'he ate it up;' yo lo sé, 'I know it,' yo me lo sé, 'I know it by heart;' ellos rieron, 'they laughed,' ellos se rieron de mí, 'they laughed their heads off at me.'

Perhaps the most common and least understood use of the reflexive to intensify an action occurs with ir (to go) and irse. For example, voy translates, "I go," or "I am going," or "I'm on my way." Me voy is more like, "I'm outta here!" And how many times in our history has a young farm hand or factory worker played out this little scene? Juanito no **fue** a su trabajo hoy. **Se fue** para California. Johnny didn't go to work today. He took off (he split) for California! The imperative also gives us a nice contrast of meaning. Vaya con Dios. "Go with God." (God be with you). Váyase. "Beat it!" "Scram!"

4. Let us now turn to the impersonal se. This is a biggie. There is nothing reflexive or reciprocal about se when used this way. It is used to indicate that the subject of the verb does not matter, that the subject is impersonal. English will often use 'one' to express this.

Another of your first Spanish phrases may have been, ¿Cómo se dice…en español? How does one (anybody, everybody, it does not matter who) say…in Spanish? Especially in cities you will see signs in store windows that say, "Se habla español aquí." "Spanish is spoken here." Exactly who speaks Spanish is not the issue. The store wants to inform the Spanish-speaking public that there are employees to wait upon them in Spanish. The impersonal se works fine for such purposes. "Se vende casa." "House for sale." "Se abre a las 9:00" "We open at 9:00." And, if you smokers want to spare yourself dirty looks, law suits, even physical attack, you better learn this one, "Se ruega no fumar." "It is urged (one begs) that you not smoke."

Instruction manuals that accompany products purchased, recipes in cookbooks, and information on the back of cereal boxes are frequently written out in this form. Any verb in the language can be used in this way. Therefore it may appear that all verbs are or can be reflexive. Not! This is simply an impersonal usage and has nothing to do with the reflexive.

5. And the se's go marching on. Here is a fifth (also non-reflexive) use of se.

This use of se we might call "se, the dispenser of indulgences"… "the grantor of immunity."

In Spanish-speaking cultures, in general, there is a deference shown to others in the course of daily life that is sometimes lacking in the United States - salutations, farewells, and other small verbal courtesies that we seem not to find time for in our busy-ness. It is an acknowledgment of our common humanity that one observes between waiters and diners, customers and store clerks, and strangers on the street. These small demonstrations of respect for the feelings of others are extended to include a curious grammatical usage that is employed with certain verbs that could otherwise be construed as assigning blame to another. Once again 'se' is trotted out, this time to create a faux reflexive by means of which blame or responsibility is shifted from the subject to the direct object, the victim becomes the perpetrator.

Q. How would you say, "John broke the teacup," in Spanish? ('To break' is romper).

A. Juan rompió la taza. Coming from a Spanish student this would be an excellent answer. However, most native speakers would probably say, "Se le rompió la taza a Juan." "The cup broke itself to John."

John - the doer, the breaker - has been changed into an indirect object only tangentially involved in the action. The cup becomes the subject and breaks itself. John has been exculpated.

Of course, what we just did for John we can do for ourselves also. I did not break the cup, se me rompió. It broke itself to me.

There is even a special word order for this:

reflexive pronoun <u>se</u>/indirect object pronoun/verb.

Other verbs that frequently employ this construction are: <u>perder</u> (to lose), <u>olvidar</u> (to forget), <u>caer</u> (to fall, but in this context meaning 'to drop'), and <u>acabar</u> (to finish, but in this context meaning 'to use up or run out of'). A few example sentences:

<u>A María se le perdieron las llaves.</u> Mary lost the keys (note that with the plural subject, <u>llaves</u>, the verb is also plural).

<u>Se me olvidó traer el sacacorchos.</u> I forgot to bring the corkscrew.

<u>Se te cayó la pluma.</u> You dropped your pen.

<u>Se nos acabó la gasolina.</u> We ran out of gas.

I recall a small incident that occurred during my Peace Corps days. A ten or twelve year old boy, running from one place to another, brushed against and knocked over a large bulletin board that we set out everyday propped against a tree. "<u>¡Epa, Luis!</u>," I shouted. Luis stopped, looked at me and then at the bulletin board. "<u>Jeem, se me cayó.</u>"

"<u>¿Qué?</u>," I asked.

"<u>Se me cayó.</u>"

"<u>¿Qué?</u>," more forcefully this time.

"<u>¿Lo tumbé?</u>" (Did I knock it over?).

"<u>Sí, señor, lo tumbaste.</u>" With no further protest Luis went back and righted the fallen board.

Clearly, as long as he was thinking of the bulletin board as having 'fallen itself,' Luis felt no obligation to correct the situation. When he re-phrased what had happened he immediately went back and un-did what he had done.

Does this grammatical slight-of-hand demonstrate an ingrained societal tendency to avoid accepting responsibility for one's actions? This question has been raised by students over the years. Does the somewhat convoluted grammar employed in these cases expose a culture-wide character flaw, a grammar-driven irresponsibility? Does the very structure of our English language hold us to a higher standard? After all, even if he had wanted to, the legendary boy George (note the lower case 'b' as in 'George Washington,' not 'Boy George') when asked about the cherry tree could not have said, "It chopped itself down to me." The language does not allow such a construction.

Gramática Apasionada
Reminiscences of a Love Affair with the Spanish Language

"No," three times, to the questions above. We gringos employ similar linguistic dodges in English. "Sweetheart, that lovely old serving platter your grandmother gave you **got broken** this afternoon." 'Got broken' is certainly the English equivalent of 'se rompió.' Or, when we say, "My car ran out of gas," do we really expect others to believe that the stupid car forgot to **get itself** some gasoline?

These are harmless evasions, in both languages, that spare others (and ourselves) the embarrassment that accompanies some of daily life's more trivial offences – "he forgot…," "I lost…," "you dropped…" At a significantly more serious level of villainy, a convicted felon's plea to the court, "Señor Juez, se me robó el banco," would convince nobody and evoke no sympathy. (Thinking a bit more about that, a judge might knock one week off a ten-year sentence just for the sheer good-humored audacity it would take to make such a statement).

6. Finally we come to what I think of as 'the cosmetic se' (we are now, finally, going to "have the last se"). Let me lead you into it this way. Applying the rules about word order and direct and indirect object pronouns, translate the following:

1. John gave me the book. _____

2. John gave it to me. _____

3. I gave John the book. _____

4. I gave it to him. _____

1. Juan me dio el libro.
2. Juan me lo dio.
3. Yo le di el libro a Juan.
4. Yo le lo di.

If you translated sentence #4 as shown above you have done everything correctly within the limits of your knowledge of Spanish grammar. Yo (I) le (to him) lo (it) di (gave). But for a reason unknown to me, Spanish does not like the combination 'le lo.'[30] Any time the happenstance of speech brings these to pronouns together you must change the 'le' to 'se.' Therefore, sentence #4 in corrected form becomes: Yo **se** lo di.

Generalizing this specific case, any time a third person indirect object pronoun (le or les) is combined with a third person direct object pronoun (lo, la, los, or las) the indirect object pronoun is changed to 'se.' In diagram form:

---

[30]The only explanation I have ever heard for this is that the two 'L' sounds so close together are unpleasing to the Spanish ear - which is why I call it 'the cosmetic se.' However, many a loving parent has nicknamed little Eduardo, Lalo, with no discernible negative impact on the boy's emotional development or social advancement.

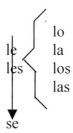

This rules applies whether the forbidden pronoun combination precedes or follows the verb.

I do not want to give it to him. Yo no quiero dár<u>se</u>lo.

To sum up this last grammatical phenomenon; a gangster on the run can **lay low** in Chicago, but he can not **le lo** in Mexico City or Madrid.

In Summary

There are six different uses for the pronoun '<u>se</u>.'

1. The true reflexive
2. The reciprocal
3. The reflexive to intensify an action

One and three accept full conjugation, the reciprocal by its nature must have a plural subject but conjugates to first, second and third person plural. The last three will conjugate only in the third person singular or plural, therefore always calling for the pronoun '<u>se</u>.'

4. The impersonal '<u>se</u>'
5. '<u>Se</u>,' the grantor of immunity
6. The cosmetic '<u>se</u>'

A Quiz

Translate the following sentences. Sentences marked with an asterisk (*) are presented to establish context and need not be translated. Familiar or formal address will also be indicated.

1. The answers are at the end of the quiz.* Cover them with a sheet of paper. (<u>usted</u>)

2. Who gave you this book? Ellen gave it to me. (Do twice - familiar and formal)

3. Have you seen the movie "Titanic"?* No, I haven't seen it. Do you want to see it?

4. We told them yesterday. They did not tell me.

5. Sit down. (usted) Don't sit there. (usted)

6. What happens to the keys?* John gives them to me every day and I give them to her.

7. Does your nephew know that story?* I was reading it to him when he fell asleep.

8. Here are the shoes.*
   Don't give them to her. (usted) Give them to me. She doesn't need them.

9. Who sent us these flowers? My mother sent them to us.

10. Do they speak Spanish well?*
    Yes. And speaking it well allows them to experience life to the fullest.

11. I forgot to pay them.

12. It is not known if the president will visit us.

The answers are on the next page.

James K. Gavin

1. Cúbralas con una hoja de papel.
2. ¿Quién te dio este libro? (familiar)
   ¿Quién le dio este libro? (formal)
   Elena me lo dio.
3. No, yo no la he visto.
   ¿Quieres verla? *or* ¿La quieres ver?
4. Les dijimos ayer. Ellos no me dijeron (a mí).
5. Siéntese. No se siente allí.
6. Juan me las da cada día y yo se las doy a ella.
7. Yo estaba leyéndoselo cuando él se durmió.
   or Yo se lo estaba leyendo cuando…
8. No se los dé a ella. Démelos a mí. Ella no los necesita.
9. ¿Quién nos mandó estas flores? Mi mamá nos las mandó.
10. Sí. Y hablándolo bien les permite experimentar la vida en toda su plenitud.
11. Se me olvidó pagarles.
12. No se sabe si el presidente nos visitará.
    or ……………va a visitarnos.
    or ……………nos va a visitar.

Chapter Fourteen

Words 'R' Us

In Roman times the conspicuous consumer did not have the Rolls Royce or Range Rover available to acquire as a status symbol. However, facing one's home with marble achieved a similar result. So the sale of marble was big business. In order to increase the profit margin some vendors would offer for sale marble of inferior quality. The flaws in the grain could be concealed by rubbing the stone with wax. (A similar tactic is used today by some supermarkets which coat apples with a waxy substance that makes them redder and shinier and, presumably, more attractive to the shoppers in the fruit department). The more reputable marble merchants caught on to this practice and began advertising their merchandise as "without wax." Of course this shady tampering with the product was going on in a place where everybody spoke Latin. Therefore the signs read "sine cera."

Two thousand years later, in a language that did not exist, being spoken in a country that did not exist at the time of these Roman pettifoggers, we are still coincidentally impugning their integrity every time we use the word 'sincere.' No wonder we got the ready-made phrase "caveat emptor" handed down to us from those times.

So, if you are in the habit of signing letters 'sincerely yours,' remember that you are really signing 'withoutwaxedly yours.' As for me, every autumn I drive up into the orchard country of northern New Mexico's Rio Grande valley and buy genuinely 'sincere' apples.

Words, like people and countries, have histories. Not all such histories are as colorful as the example above, but words should not be viewed as just globs of letters. Not only are they used to tell stories, many words have stories of their own to tell.

The Spanish word for sniper, francotirador, has a story to relate.

In 1808 when Napoleon sent his troops into Spain the vast Spanish empire built by Carlos V and Felipe II was in disarray. The royal portraits painted by Francisco Goya at this time reveal a family declining toward idiocy through generations of royal in-breeding. And it might be assumed that even as great a truth teller as Goya may have employed touches of flattery in depicting his powerful patrons.

In any event, the Spanish government was in no condition to mount an effective defense of the country. But Spain did resist. The invading French were shot at from behind rocks and trees, from behind corral walls and farm houses by small bands of patriots. It turned into a very bloody conflict. And the person who shoots his unsuspecting target from a hiding place is still called a shooter (tirador) of the French (franco).

The Spanish resistance to Napoleon's army was indeed fierce. The Spanish government was incapable of waging war effectively. So Spanish patriots waged their own war. They did not invent the hit-and-run strategy they employed. The indigenous people of my native state of Massachusetts, almost forgotten people called the Pequot and the Wampanoag, used similar tactics against European colonizers (invaders) of their lands in the 17th and 18th centuries. And, undoubtedly, native peoples before and since them have employed like methods in defense of their lands when facing better-armed invaders.

The Spanish did not invent the strategy but the name they gave to it has stuck. Perhaps this is because the images that Goya left us of that horrific struggle were etched not just on copper plates but in the minds of the millions of people who have since seen them. The Spanish crown could not fight a real war (guerra) so the Spanish people fought what they called a 'little war' (guerrilla). Americans have become all too familiar with the term in recent decades.

There is so much history in words.

It is common knowledge that the indigenous peoples of our continent are called Indians because Columbus believed that he had reached India when he finally bumped into land. That historically revealing misnomer has been with us for over five hundred years now. Perhaps less well known is the fact that the two continents of the Western Hemisphere are named after the Italian cartographer and occasional explorer Amerigo Vespucci. He made one of the first maps of the New World and, in one of histories most enduring displays of *chutzpa,* named this half of the planet after himself. Amerigo, by the way, is a form of Henry. Therefore, every morning we have thousands of our children pledging allegiance to the flag of the United States of Henry.

It loses, as they say, something in the translation.

Curiosity about the origins of words and names can from time to time be of practical value - not just a hobby for idle minds. Some years back while traveling in the Jackson Hole area of Wyoming I came upon a lovely Catholic chapel tucked into a hillside and dedicated to Our Lady of the Grand Tetons. I suspect that the devotees of the Blessed Lady who named the church were unaware of the origins of the name they chose for her.

The majestic Grand Teton mountains were so named by French trapper/explorers. These rugged adventurers spent months or years in the wilds in exclusively male company. The spectacular prominences of stone recalled to their minds the lovely bosoms of the mademoiselles of faraway St. Louis and New Orleans. It was with such fond memories swirling about in their heads that the mountains were named. But it was probably not the intention of the church community of a later time to call so much attention to that portion of the good lady's anatomy.

The history of individual words is fascinating but words can and should also be appreciated for the inherent aesthetics of letters and sounds.

One man building a stone wall may simply grab the nearest rock of approximately the right size and place it in its mortar bed. Another will actually look at the rock before he sets it in place. Perhaps he will appreciate for a moment a certain subtlety of form, or a few flecks of mica, or a streak of greenish mineral in an otherwise gray stone.

Words are the building blocks of language. We usually just grab the one that fits and shove it into its place. But there are rewards to be had if one looks for the inherent beauty of individual words.

Chihuahua is a particular favorite of mine. I like the stately march of the 'h's across its length. I like the way the citizens of this city and state soften the initial 'ch' to 'sh' (a sound that does not even exist in the Spanish sound system) turning the name of their home state into a caress (Shee-wua-wua). I like the fact that the word is used as an exclamation of surprise or delight. The word even looked, until recently, like the skyline of the city that uses it for its name, a flat city of one-storied adobe buildings broken by a church steeple here and there.

Sonorous ferrocarril is such a word. Its rare twin set of rumbling double 'r's evokes images of trains crossing the vast Mexican desert or disappearing into sinuous canyons of the Sierra Madre.

Another special favorite of mine is ajonjolí. It is a delight to look at. In the lower case Spanish alphabet 'j' vies with 'ñ' for the title of most graceful letter. Here we have two 'j's. The two dots floating above plus the dramatic slash of accent at the end create a visually exotic and interesting word. Aurally, as well, it is a pleasing experience. All the aspirations give the word a breathless whispered quality - this is not a word that should be shouted. Perhaps it is the secret name for a loved one.

Words can be objects of beauty, but whether they are pleasant to behold or as plain as fried hamburg, words matter. We must respect the power of words without allowing them an unwarranted authority over us.

We tend, I think, to underestimate the power of words. And here I do not mean the power of persuasion that a clever speaker wields through the skillful use of words; rather the power inherent in the physical reality of individual words. We think of words as convenient labels for reference purposes. Instead of having to jump about pointing and grunting, we can simply say 'door' or 'window.' But words are so important they can take on a reality of their own. They become a 'thing' in themselves, independent of the thing they are intended to reference.

Relatively few Americans under the age of thirty have ever been in a classroom where the blackboards were actually black. The teacher says, "Johnny, go to the blackboard and divide 6 into 35." Johnny gets up and walks up to a vertical surface that is just as green and almost as big as the lawn he has to mow in the summer and rake in the fall. He does his division. He gives no thought to the fact that the blackboard is not black. Nor does any student ask the teacher why an object so thoroughly green is labeled as black. If asked all the students would agree that the blackboard is green but none would think to call it the greenboard.[31]

Or, how many times have you asked for a glass of water and actually been given a 'plastic' of the liquid? The word itself has taken on a physical reality that to some extent transcends the reality of the object it is supposed to represent.

There is soft-edged antipodean irony in the Spanish verbs used to describe the acts of entering and exiting a vehicle.

You are hitch-hiking along a road in Spain. A driver in his little European compact pulls over, beckons to you and says, "Suba." You open the door, scrunch down onto the seat and assume a position that has your knees three inches from your chin and your head about two and a half feet above the pavement. Approaching your destination you say to your benefactor, "Quisiera bajar aquí." As you step out of the car you experience a momentary dizziness when your head soars back to its accustomed height.

The verbs used in this vignette take us back to a time when a passenger had to use hands and arms as well as legs and feet to climb up (subir) into a horse-drawn coach. At the end of the journey the process was reversed and he climbed down (bajar). But centuries later the Spanish are in an age of travel in which, due to narrow medieval streets and the high price of fuel, there is a prevalence of mini-economy vehicles. The verbs in question now describe the opposite of what you actually do. The persistence of this contradiction may be due to the fact that Spaniards still refer to their automobiles as coches. Perhaps they will switch the verbs around if the term carro, which is more common on this side of the Atlantic Ocean, ever catches on over there. Or, if "bájese" (lower yourself) seems too inelegant a way to invite someone into your car, they could use other altitude-neutral verbs like the English 'get in' and 'get out.'

A word can negate itself and we accept this self-denial or we do not even notice. The cases cited above may seem trivial. But this concept takes on a more menacing aspect if one uses a different word, for example 'liberty.'

A government may present a certain set of circumstances to the people as 'liberty.' The people may accept the physical thing that is the word 'liberty' as liberty, without comparing it carefully enough to the rules and restrictions that are being labeled 'liberty' by the

---

[31] The Spanish word for 'blackboard', pizarra, also contradicts itself in the modern classroom, but it gives us more information in the process. Pizarra means 'slate.' That is what blackboards were originally made from and the source of their blackness.

government. The reality and authority of the word, existing in our minds, may carry as much weight as the external object or thing to which it is supposed to refer.

So we must respect words but we should not give them undue power over us. One way to limit their sway is to play with them. Words do make wonderful playthings.

As a matter of fact this seems an appropriate place to admit that the etymology of francotirador that I gave you is pure speculation on my part. It fits the historical circumstances nicely but I do not know if that is the origin of the word. But, true or not, such speculation is fun and helps to fix the word in my mind, makes it more 'rememberable' if and when I might want to use it. One never knows when one might want to talk about snipers in Spanish.

And in the vein of playing with words a student once said to me, "Me descasé hace cinco años." We were working on the preterit tense so I was asking him questions about his past - Where was he born? How long did he live there? What did he study in school? When did he get married? etc. He did not have in his vocabulary the verb he needed for what he wanted to tell me. But he did know that when the students were tired (cansados) we took a descanso (a break or rest). He also knew that cansado comes from the verb cansarse (to get tired) and that by adding the negative prefix des- to that verb you got descansarse, (to un-tire yourself, in other words, to rest, whence descanso also).[32] So he did the same thing to the verb casarse (to get married) to tell me that he had gotten divorced some years back.

I presented the verb divorciarse to the class and we all had a good chuckle. We were not laughing at the student, we were laughing with delight at his inventiveness. That student's willingness to play with words bodes well for his future progress in Spanish. He did not view Spanish words as obstacles in his path, rather as things to be played with, to be put to his service. This student gets an 'A' in lexi-frolicking.

That incident brings to mind another class I once worked with. It was a group of five adults. As they talked they discovered that all of them had been divorced. I had been waiting for our conversation to present us with a multi-syllable reflexive verb to pounce upon for some preterit conjugation drill. It soon became apparent that they all felt that, in the long run at least, divorce had led to better things. So we spent a jolly interval conjugating the verb divorciarse: I got divorced, she got divorced, did he get divorced?, yes, he got divorced, they got divorced, did you get divorced?, yes, we all got divorced!

---

[32]There are many interesting pairs to be created by adding the prefix des- to a verb: cansar and descansar (mentioned above); hacer and deshacer, ('to do' and 'to undo'); cubrir and descubrir, ('to cover' and 'to uncover,' also 'to discover'); pegar ('to hit' but also 'to stick' in the sense of 'to adhere') and its opposite, despegar, ('to detach' or 'to unfasten' and 'to un-stick,' thereby becoming the verb used to describe an airplane taking off); ayunar ('to something?')and desayunar, ('to eat breakfast,' i.e. 'to break your fast' or 'to un-fast,' therefore ayunar is 'to fast'); and many more.

James K. Gavin

Then I told them about the previously mentioned student who had made up his own verb for divorce and we spent another few minutes conjugating the non-existent reflexive verb descasarse in the preterit, imperfect, present, and conditional tenses.

Every new word that you encounter is also a potential rompecabezas waiting to be solved. If you, dear reader, are beyond the most basic level of Spanish you might take the example of rompecabezas itself as a case in point. Take the time now to look at the word again. After the most cursory study of it surely -cabezas (heads) will jump out at you. That leaves you with rompe-. If you happen to know the verb romper (to break) you are moving closer to figuring it out. Rompe- (break) -cabezas (heads), or perhaps 'headbreaker.' That might call to mind a hoodlum's blackjack or a policeman's nightstick. But these possible translations do not fit the context in which the word was used in the first sentence of this paragraph. Re-read the first sentence of this paragraph. Look at the context in which the word was used - 'nightstick' or 'blackjack' just does not fit.

Context is very important - crucial - to understanding. Even on the familiar terrain of our native language we might need a minute or two to catch on to the conversation if we come upon a group of friends in the middle of a discussion. So what do we do in such a situation? One can interrupt and ask what the topic is or, more likely, just keep listening knowing that eventually it will become clear what is being discussed. The key is to keep going. As you are reading or listening to Spanish do not let an unknown word or phrase stop you in your tracks.

A new word, an unknown phrase, is not a red light. Do not stop. Go right on through it. Then, at a little distance beyond, look back at the unknown entity. See it in its environment, its context. Your mind, the totality of your life experience, will eliminate all sorts of impossibilities. You will not, for example, see an elk on a busy Manhattan street nor will you encounter a tow truck at 10,000 feet in the Pecos Wilderness of New Mexico. Some things simply do not go together. That is as true of words as it is of elk and tow trucks. And, getting back to the problem of rompecabezas as it was first used three paragraphs ago, a policeman's nightstick will not ever be "waiting to be solved." A 'headbreaker' that is "waiting to be solved" is a… good for you! you figured it out!… a puzzle or riddle.

Think of every new word as a riddle waiting to be solved. Each time that you solve one it will be another small victory to celebrate in the long struggle to learn to speak Spanish well.

Here is a list of words and phrases for you to look at. Presumably they will be new words for you. Approach them as puzzles to be solved. They vary in level of difficulty from rompecabezas that someone with no Spanish but a good feel for words, their roots, prefixes, suffixes, etc. might be able to solve, to items that would require a fairly advanced knowledge of Spanish to decipher. First they will be presented simply as a list. Then they will be put in a context to give you a more realistic situation to deal with. Translations and a brief explanation of each item will follow.

Gramática Apasionada
Reminiscences of a Love Affair with the Spanish Language

1. Portaaviones
2. Imprevisto
3. Guardaespaldas
4. La Vía Láctea
5. Aguafiestas
6. La Cuenta Regresiva
7. Parabrisas
8. De Antemano
9. Aguardiente
10. Hechizado, Perturbado, y Desorientado

1. El portaaviones es demasiado grande para usar el Canal de Panamá.
2. La presencia imprevista del presidente en la reunión causó mucha confusión.
3. Los guardaespaldas del presidente esperaron fuera del salón.
4. En una noche despejada La Vía Láctea es una vista gloriosa.
5. Mi papá es un aguafiestas, nunca quiere que nos divirtamos.
6. Detuvieron la cuenta regresiva cuando descubrieron un problema con un computador del cohete.
7. Es muy importante mantener el parabrisas limpio para poder manejar con seguridad.
8. Avísame de antemano si quieres que te incluya en la cena.
9. El aguardiente de cada país es diferente pero todos causan dolor de cabeza el día siguiente.
10. "Hechizado, Perturbado, y Desorientado" es el título de una canción famosa de un famoso "show" de Broadway.

1. Break this compound word into its two components 'porta-' and '-aviones.' We have the English words 'porter,' one who carries things; 'portable,' capable of being carried; 'portage,' a place where it is necessary to carry a boat from one navigable body of water to another - a word much used when reading accounts of the adventures of the first European explorers of the Great Lakes region of North America. The second part of the word might suggest 'aviation' or 'aviary,' both words related to flight. So what is this thing that is about flight and carrying and is too big to use the Panama Canal? An aircraft carrier, of course.

2. Here we have the root word 'visto(a)' which suggests a view, or vision, and two prefixes. 'Im-' is a negative prefix as in 'impossible,' i.e. 'not possible;' and 'pre-' which means 'before' as in the word 'prefix' itself, to attach or fix before or in front of. The President's presence caused confusion because it had not been expected, it was unforeseen.

3. 'Guarda-' is just like its English equivalent 'guard,' and 'espalda' means 'back' in the anatomical sense. They accompany the President and the guard his back. They are bodyguards.

4. 'Vía' suggests 'way' - we went to Cape Cod via (by way of) Providence. Does any English word come to mind when you look at the root word 'lact-?' The words that I think of are 'lactate,' 'lactic,' and 'lactose,' all words related to milk. So on a clear night what glorious sight is overhead? ...the Milky Way.

5. This compound word is made up of two words that even non-speakers of Spanish may know. 'Agua' is 'water' but it can also be a verb, aguar, 'to water down.' A 'fiesta' is a

party. Someone who does not want us to have fun, who 'waters down the party' is a spoilsport or party pooper.

6. 'La cuenta' is what one asks for in a restaurant when it is time to leave. It is 'the bill' but it comes from the verb contar, 'to count' and it is 'the count' of the amount of money you owe. Regresiva surely suggests 'regressive.' To regress is to go back. The count that regresses or goes back(ward) and has to do with computers and rockets is the countdown.

7. 'Para' could be the preposition 'for' but in this context it is more likely that it is from the verb parar, 'to stop.' 'It stops' the brisa, 'the breeze.' Safe drivers keep it clean. It is the windshield.[33]

8. 'Ante-' means 'before' as in 'antecedent,' 'that which comes before' (something else), or 'antebellum,' 'before the war' (Latin bellum means 'war' whence English gets 'bellicose' and 'belligerent' meaning warlike) - of course, when used in the context of United States history, antebellum means 'before the Civil War' as in 'the lovely antebellum mansions of Charleston.' 'Mano' is 'hand' - when something is done manually it is done by hand. The expression 'de antemano' means 'beforehand.'

9. In this compound word the first component, 'agua-', shares its last letter with the second component, '-ardiente.' 'Agua' is, of course, 'water.' 'Ardiente' perhaps brings to mind the English word 'ardent.' An ardent desire is a burning desire. Other related words are 'ardor' and 'arson' from the Latin 'ardere,' 'to burn'. So we have 'burningwater' which causes a headache the next day. This is the firewater of many a cowboy movie.

10. It is unlikely that hechizado is in your vocabulary unless you are a fairly advanced student of Spanish. Nor does the word trigger associations with any English word that I can think of. So skip over it. We have a three word song title, "———, Perturbed and Disoriented." Does it help if I tell you that hechizado means 'bewitched?' That the song is from the musical "Pal Joey?" Now you have it. "Bewitched, Bothered and Bewildered." (It probably also helps if you were born before 1950).

---

[33]The two meanings of para recall a small triumph scored by a linguistically alert leftist in Venezuela during the Cold War era propaganda battle between Capitalism and Communism. The Peace Corps was a small part of a large diplomatic initiative in Latin America called The Alliance for Progress, La Alianza para el Progreso. There were posters all over Caracas hailing this new relationship between Venezuela and its benevolent brother to the north. A Venezuelan "Communist" – i.e. "Nationalist" with a strong anti-American bias as a result of a history of heavy-handed American interference in their affairs -- noticed that underlining para would give it spoken emphasis changing it from a preposition to a verb. So the U.S. propaganda blitz was effectively countered by party henchmen running around the city with a can of black paint in one hand and a brush in the other. "La Alianza para el Progreso" The Alliance Stops Progress.

Like hechizado not all words lend themselves to solution by the word sleuth. But the mind that will look at the unknown as a challenge rather than an obstacle will have many successes. Let your mind play with new words, do some free association. Look at the word up close, break it down into its sub-parts. Look at the word from a distance, view it within the context in which you encountered it. There will be rewards.

And this is a two-way street. Not only will applying your knowledge of English speed the learning of Spanish; as you learn Spanish it will, in its turn, teach you things about English. 'Exigent' became a part of my English vocabulary only after I had started using the Spanish verb exigir, 'to demand.' 'Perdition,' a word much used by bible-thumping preachers, took on real meaning only after I had connected it to the Spanish perder, 'to lose.' In the course of learning what Spanish I do know, I have learned a lot about English as well.

As you become more word-aware there will be occasional surprises that will give delight and sometimes even bring insight. I was reading Gabriel García Márquez's fine novel about love, El amor en los tiempos del cólera, when I came upon a new word for me, 'adolecía.' In context it was obviously the verb. Dictionaries do not list conjugated verb forms, they have only the infinitive of the verb. So converting the verb form back to the infinitive is a necessary, albeit simple, step. The ending, -ía, indicated that the infinitive was either adolecer or adolecir. As there is a sizeable group of verbs that end -ecer that seemed the better bet. While flipping through the dictionary, zeroing in on the page, column and word I was doing some word-sleuthing. In my mind I discarded the ending, -ecer, to focus on the root word, adol-, which told me nothing. However, a- is a fairly common prefix when generating a verb from an adjective, (delgado, adelgazar, for example). Dropping the prefix leaves -dol- which suggested dolor, doler, and doliente, all words relating to pain.

There it was, adolecer. We have no equivalent verb in English. So the dictionary gave short phrases to explain the verb, "to suffer from a disease," "to struggle on in affliction." Those meanings fit well in the context of the story and I resumed reading. Then it hit me - "Adolescente!" That moment of recognition of the word was pure delight. Then came the insight, "one who is in pain." With it came the realization that the word itself calls to us for compassion and understanding when dealing with people who fall in this category. Teen-agers can be very difficult to live with. But the name given to this time of life is itself a reminder to us that we are dealing with "someone who struggles on in affliction," an adolescent. How many of us, dear reader, recalling our own teen-age years, would dispute the appropriateness of this word.

The stories within words, there are so many of them.

The first time that I consciously and consensually engaged in an act of sesquipedalianism was in a hotel in Mexico. I was sitting in the lobby reading the local newspaper. There on the page appeared the word 'desnuclearización.' First of all it made a neat rompecabezas - although in the context of the article it was easily solved. Then I thought, "My goodness, what a long word." I counted the letters - 17. At that moment, without my realizing it, a small cluster of brain cells put itself on alert for any future encounter with a word that would contain more than 17 letters. Thus began a modest word-related project that has entertained me from time to time for many years. Although I did not think of it in these terms until later, my mind wanted me to be more "word-aware".

Time passed. Life went on apace. Suddenly one afternoon while walking down a street in Chihuahua my cerebral SWATL-Team (Spot Words And Tally Letters) leapt into action. Alarum! Over my head was a sign, "Doctor Fulano, Otorrinolaringólogo."[34] I confirmed the SWATL-Team's acuity - 18 letters. (If you took the time to count the letters for yourself and came up with 19 it is because you have forgotten or, perhaps, did not know that 'rr' is one letter of the Spanish alphabet coming between 'r' and 's'). Dr. Fulano was an otorhinolaryngologist. In all probability you have consulted one yourself at some time in your life. Although in our preference for shorter rather than longer words you may have called him (or her) an Ear (oto-) Nose (rhino-)[35] and Throat (larynx-) Specialist.

Some years ago I was doing a two week intensive conversational Spanish program at Ghost Ranch in northern New Mexico, a place best known to Presbyterians and admirers of Georgia O'Keeffe. Among the students we had a genuine otorhinolaryngologist. He was a very personable young man but he soon became the object of undeserved derision. His presence perforce required that all the students learn to pronounce properly his occupation. Much time and effort, that might otherwise have been spent learning the present tense, was going into this endeavor. He was saved from seemingly inevitable pariah-dom when a fellow student had the idea of setting the word to music. In a special session of the entire group the composer taught everyone to sing his little ditty. In fifteen minutes the problem was solved. The otorhinolaryngologist was restored to his rightful place in the hearts of his companions and we got on with the business of teaching the rest of the language. Many years later I still find myself occasionally humming the pleasant tune that got our program moving forward again.

My quest for lexical lengthiness had two self-imposed limits (you may, of course, make your own rules): first, 'ch,' 'll,' and 'rr' would count as one letter; second, the discovery must be the result of casual conversation or reading - I could not, for example, deliberately read an article about the latest DNA research in the hope of coming upon the 37-letter name of a chemical compound.

Eventually I got up to 21 letters, desproporcionadamente. I was stuck there for a long time.

Then one evening the phone rang.

---

[34] When out and about in Spanish-speaking places there is much to be learned from reading billboards, political posters and slogans scrawled on walls, advertisements for cigarettes and beer in store windows, etc. Develop the habit of visually prowling the neighborhood.

[35] 'Rhinoceros' probably came to mind - it means 'horned nose'. You may also have thought of 'rhinoplasty', more vulgarly known as a 'nose job.'

The caller was old friend who lives in Mexico City. A businessman with a talent for telling a tale and dramatizing the humdrum, he was relating his latest attempt to find his way through the bureaucratic labyrinth of governmental regulations that has grayed his hair but not his spirit. Groping for words as he tried to adequately describe the extremely vexatious actions of one pompous official with whom he has to deal, he used the word desproporcionadísimamente. He had taken my longest word and added the superlative suffix -ísimo to it. I lost track of his story as the SWATL-Team stormed my brain. 25 letters!

And that is where things have stood for some time now. I have recently noticed a growing personal fascination with the discoveries being made in the field of genetic engineering. I may have to do some reading in that exciting new field.

Words, words everywhere and many a thought to think. Words. Words. Words. No one ever really has the last one.

Chapter Fifteen

Junk Is My Middle Name

The troubled romance of Ramón Montaglione and Julia Capuletski, whose misfortunes of the heart we have been following, will finally come to happy fulfillment. Driven asunder by the grammatical bumbling of Ramón, they will be reunited thanks to the linguistic acuity of Julia.

Here, then, is the final episode of "The Stair-crossed Lovers."

Vowing never again to be the cause of a frown of sorrow or hurt on Julia's beautiful brow, Ramón has returned to the Arizona desert. There he will live out his years with only cactus and lizards for companions. As Fate would have it, however, the weather-beaten one-room shack that will be his home does have internet link-up capability. He sends one last e-mail to Julia telling her of his decision and pledging eternal love. He ends the letter saying, "Aunque viva otros cien años nunca dejaré de amarte."

Julia read her e-mail with tear-blurred vision. Was she not duty-bound to accept and respect Ramón's personal life-style choice? Yes, she must give him his space. Perhaps someday…

Then, suddenly, her eye and mind focused on the subjunctive verb form (<u>viva</u>) that Ramón had used in that last touching sentence. That use of the subjunctive made her realize once again how tenuous is our hold on life, how uncertain even tomorrow is.

Her heart took charge. She e-mailed back to Ramón immediately telling him to come home to her. He did. And, as they say in Spanish, "Vivieron felices y comieron perdices." (They lived happy and ate partridge.)

What is this thing called the subjunctive?

Unlike Julia, we English-speakers are not on the whole well attuned to the linguistic and grammatical nuances of our language. Most of the people who study with me can look at a sentence and point out the subject and the verb. Those who actually paid attention in high school English class might correctly identify a direct or indirect object. But even these people will probably find their thoughts wandering toward the always interesting question of what to have for lunch if the discussion turns to arcana such as the passive voice, the pluperfect, and predicate nominatives

Gramática Apasionada
Reminiscences of a Love Affair with the Spanish Language

Perhaps the least understood grammatical concept I have to deal with in teaching Spanish is the subjunctive. Articulate, even eloquent, speakers of English who are excellent Spanish students throw up their hands in dismay or threaten to quit the class when it is suggested that it might be time to tackle this important aspect of the language. This reaction is quite human – we distrust and fear the unknown. Like arranged marriage, fried ants for munchies, and dental work without Novocain, the subjunctive is simply not part of our culture.

But is that really true? Before going any further please do a brief exercise in English. Complete each of the following sentences using the verb 'to eat' in the present tense.

1. My mother is pleased that I _____ all of my broccoli.
2. My mother demands that I _____ all of my broccoli.
3. My mother is pleased that my brother _____ all of his broccoli.
4. My mother demands that my brother _____ all of his broccoli.

Let's assume that you answered as follows: 1. eat, 2. eat, 3. eats, 4. eat. The question then arises, why "my brother eats" in sentence #3 but "my brother eat" in sentence #4?

Your response is probably, "It just sounds right that way." And that is a perfectly good answer. For that is how we learned to speak English in the first place. We imitated what we heard the people around us saying. So even though 'my brother eat' sounds wrong when isolated, it sounds right in the context of sentence #4 above.

Now complete each of the four sentences below using the verb 'to work' in the present tense.

1. The boss believes that he _____ hard.
2. The boss requests that he _____ harder.
3. The boss says that he _____ hard.
4. The boss urges that he _____ harder.

Again we have the question, why 'he work' in sentences #2 and #4?

Note that in each of the cases where the final 's' was dropped from the third person singular of the verb ('my brother eat' and 'he work') the subject of the main clause of the sentence ('my mother' in the first instance, and 'the boss' in the other two) was trying to influence the actions of the subject of the second or dependent clause. This attempt by one entity to influence the behavior or actions of another entity created the subjunctive mode. Therefore the verb in the dependent or subjunctive clause had to be conjugated in its subjunctive form. 'My brother eat' and 'he work' are the subjunctive forms of the verbs 'to eat' and 'to work.' They sound right and are, in fact, grammatically correct only when they occur 'sub-joined' to a main clause whose subject is exerting or trying to exert influence over them. The subjunctive does not and cannot exist on its own.

James K. Gavin

In the sentence, 'my mother demands that I eat all of my broccoli,' 'I eat' is also subjunctive. But in English we only hear or see the difference between the indicative and subjunctive forms of a verb in the third person singular. Spanish, on the other hand, has a separate and fully developed subjunctive conjugation for all verbs in both the present and past tenses.

What is the subjunctive mode? It is a mode or way of speaking that is different than the usual way we speak. This 'normal' way of speaking is called the indicative mode. The difference in the two ways of talking shows up in the manner in which we handle the verb - it is the difference between 'he eat' and 'he eats' or 'he work' and 'he works'.

What is the subjunctive mode? *Think of the subjunctive as a grammatical change in the tone of your voice.* We change our tone of voice to say different things. As circumstances and subject matter change we are continually adjusting our tone of voice. We do not say, "Good night, sweetheart," in the same tone of voice that we use to say, "Get those dirty socks off the dining room table!" Even the same sequence of words can be loaded with a positive or negative charge. The simple phrase, "Isn't that nice!" can be a comforting reassurance, a neutral indicator that you are still listening, or a scathing condemnation. Adjustments of tone are as integral and automatic a part of our speech as is pronunciation. Therefore it should not really come as a great surprise that this important aspect of verbal communication has worked its way into the ground rules of speech, i.e. grammar.

Think of how you alter your tone of voice when you tell someone to do something. Either you will soften your tone to sound less bossy ("Have a good trip!") or you will harden your voice to exert authority ("Give that back to me!"). Depending on circumstances you do one or the other, but your voice does change. That change of tone is also built into the grammar of both English and Spanish by means of the imperative mode or command form of the verb.

Just so, when the subject of the main clause of a sentence wants to affect the behavior or actions of the subject of the dependent clause there is a grammatically mandated change of tone. This change is manifested in the handling of the verb of the dependent clause.

It is called the subjunctive mode or mood. I find it more useful to think of it as the subjunctive mood. When some one says, "I suggest that..." or "he wishes that..." or "they insist that...," the mood suddenly changes. The usual incandescent white light of daily (indicative) life shifts to a soft red glow. A different mood is created. While bathed in this rosy light we conjugate verbs differently, we conjugate in the subjunctive mood.

But let us go back to the allegation made above that "the subjunctive is simply not part of our culture." Clearly it is. You may not have been able to put a label on it but you have been using it frequently and correctly most of your life. In contrast to Spanish, however, the subjunctive in English is almost invisible. It stands apart from its indicative counterparts only in the third person singular of the verb. There is only one English verb with its own complete subjunctive conjugation. Conjugate the verb 'to be' in the present indicative:

I am, you are, he/she is, we are, they are. Now read the variations of the sentence below to confirm that each sounds right.

In spite of this exception our subjunctive does seem to be languishing in a lingering linguistic sunset. Not only is the English subjunctive all but indistinguishable from the indicative, we often dodge the necessity of using it by substituting an infinitive phrase for the subjunctive clause. For example, the model sentence "the boss urges that he *work* harder," could just as well be said, "the boss urges him *to work* harder," neatly side-stepping the need for the subjunctive. With the verb 'to want' English no longer even offers the subjunctive clause as a possibility. What native speaker of English would say, "I want that he help me" (note the subjunctive 'he help') instead of, "I want him to help me"? Spanish much less frequently offers the speaker this substitute for the subjunctive clause. English also has the auxiliary verbs 'may,' 'might' and 'should' as ways to duck the need for the subjunctive - for example: "I **may** have spotted Elvis yesterday!" "Es possible que yo **haya** visto a Elvis ayer."

With the exception of phrases such as, "If I were president…," and, "If he were a gentleman…," English does not have a past subjunctive verb form. And given the frequency with which one hears people in high-profile positions (news broadcasters, government officials, and the like) saying 'was' in this context it may not be long before the subjunctive 'were' is banished to the secret lexical garden wherein reside 'thou,' 'anon,' 'wouldst' and other such archaisms and where only preachers, professors and poets occasionally stroll.

Although the subjunctive in English is gray and, quite possibly, moribund its Spanish counterpart is vital and vibrant with hues and nuances. As will be seen later it encompasses all of the syntactical happenings of the English subjunctive and much more. It is an integral part of everybody's everyday speech. I make this assertion boldly. This, in spite of the fact that in different places and times, as a field evaluator of linguistic progress, I have had a number of Peace Corps volunteers (who spoke a quite adequate but subjunctive-less Spanish) look me straight in the eye and report that where they lived and worked nobody used the subjunctive.

As a matter of fact, in direct refutation of that declaration, my first brush with this grammatical phenomenon came in what might seem unlikely circumstances. It happened during a break in a half-court basketball game - three on three under a strong Venezuelan sun. One of the players had gone off in search of water or, perhaps, shade.

Sensing that enthusiasm for the game might quickly diminish I said to the other players, "Hey, wait a minute, we'll finish the game when José comes back (cuando vuelve José)."

"No, no, Jeen, cuando *vuelva* José."

The speaker was a young man about my age named Juan Ramón. He spent his work time down at the docks hoping to earn an occasional bolívar helping to load and unload cargo. He spent a lot of his free time at our center always available for a pick-up game of básquet. He wore the same threadbare clothes day after day, but he would show up in 'new' threadbare shirt and pants just before one started thinking of what he had been wearing for the last few months as rags. On his feet were alpargatas, the national footwear of the country. The sole cut from a discarded tire, the open-toed upper part of the 'shoe' made of a woven fabric, the alpargata was at the same time something more and something less than a sandal. One could identify the region of the country whence came the wearer by the color and design of the woven upper. But the alpargata told more than where one came from, its presence on the foot stated that the user was of the lower class, one of the great mass of Venezuelan poor. No one who could afford real shoes would be seen in public in alpargatas. What was on your feet classified you in much the same way that what kind of car you drive classifies you in the United States.

Juan Ramón proceeded to explain to me that because there was no certainty that José would ever come back, that only God can know the future, I must say 'vuelva' instead of 'vuelve.' He made me aware for the first time that things could happen to verbs beyond the vuelvo, vuelves, vuelve, I had struggled so doggedly to master.

That brief lesson by Juan Ramón as we stood sweating at the edge of the basketball court was a definite beginning for me, the first slim ray of light cast into a vast unexplored grammatical cavern. I cannot now recall if he actually used the word 'subjunctive' in his lecture. In either case, that is what he was talking about. I had heard the term 'subjunctive' before. I knew it had something to do with language but that was it. Until that moment it had had nothing to do with my life. Let us, then, do some spelunking. But before we get into all the uses of the subjunctive let's take care of the mechanical part, conjugation.

Present Subjunctive

-AR verbs	-ER,-IR verbs
Stem + -e -emos	Stem + -a -amos
-es -en	-as -an
-e -en	-a -an

The stem for the present subjunctive is the first person singular of the present indicative of the verb minus the final 'o.'

There are four irregular verbs - ser, ir, saber, haber. They will be dealt with below.

Gramática Apasionada
Reminiscences of a Love Affair with the Spanish Language

Examples: Hablar (yo hablo)   Comer (yo como)   Vivir (yo vivo)
              stem = habl-   stem = com-   stem = viv-
              present subjunctive   present subjunctive   present subjunctive
              hable   hablemos   coma   comamos   viva   vivamos
              hables   hablen   comas   coman   vivas   vivan
              hable   hablen   coma   coman   viva   vivan

As was true of the pronunciation of verbs in the present indicative, the accent will always fall on the next-to-the-last syllable.

HA-ble   ha-BLE-mos   CO-ma   co-MA-mos   VI-va   vi-VA-mos
HA-bles   HA-blen   CO-mas   CO-man   VI-vas   VI-van
HA-ble   HA-blen   CO-ma   CO-man   VI-va   VI-van

(You will recall that when you studied Chapter 2, the present indicative, you learned that there are a number of verbs that have an irregular first person singular. Now comes the payoff for having taken the time to learn those irregular forms).

Tener (yo tengo)   Conocer (yo conozco)   Hacer (yo hago)
stem = teng-   stem = conozc-   stem = hag-
present subjunctive   present subjunctive   present subjunctive
tenga   tengamos   conozca   conozcamos   haga   hagamos
tengas   tengan   conozcas   conozcan   hagas   hagan
tenga   tengan   conozca   conozcan   haga   hagan

And you will recall the phenomenon of stem-changing verbs that was presented in Chapter 2. The stem change is a present tense phenomenon, not just a peculiarity of the present indicative. It happens in the present subjunctive as well.

Recordar (yo recuerdo)   Entender (yo entiendo)
stem = recuerd-   stem = entiend-
present subjunctive   present subjunctive
recuerde   recordemos   entienda   entendamos
recuerdes   recuerden   entiendas   entiendan
recuerde   recuerden   entienda   entiendan

Note that in these two examples the stem change of 'o' to 'ue' and 'e' to 'ie' follows the present tense model. The stem change does not occur in the first person plural (<u>nosotros</u>) of the verb. The rules about stem change and accent patterns that were learned in the chapter on the present indicative also apply to the subjunctive of the present tense.

However, there is one additional twist to present subjunctive conjugation that must be learned. It relates to third conjugation (-IR) verbs that have a stem change in the preterit tense (see Chapter 6). You still use the present indicative stem change in the usual places, i.e. 1st, 2nd and 3rd persons singular, and 2nd and 3rd persons plural, as you conjugate in the subjunctive. But the stem change that occurs in the preterit shows up as well in the first person plural of the present subjunctive. That may sound confusing but study the examples below for all but instantaneous clarification.

Sentir (yo siento)		Dormir (yo duermo)		Pedir (yo pido)	
stem = sient-		stem = duerm-		stem = pid-	
present subjunctive		present subjunctive		present subjunctive	
sienta	sintamos	duerma	durmamos	pida	pidamos
sientas	sientan	duermas	duerman	pidas	pidan
sienta	sientan	duerma	duerman	pida	pidan

Sintamos instead of sentamos, durmamos instead of dormamos. These are small things. The foundations of Western Civilization will not be imperiled if you forget this detail, but our discussion of the conjugation of the present subjunctive would be incomplete without it.

There are six verbs that cannot comply with the guideline for finding the stem of the present subjunctive as outlined above.

The stem for the present subjunctive was defined above as the first person singular of the present indicative minus the final 'o'. There are six verbs that do not have a final 'o' to drop. They must be considered separately. The six verbs are: estar (yo estoy), dar (yo doy), saber (yo sé), haber (yo he), ser (yo soy), and ir (yo voy).

In the case of dar you drop the '-oy' of the present indicative and proceed as with any -AR verb: dé, des, dé, demos, den, den. Note the written accent in the first and third persons singular (dé) which serves to distinguish the verb form from the preposition (de). With estar you also drop the '-oy' of yo estoy to get the stem for the subjunctive. Referring again to the chapter on the present indicative you will recall that, unlike dar, estar is not listed as a verb that is irregular only in the first person singular. Estar is listed with the handful of totally irregular verbs. That is because it violates the accent pattern of the present tense (which, as was noted above, applies to all three modes of the present). Estar goes right on merrily breaking the rules in the subjunctive. Therefore the present subjunctive of estar is:

yo esté	nosotros estemos
tú estés	ustedes estén
él/ella esté	ellos estén

The spoken stress will be as follows:

es-TE	es-TE-mos
es-TES	es-TEN
es-TE	es-TEN

The other four verbs require that you learn a separate irregular stem for the present subjunctive. Then use the subjunctive endings for -ER,-IR verbs listed above.

Saber
regular stem: sep-
present subjunctive
sepa   sepamos
sepas sepan
sepa   sepan

Haber
irregular stem: hay-
present subjunctive
haya   hayamos
hayas hayan
haya   hayan

Ser
irregular stem: se-
present subjunctive
sea   seamos
seas   sean
sea   sean

Ir
irregular stem: vay-
present subjunctive
vaya   vayamos
vayas vayan
vaya   vayan

Spanish also has a fully developed past tense for the subjunctive. Its conjugated forms may, at first sight, look threateningly resistant to conquest. In fact there is one simple rule with absolutely no exceptions for achieving past subjunctivity. With a little practice these forms will flow like linguistic gold from your silver-tongued conjugating orifice.

Imperfect Subjunctive

-AR, -ER, -IR verbs
stem   +   -a   -amos**
           -as   -an
           -a   -an

The stem for the past subjunctive is the third person plural of the preterit of the verb minus the final –on.

**Please note: the accent pattern of the imperfect past tense holds for the subjunctive as well. So in the first person plural (nosotros) the accent falls on the third-to-the-last syllable as in the imperfect indicative, i.e. on the syllable before the ending itself. It also requires a written accent mark. See examples below.

Hablar (ellos hablaron)
stem = hablar-
imperfect subjunctive
hablara   habláramos
hablaras   hablaran
hablara   hablaran

Comer (ellos comieron)
stem = comier-
imperfect subjunctive
comiera   comiéramos
comieras   comieran
comiera   comieran

Ha-BLA-ra	ha-BLA-ra-mos	co-miER-a	co-miER-a-mos
ha-BLA-ras	ha-BLA-ran	co-miER-as	co-miER-an
ha-BLA-ra	ha-BLA-ran	co-miER-a	co-miER-an

Vivir (ellos vivieron)
stem = vivier-
<u>imperfect subjunctive</u>
viviera	viviéramos
vivieras	vivieran
viviera	vivieran

Tener (ellos tuvieron)
stem = tuvier-
<u>imperfect subjunctive</u>
tuviera	tuviéramos
tuvieras	tuvieran
tuviera	tuvieran

Decir (ellos dijeron)
stem = dijer-
<u>imperfect subjunctive</u>
dijera	dijéramos
dijeras	dijeran
dijera	dijeran

Leer (ellos leyeron)
stem = leyer-
<u>imperfect subjunctive</u>
leyera	leyéramos
leyeras	leyeran
leyera	leyeran

Pedir (ellos pidieron)
stem = pidier-
<u>imperfect subjunctive</u>
pidiera	pidiéramos
pidieras	pidieran
pidiera	pidieran

Ser and Ir (ellos fueron)
stem = fuer-
<u>imperfect subjunctive</u>
fuera	fuéramos
fueras	fueran
fuera	fueran

In centuries past you would have had to make preterit/imperfect distinctions in the past subjunctive just as you still must in the indicative past. But over time this distinction blurred and eventually disappeared all together. In the duel to the death between the two past forms of the subjunctive the imperfect won. It is still called the imperfect subjunctive but it is in fact the past subjunctive, it covers all your subjunctive needs in the past.

In the life or death struggle between the imperfect and the aorist (preterit) subjunctive the victory of the imperfect was decisive but not absolute. The aorist subjunctive was vanquished, driven forever from the broad open fields of conversational Spanish, but not annihilated. It lurks about in the literary underbrush, ready to jump out and startle the unwary student. Its use is no longer a question of preterit/imperfect distinctions, rather it is a matter of style. Some writers simply choose to use it instead of the imperfect - perhaps its use is intended to elevate the tone of the writing.

On very rare occasions I have actually spoken to someone who uses this alternative past subjunctive in speech. To me it has the feel of someone putting on airs - as if a beer drinking buddy or a member of your coffee klatch went off to Boston one summer to take a remedial course in composition at Harvard and came back talking like an Oxonian don (for those of you who don't speak British that's a tutor at Oxford University).

As for me, I'll (and I humbly suggest that you) stick with the imperfect (-ra) form of the subjunctive. But you will definitely encounter the alternate (-se) form of the past subjunctive in your Spanish readings.

The conjugation is done by dropping the final -ron of the ellos form of the preterit and adding the endings -se, -ses, -se, -semos, -sen, -sen. Thus you get verb forms that look like these:

Hablar		Comer	
hablase	hablásemos	comiese	comiésemos
hablases	hablasen	comieses	comiesen
hablase	hablasen	comiese	comiesen

Tener		Ser and Ir	
tuviese	tuviésemos	fuese	fuésemos
tuvieses	tuviesen	fueses	fuesen
tuviese	tuviesen	fuese	fuesen

In coming to grips with the subjunctive, as with many of the difficulties we encounter in life, the first step toward a solution is simply recognizing or acknowledging that we have a problem. If you have read this far, you have taken this first important step. Unlike the Peace Corps volunteers alluded to earlier, you are no longer in denial of the existence of the subjunctive. And more than this, you have already entered phase two. You have studied the conjugation of verbs in the present and the past subjunctive. To complete phase two you must substitute other verbs and practice conjugating them in the subjunctive. If you have not yet done this I urge that you do so now. When you can conjugate in the subjunctive fairly comfortably, you will be ready to start phase three.

Phase two may be as far as you want to go with the subjunctive right now. This is a good place to stop if you are still struggling with other basic aspects of the language. If you are still on shaky ground when trying to sort out preterit/imperfect usage, for example, set the subjunctive aside for now. It is sufficient that you know that the subjunctive exists and that you will recognize it when you come upon it in your readings or hear it used in conversation. It is not possible to do all things at once.

What you have learned about the subjunctive up to this point will not go away. As a matter of fact, now that there is a base upon which to build, your mind will continue to acquire bits of information about the subjunctive even as you consciously focus on other elements of the language. Slow absorption and digestion of information are an integral part of the process of learning a language.

You have to allow time for that to happen. ¡Paciencia y persistencia!

Chapter Sixteen

It Takes Two to <u>Tenga</u>

The subject is the subjunctive. And as we try to arrive at an understanding of this thing called the subjunctive the name itself gives us a clue - subjunctive or sub-joined. It is attached to something else. Like mistletoe it does not exist alone or on its own. This grammatical parasite draws its sustenance from the main clause of the sentence. It feeds on, and cannot exist without, one of the following: indirect command (an attempt to influence what others do), or emotion, or doubt, or denial, or unreality, or non-experience.

In slightly less unscholarly terms this is how it works. The verb of the main clause of the sentence creates the subjunctive mode (or 'mood,' if you wish) by expressing one of the items from the 'menu' just listed. That mood created, the verb of the attached clause must then 'get into the mood' by being conjugated in its subjunctive form. Please note that there are two conditions that must be met for the subjunctive to exist. First, the main clause must express one of the items from our subjunctive menu. Second, there must be an attached or subordinate clause. Not all subordinate clauses are subjunctive clauses. Some examples:

'The boss believes that he works hard.' This sentence meets the second requirement. It has a subordinate clause – 'that he works hard' - but it does not meet the first requirement. 'Believes' does not express emotion or doubt or any other item on the subjunctive menu. The sentence does not meet both requirements. Therefore there is no subjunctive

'The boss demands many things of his workers.' This sentence fulfills the first requirement – 'The boss demands' implies command, the boss is trying to influence what the workers do or how they behave. There is, however, no subordinate clause with its essential component, a conjugated verb, so there is no subjunctive.

'The boss requests that he work harder.' This sentence meets both requirements for the subjunctive. The verb of the main clause, 'requests,' implies command or the desire to influence the actions or behavior of the employee. And there is a subordinate clause – 'that he work harder.' Thus the verb of the subordinate clause is conjugated in the subjunctive mode, 'he work.'

Now let us look at some other verbs that create the subjunctive mood.

1. There are a number of verbs that imply command or the desire to influence: to suggest, to insist, to implore (beg), to tell (in the sense of 'to order to…'), to demand.

> A. Sugiere que **estemos** allí.
>   He suggests that we be there.
> B. Insisto en que **tomes** una taza más.
>   I insist that you have another cup.
> C. Ruegan que no lo **haga**.
>   They beg him not to do it.
> D. Dígale que me **escriba**.
>   Tell him to write to me.
> E. La situación exige que nos **callemos**.
>   The situation demands that we be quiet.

You will have observed that not all the English translations of the Spanish example sentences require the subjunctive mode. But in Spanish this desire to influence actions or behavior always creates the subjunctive mode. When one person or entity suggests or insists or begs or orders or demands that another person do something there is indirect or implied command, an attempt to influence what the subject of the subordinate clause will do and the subjunctive mood is created.

2. When the verb of the main clause of the sentence expresses emotion (joy, fear, sorrow, hope, desire, surprise, etc.) the subjunctive mood is created and the subjunctive mode is invoked for the verb of the subordinate clause.

> A. Quiero que **vengas** a mi casa esta noche.
>   I want you to come (I want that you come) to my house this evening
> B. Esperamos que no **llueva**.
>   We hope it doesn't rain.
> C. Temo que **se haya** perdido.
>   I am afraid it has been lost.
> D. Les sorprende que él **sepa** hablar español.
>   They are surprised that he knows how to speak Spanish.
> E. Sentimos que **estés** enfermo.
>   We are sorry that you are sick.
> F. Se alegran de que yo **pueda** ir.
>   They are happy that I can go.

The intensity of the emotion expressed is immaterial - from the mildest surprise to the most heart-wrenching anguish, all expressions of emotion create the subjunctive mode. But, don't forget, it takes two to <u>tenga</u>. There must be a verb of emotion in the main clause and a subordinate clause. The subjunctive is like a room inside of a bigger room. It cannot be entered directly. You must first pass through the outer room.

A. Yo quiero ir al cine.
   I want to go to the movies. (Emotion is expressed but no subordinate clause).
B. Sabemos que estás enfermo.
   We know that you are sick. (There is a subordinate clause but no emotion is expressed in the main clause).

3. When the main clause casts doubt or expresses uncertainty, if it denies that the action in the subordinate clause occurred, the questionable reality of the information in the subordinate clause is indicated by the subjunctive.

A. No es verdad que **se vaya**.
   It is not true that he is leaving.
B. Dudo que **vengan**.
   I doubt they are coming
C. No estamos seguros de que **se conozcan**.
   We are not sure that they know each other.
D. Niegan que ella lo **haya** dicho.
   They deny that she has said it.
E. No creo que **pueda** hacerlo.
   I do not believe he can do it.

BUT...

A. Es verdad que se va.
   It is true that he is leaving.
B. No dudo que vienen.
   I do not doubt that they will come.
C. Estamos seguros de que se conocen.
   We are sure that they know each other.

If there is no doubt, no uncertainty, no denial, there is also no subjunctive.

4. When the reference in the subordinate clause is to an unknown, uncertain, or indefinite entity, that is to some one or some thing that has not yet been experienced by the subject of the main clause, the subjunctive is used to indicate the tenuous quality of the existence of that entity. This may be the most elusive subjunctive concept to grasp. But study and think about the examples below. In these cases it is not the verb of the main clause that creates the subjunctive mood. It is the reference to a person or thing that has not yet been experienced.

A. Voy a dar mil pesos al primero que **venga**.
   I'll give one thousand pesos to the first person that comes (whoever that may be).
B. Juan quiere una esposa que **esté** dispuesta a planchar sus calcetines.
   John wants a wife who is willing to iron his socks (is there such a woman?).

Going from the ridiculous to the sublime, there is a segment of the Federico García Lorca poem, *"Llanto por Ignacio Sánchez Mejías,"* that beautifully illustrates this subjunctive concept. The poem is a lament for a well-known bullfighter killed in the ring. The poet is transfixed by the sight of the blood of the <u>torero</u> on the ground:

¡Que no quiero verla!/Que no hay cáliz que la **contenga**,/que no hay golondrinas que se la **beban**,/no hay escarcha de luz que la **enfríe**,/no hay canto ni diluvio de azucenas,/no hay cristal que la **cubra** de plata./No./ ¡¡Yo no quiero verla!!

Returning to our mundane grammatical musings we trudge on:

   C. Quieren comprar la computadora más sofisticada que **haya.**
      They want to buy the most sophisticated computer that there is.
   D. Busco alguien que **hable** ruso.
      I am looking for some one who speaks Russian.

However, taking the last sentence as a case in point, if you were to enter a room full of people and be told that there is a man in the room who speaks Russian you would then say, "Busco al señor que habla ruso." Even though you have not yet met this man his existence has been confirmed.

   E. Uno debe hacer lo que **quiera**, cuando **quiera**, donde **quiera**, con quien **quiera**.
      One ought to do whatever he wants, whenever he wants, wherever he wants, with whomever he wants.

The '<u>lo que</u>,' '<u>cuando</u>,' '<u>donde</u>' and '<u>con quien</u>' all make reference to events, times, places, and people that are as yet unknown, that have not yet been experienced. Therefore each in turn creates the subjunctive mode.

5. There are a number of impersonal expressions with the verb <u>ser</u> which also create the subjunctive mode. It will be seen, however, that these expressions, by their very nature, evoke the subjunctive mood.

   A. Expressions of emotion:
     Es bueno que **venga**.
        It's good that he's coming.
     Es sorprendiente que **venga**.
        It's surprising that he's coming.
     Es una lástima que **venga**.
        It's a pity that he's coming.
     Es triste que **venga**.
        It's sad that he's coming.

B. Expressions of implied command or desire to influence:
   Es necesario que lo **aprendas**.
   　　It's necessary that you learn it.
   Es preferible que lo **aprendas**.
   　　It's preferable that you learn it.
   Es mejor que lo **aprendas**.
   　　It's better that you learn it.
   Es importante que lo **aprendas**.
   　　It's important that you learn it.

C. Expressions of doubt, uncertainty and denial:
   Es dudoso que **sepan** eso.
   　　It's doubtful that they know that.
   Es posible que **sepan** eso.
   　　It's possible that they know that.
   No es cierto que **sepan** eso.
   　　It is not certain that they know that.
   Es imposible que **sepan** eso.
   　　It's not possible that they know that.

But remember that there are two pre-conditions for the subjunctive, an expression that evokes the subjunctive 'mood' in the main clause and a subordinate clause.

A. Es necesario estar allí.
   　　It is necessary to be there. (Implied command but no subordinate clause)
B. Es cierto que me quiere.
   　　It is certain that she loves me. (Subordinate clause but the main clause does not create the subjunctive mode)

6. The last broad category that needs to be studied is made up of conjunctions that carry in their meaning desire or denial or uncertainty or non-experience. These conjunctions may create the subjunctive on their own. It is still necessary that the sentence have two clauses but the main clause does not create the subjunctive 'mood.'

First we will look at some common conjunctions that always create the subjunctive mode:

a menos que-	unless-
en caso de que-	in case-
con tal que-	provided that-
antes de que-	before-
para que-	in order that-
sin que-	without-

A. Ella no asistirá a la fiesta a menos que me **inviten** también.
   She will not attend the party unless they invite me too.
B. En caso de que **llueva** jugarán mañana.
   In case it rains they will play tomorrow.
C. Creo que él ganará la elección con tal que los pobres **voten**.
   I believe that he will win the election provided that the poor people vote.
D. Debemos fortalecer los muros antes de que **llegue** el enemigo.
   We must strengthen the walls before the enemy gets here.

In each of the four examples above the conjunction makes reference to an action that has not yet occurred and may or may not ever occur. Because of the meaning of these conjunctions a fog of uncertainty enshrouds the events to which they refer thus calling for the subjunctive.

E. Te digo para que **aprendas.**
   I'm telling you in order that you learn.

This conjunction expresses intention or will that something happen, hence we have the desire to influence or implied command.

F. Los viejos aprecian cada hora pero los años pasan sin que los jóvenes **se den** cuenta.
   Old people value every hour but the years pass without young people noticing.

The conjunction sin que denies the action of the attached clause; therefore the subjunctive is called for.

Please note that although antes de que, para que, and sin que create the subjunctive, the prepositions antes de, para, and sin do not.

A. Estamos fortaleciendo los muros antes de la llegada del enemigo.
   We are strengthening the walls before the arrival of the enemy.
B. Estudio para aprender.
   I study in order to learn.
C. Me envejezco sin darme cuenta.
   I grow old without realizing it.

The second group of conjunctions that we will look at is made up of conjunctions that bring on the subjunctive only under certain conditions. They are:

aunque — although
dado que — given that
a pesar de que — in spite of (the fact that)

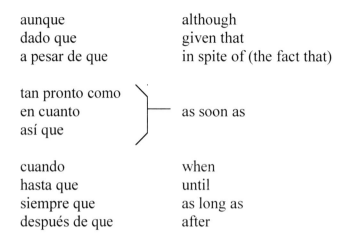

tan pronto como
en cuanto   — as soon as
así que

cuando — when
hasta que — until
siempre que — as long as
después de que — after

In the case of the first three conjunctions listed above the subjunctive is needed if the information conveyed in the subordinate clause is stated as a supposition, therefore uncertain or unknown; the indicative is used if the information is known or believed to be true. Compare the following examples:

A1. Aunque **sea** buena persona, lo que hizo trajo malas consecuencias para mí.
    Although he may be a good person, what he did brought me bad consequences.
A2. Aunque es buena persona, lo que hizo trajo malas consecuencias para mí.
    Although he is a good person, what he did brought bad consequences for me

B1. Va a asistir a universidad en setiembre dado que **tenga** el dinero.
    He is going to attend college in September granted that (if) he has the money.
B2. Va a asistir a la universidad en setiembre dado que tiene el dinero.
    He is going to attend college in September granted that (seeing as how) he has the money.

C1. A pesar de que **sea** fea, la llevaré al baile.
    In spite of the fact that she might be ugly (a blind date) I will take her to the dance.
C2. A pesar de que es fea, la llevaré al baile.
    In spite of the fact that she is ugly (I've seen her) I will take her to the dance.

The rest of the conjunctions listed above create the subjunctive mode only if the action of the main clause is in some fashion pending upon something happening in the subordinate clause. The action of the subordinate clause is an as yet not experienced event which may or may not ever occur. If the verb of the main clause is in the past the action of the subordinate clause has to have been pending at the time referenced in the main clause. The uncertainty as to whether the action referred to in the subordinate clause will ever take place requires the subjunctive.

A1. Comeremos tan pronto como **llegue** mi papá.
   We will eat as soon as my father gets home. (He has not yet arrived and there is no guarantee that he ever will).
A2. Siempre comemos tan pronto como llega mi papá.
   We always eat as soon as my father gets home. (This sentence reports habitual action - nobody is waiting for father to get home as the statement is made).

(Music, maestro, please!)

B1. "Cuando **sea** la primavera en las montañas Rocosas estaré regresando a casa y a ti."
   "When it's springtime in the Rockies I'll be coming home to you." (This is what will happen whenever springtime comes – who knows when that will happen).
B2. "Cuando la luna sale sobre la montaña cada rayo trae un sueño, querida, de ti."
   "When the moon comes over the mountain every beam brings a dream, dear, of you." (This is what happens every time the moon comes up - no action is pending as Kate Smith sings).
C1. No recibirá el dinero hasta que **cumpla** cincuenta años.
   She will not get the money until she turns fifty. (Getting the money depends on her making it to fifty and she is not there yet.)
C2. No recibió el dinero hasta que cumplió cincuenta años.
   She did not get the money until she turned fifty. (She made it to fifty and got the money - those things happened.)
D1. Siempre que ustedes no **saquen** fotos pueden presenciar la ceremonia.
   As long as you do not take photogragshs you may be present at the ceremony.
D2. Siempre que los turistas sacan una foto les exigen un dólar.
   Whenever the tourists take a picture they demand a dollar from them.

(Note that English must give different translations for the conjunction siempre que in these two sentences whereas in Spanish the difference in meaning comes with the shift from the subjunctive to the indicative mode.)

E1. Todos los problemas de la vida desaparecerán después de que **aprendas** el subjuntivo.
   All life's problems will vanish after you learn the subjunctive.
E2. Después de que aprendió el subjuntive fue elegido presidente del país y Miss Universe se enamoró de él.
   After he learned the subjunctive he was elected president of his country and Miss Universe fell in love with him.

At this point in our survey of the uses of the subjunctive let us recapitulate.

The subjunctive is a grammatically mandated change in your tone of voice. The subjunctive is a mode or way of speaking (which shows up in the handling of verbs) when a certain mood is created. This mood is created by expressions of emotion, doubt, denial, the desire and/or attempt to influence what others do, or references to things that have not been experienced or are contrary to fact. Therefore the subjunctive is not a 'self-made man.' It is dependent upon and comes into existence only if some other part of the sentence creates the conditions for its appearance.

There are several ways in which the conditions for the subjunctive to appear are created. First, if the verb in the main clause of the sentence expresses doubt, emotion, implied command, etc. Second, if the main clause of the sentence is an impersonal expression (with the verb ser) that none-the-less conveys a sense of emotion, doubt, implied command, etc. Third, if the conjunction joining two clauses in a sentence carries in its meaning the desire to influence or denial or makes reference to a specific event or condition which has not yet happened or come to be and therefore is uncertain of ever occurring.

The guidelines outlined above will account for most uses of the subjunctive in Spanish. But from time to time you will also stumble upon the subjunctive outside of these boundaries.

1. The adverbs of possibility quizá and its variant quizás, and the expression tal vez, all translate 'maybe' or 'perhaps.' They express uncertainty and take you directly to the subjunctive without the need of passing through a main clause and conjunction to get there.

>Tal vez **venga**.
>>Maybe he'll come.
>
>Quizás **sepa** Elena.
>>Perhaps Ellen knows.

2. Ojalá is neither a verb nor a conjunction but it creates the subjunctive mode. It is the remnant of an Arabic supplication to God, (Allah, or Alá in Spanish). Ojalá means "God grant..." It expresses a desire that something happen or come to be (or not happen or not come to be), therefore its use creates the subjunctive mode. In the secular language of late twentieth century America ojalá translates as a rather bland "I hope that...," or "I wish that..." For example:

>Ojalá que no **llueva** sobre tu desfile.
>>I hope that it does not rain on your parade.

In light of the long history of conflict between Christianity and Islam (and especially given the almost eight centuries long struggle between los cristianos and los moros for control of the Iberian Peninsula!) one might find a certain irony in the fact that Spaniards regularly invoke the power of the God of the Mohammedans. [An author recently described Spain as the place where God (i.e. the Christian God) would feel most at home if He came down to Earth. Did the writer simply overlook this everyday affront? Would God even be offended? Ojalá que no (One hopes not)] Or does the persistence of this expression reflect a grudging respect for and acceptance of an age old adversary? Present day Spain and its language are in large part the product of the forced union between Medieval Christian tribes and invading Moors. It was a 'shotgun wedding' and a stormy marriage but the offspring is much to be admired.

The most obvious influence that Arabic had on the Spanish language is in its vocabulary. I have read varying estimates of the percentage of Spanish words having an Arabic root – from ten to twenty five per cent. The grammar, however, has come directly from Latin. But I suspect that there is another much more subtle influence of Arabic on Spanish. Given the long propinquity of the two languages, the great body of learned writings by Arab scholars and the emotive power of Arabia's poetry must have a lingering effect as manifested in the eloquence and erudition found in Spanish letters going back centuries.

Of course Arabic has found its way into English as well. One interesting example is the term used to end a game of chess. The Moors introduced chess (the Spanish, ajedrez, is itself of Arabic derivation) on the Iberian Peninsula whence it found its way to the rest of Western Europe. When the king is inextricably trapped the triumphant Moslem cries, "Shah'akh maat!" The Spaniard turned this into jaque mate, and English further corrupted the Arabic expression into the enigmatic 'checkmate.' Mysterious no longer, "Shah'akh maat" means "Death to the shah!"

End of digression.

3. In the case of three verbs, querer, poder, and deber, Spanish permits the use of the imperfect or past subjunctive to soften a statement. This is not the subjunctive mode per se, rather the borrowing of a subjunctive form to achieve a gentler tone when making some requests or admonishing a friend.

Quisiera usar tu cepillo dental.
I would like to use your tooth brush.

¿**Pudieras** hacerme un favor?
Could you (possibly) do me a favor?

No **debieras** haberlo hecho.
You should not have done that.

4. "¡Qué me **entierren** en Bilbao!" ("Let me be buried…" or "Have me buried in Bilbao!")

The student of the subjunctive might look at this quotation and wonder what could have created the subjunctive mode in this case. The subjunctive mode is created in this instance by an unstated but understood "Quiero…" The speaker achieves more insistent force or dramatic impact by the omission. The quote is from a joke that plays upon the legendary cabezudez peninsular, to use Gabriel García Márquez's term for Spanish obstinacy. The speaker is an old patriarch on his deathbed, surrounded by his family, making and repeating this last wish. As the family lives in southern Spain and has no friends or relatives in the northern city of Bilbao his oldest son dares to ask why he wants to be buried there. His response as he expires, "¡Pa' joder!" (Rough translation: "Just to be a pain in the — one last time!")

Here is one slightly more run of the mill example of this usage:

Yo no quiero decirle. ¡Qué le **diga** su hermano!
   I don't want to tell him. Let his brother tell him!

5. There is one more instance in which the past subjunctive is used where the student of the language will find nothing in the sentence that would seem to warrant its use. For years I was puzzled by these inexplicable encounters with the imperfect subjunctive. As they came from the pens of competent authors writing for respected publications I had to assume that the usage was legitimate, albeit mysterious to me. I finally dismissed it as a literary affectation.

Up to a point, perhaps, I was right. But if it is an affectation it is not haphazard nor without solid grammatical footing. I finally found the explanation in a very detailed hundred-year-old grammar in which I was browsing one evening. Spanish grammar permits the substitution of the imperfect subjunctive for the pluperfect. This is a literary and not a conversational usage. It probably has its origins in a confusion dating back to the earliest years of the emerging Spanish language (in the 10th and 11th centuries) between the Latin pluperfect and the Spanish imperfect subjunctive - the forms are very similar. In any case, it is now an accepted stylistic practice. An example by way of illustration:

Colón se atrevió a navegar hacia el oeste porque **estudiara** (había estudiado) por muchos años las direcciones contrarias de los vientos alisios en diferentes latitudes.

Columbus dared to sail west because for many years he had studied the opposing direction of the trade winds at different latitudes.

Time Out

You have been given many rules to guide you through this grammatical maze. The great majority of the native speakers of Spanish is only vaguely aware, if aware at all, of these rules. For the Peruvian or the Costa Rican or the Spaniard the subjunctive is more like a sixth sense than a set of rules. It helps to shape his or her thoughts and his or her view of this world we all live in together. But the rules are there, and not just for students for whom Spanish is a new language. On a few occasions I have listened to native speakers of Spanish discuss a disagreement among themselves about whether to use the subjunctive in a particular instance. The subjunctive is not a grammatical monolith. Read four or five different grammar books and you will find minor discrepancies and conflicting opinions on small points. The rules do have their limitations.

The subjunctive is also part of the English-speaker's linguistic heritage. But the subjunctive clearly is a much more crucial part of the Spanish language than it is of English. The English-speaker does not have a well-developed sixth sense about the subjunctive as does his Spanish-speaking counterpart. So the student of Spanish as a second language has rules instead of a culturally set inner compass to guide him.

Here is an exchange typical of many that I have had with students over the years:

Prof. - <u>Perdónenme. Necesito un *kleenex*. Continuaremos la lección cuando yo vuelva.</u>
Estud. - Why did you use the subjunctive?
Prof. - Because I have to go get a kleenex…
Estud. - Yes, but…
Prof. - Perhaps I'll never come back.
Estud. - But the kleenex is right over there. I can see the box.
Prof. - But there is no guarantee that I'll ever get back to the table.
Estud. – It's only five steps away.
Prof. - Maybe I'll drop dead.
Estud. - No you won't!
Prof. - How do you know?
Estud. - I don't get this!

Is language destiny? Is the Latino more fatalistic because the subjunctive is constantly reminding him of doubts, uncertainties and unknowns of this life? Is the Gringo fatuously optimistic because his language downplays or hides these realities? Are we the way we are because of the different languages we speak or have different histories shaped the languages we used in making those histories? These are very interesting questions, and beyond the purview of this exposition of rules governing the subjunctive. But one cannot study language without also thinking about those who use that language. Language, human nature, cultures, history are hopelessly tangled up together.

The Subjunctive in the Past

Here is one more rule to guide you until that 'sixth sense' kicks in. Given the discussion above about conjunctions that can create the subjunctive mode because their meaning conveys doubt or uncertainty or refer to some as yet un-experienced event or condition it would seem logical to find <u>'si' condicional</u>, i.e. 'if,' (as opposed to <u>'sí' afirmativo</u>, 'yes') on that list. However, the subjunctive is never used after <u>'si' condicional</u> in the present tense.[36] For example:

"Si hoy es jueves, esto debe ser Bélgica."
"If today is Thursday, this must be Belgium."

---

[36] A bi-lingual friend who spent several years teaching in the northern Mexican state of Sonora reports that among his acquaintances there this rule was regularly ignored. This may be a regional idiosyncrasy or the start of a small grammatical revolution. Time will tell. For now, I'd follow the rule as is.

However, the past (imperfect) subjunctive is used after si when the 'if clause' contains a statement that is contrary to fact. English has an equivalent subjunctive usage. For example:

Si yo **fuera** dictador del mundo sometería a cadena perpetua a las personas que arrojan chicle usado en las vías públicas.
   If I **were** dictator of the world (but I am not) I would give life imprisonment to people who throw used chewing gum onto sidewalks and streets.

or, in a more humane and tolerant frame of mind, but still contrary to fact:

"Si yo **tuviera** un martillo yo martillaría en la mañana…"
"If I had a hammer, I'd hammer in the morning…"

Please note, however, that if the information that follows si is unknown or uncertain, as opposed to contrary to fact, there is no subjunctive.

No sabíamos si venían por avión o a camello.
   We didn't know if they were coming by airplane or on camels.

The mention of the 'if clause' leads us neatly into a discussion of the past subjunctive. With the exception of the 'if clause' the subjunctive mode is created in the past in the very same ways that it is created in the present. Implied command, emotion, doubt, uncertainty, denial, non-experience all create the subjunctive mood in the past just as in the present.

If the verb of the main clause is in the past - preterit, imperfect or pluperfect - the subjunctive clause must also be in the past. This is not so with our bush league English subjunctive. For example:

Present tense: The boss requests that he *work* harder.
   Past tense: The boss requested that he *work* harder.

In both cases the subjunctive 'he work' is present tense. But:

Present: El jefe pide que se **esfuerce** más.
   Past: El jefe pidió que se **esforzara** más.

There now follows a brief exercise to allow you an opportunity to dabble in past subjunctive. Translate the English sentence given, then backshift that sentence to the past tense as in the example set of sentences below.

I want you to come to my party.
   Quiero que **vengas** a mi fiesta.
     backshift: Quería que **vinieras** a mi fiesta.
       (I wanted you to come to my party)

Gramática Apasionada
Reminiscences of a Love Affair with the Spanish Language

Now translate and backshift the following sentences. Model sentences will be found at the end of the exercise.

1. Duke Ellington suggests that you take the A train.

_____

backshift: _____

2. Without Pedro I doubt that the Red Sox will win the pennant this year.

_____

backshift: _____

3. It is not possible that it is raining on the Atacama Desert. (It hasn't rained there for 25 years).

_____

backshift: _____

4. His parents work in order that he have a better life.

_____

backshift _____

5. He knows that we are sick

_____

backshift: _____

6. I think that she will go on talking until the cows come home.

_____

backshift: _____

7. "I never met a man I didn't like."

_____

forwardshift: _____

Now check your translations and conjugations against pure truth.

1. Duque Ellington sugiere que **tomes** el tren A.
    backshift: Duque Ellington sugirió que **tomaras** el tren A.

2. Sin Pedro dudo que las Medias Rojas ganen el campeonato este año.
    backshift: Dudaba que las Medias Rojas **ganaran** el campeonato este año.

3. No es posible que **esté** lloviendo en el desierto Atacama.
    backshift: No fue posible que **estuviera** lloviendo en el desierto Atacama.

4. Sus padres trabajan para que él **tenga** una vida mejor.
    backshift: Sus padres trabajaron para que él **tuviera** una vida mejor.

5. El sabe que nosotros estamos* enfermos.
    backshift: El sabía que nosotros estábamos* enfermos.
    *(I hope that you noticed that no subjunctive is required!)

6. Creo que ella continuará hablando hasta que las vacas **vuelvan** a casa.
    backshift: Creía que ella continuaría hablando hasta que las vacas **volvieran** a casa.

7. Jamás (nunca) conocí a un hombre que no me **gustara**.
    forwardshift: Nunca conozco a un hombre que no me **guste**.

One more twist of the screw

There used to be a future subjunctive. In modern Spanish its function has been completely taken over by the present subjunctive. Note the examples that follow:

I doubt that he works on Saturdays.
    Dudo que él **trabaje** los sábados.

I doubt that he will work next Saturday.
    Dudo que él **trabaje** el sábado próximo.

It is truly a rare thing these days to stumble upon the future subjunctive. It does still linger on in some old proverbs and expressions. But if it does appear it comes before you redolent of times long gone by. One example:

Fuere lo que **fuere** seguiremos en la lucha.
    Be what will (be) the struggle will go on.

Gramática Apasionada
Reminiscences of a Love Affair with the Spanish Language

The End

Having finished this survey of the subjunctive, the question becomes, where to go from here?

Here are three suggestions:

First, study and practice the conjugations (out loud) so that you can easily produce them when you are speaking and so that they will be recognizable to you as you are reading or listening.

Second, look at several different grammar books. The variety of example sentences and varying ways of explaining what the subjunctive is will expand your understanding of this concept. I highly recommend the first or second editions of <u>A Concept Approach to Spanish</u>, by Da Silva and Lovett, published by Harper and Row. Unfortunately these two editions are out of print. If you happen to stumble upon this book at a garage sale or in a used bookstore, buy it! It has an excellent presentation of the subjunctive and is the best overall Spanish grammar book I have seen. A good portion of the structure of this chapter is beholden to the fine presentation of this material by <u>los señores</u> Da Silva and Lovett

Third, read as much as possible in Spanish. Spanish newspapers and magazines are available in most American cities these days. Most libraries will have a selection from the rich literature of Spain and Latin America. As you read try to spot subjunctive usages, then stop and analyze what it is in that sentence that created the subjunctive mode. This is an excellent exercise. Any subjunctive that you find can be explained within the framework of what has been presented in this chapter. It may take extra thought but it will have its explanation. For example, what makes this subjunctive?

Es lógico que ella **haga** eso.
It is logical that she do that.

What creates the subjunctive in this case? There is no emotion, no doubt or denial, the action of the subordinate clause is not pending or perhaps to happen in an unknown future. What makes this subjunctive is the desire to influence - logic demands that she do that. And on it goes, every new encounter with a subjunctive usage will be a new challenge.

A Mysterious Malady

As a serious student of the subjunctive mode it is very likely that you will eventually come down with a case of subjunctivitus. Medical science does not yet fully understand this affliction. The most promising theory so far believes it to be an inflammation of the synapses adjacent to the brain cells where knowledge of the subjunctive is stored. The symptoms are overuse of the subjunctive driven by an unfounded suspicion that the meaning of almost every verb and conjunction can somehow be twisted to create the subjunctive mode. Diagnosis is confirmed if the patient is observed to use the subjunctive mode in 90%

of his or her sentences over a three- day period. There is, as yet, no miracle remedy; but time and additional study have proven remarkably effective in curing this malady.

<u>Paciencia y persistencia</u>.

Gramática Apasionada
Reminiscences of a Love Affair with the Spanish Language

Chapter Seventeen

Add Some Stress to Your Life

Here are two presidential trivia questions. The first one you will probably consider rather easy, but the second question more truly fits the definition of trivia.

The first question: Which president do you associate with a Gettysburg address?

The second question: Which president do you associate with a Gettysburg address?

Oh dear! How silly of me. Of course you cannot tell the two questions apart. If I were speaking these questions to you rather than writing them there would be no confusion. These are two distinct questions. The reason for the seeming repetition is that English, unlike Spanish, does not have a system by which the stressed syllable of every word can be identified in its written form. Let me re-phrase the two questions.

First, which president is associated with a speech made in Gettysburg? (a Gettysburg ad-DRESS).

The second question: Which president is associated with a residence in Gettysburg? (a Gettysburg AD-dress)[37]

Shifting the stress within an English word from one syllable to another does not often change its meaning. In Spanish, however, shifting the accent from one syllable to another changes the meaning of thousands of words. The accent mark, tilde[38] as it is called in Spanish, is not simply a device for adding visual pizzazz to the written language. It carries meaning in itself just as each letter does. The difference between 'o' and 'ó' in a word is just as significant as the difference between 'm' and 'n' or 'a' and 'z.'

For the English-speaker, whose language requires a low level of awareness of accentuation, the shift to speaking Spanish calls for significantly increasing the attention paid to stress. English leaves the speaker, who does not happen to be carrying a dictionary around with him, to make his best guess as to where to put the accent on any new multi-syllabic word he encounters. In fact, many years after the Clarence Thomas-Anita Hill

---

[37] The answers: Abraham Lincoln, who made his famous speech dedicating the National Cemetery in Gettysburg on November 19, 1863, four and one half months after the crucial battle fought there; and, Dwight Eisenhower, who lived on a farm in Gettysburg from his retirement in 1961 until his death in 1969.

[38] Many people believe that the tilde refers only to the squiggle part of the 'ñ.' The Royal Academy defines it as denoting accentuation as well and it will be so used in this chapter.

James K. Gavin

confrontation, news broadcasters still do not seem to have decided whether the word central to those hearings is 'HA-rass-ment' or 'ha-RASS-ment.' (At the height of that drama one well-known announcer was so flummoxed by the problematical word that it came out 'ha-rass-MENT'). Spanish, neat and orderly in all things, will never do this to you.

Of course you must know the rules. There are only three.

The last letter of the word is the key.

Rule #1. If the word ends with a vowel or 'n' or 's' the accent falls on the next-to-the-last syllable.

Rule #2. If the word ends with a consonant other than 'n' or 's' the accent falls on the last syllable.

Rule #3. Any word that violates Rule #1 or Rule #2 will have a written accent mark that shows you where to put the stress.

There you have it! Three simple rules to learn. Of course one must be know how to break a word down into syllables, so a few words about syllabification (where does the accent go in that word!?) are in order. As long as each vowel in a word is bracketed by consonants there is no challenge involved in counting the syllables in a Spanish word. Problems do arise, however, when a word contains successive vowels.

Again there are rules.

We must divide the vowels into two groups. 'a,' 'e' and 'o' are classified as strong vowels; 'i' and 'u' (also 'y' when acting as a vowel) are weak vowels. Any combination of a strong and weak vowel, e.g. <u>pue</u>do, a<u>cei</u>te, <u>cual</u>, <u>rey</u>, or two weak vowels, e.g. <u>fuis</u>te, <u>ciu</u>dad, will generate only one syllable. These combinations, there are fourteen possibilities, are called diphthongs. When counting syllables to determine where to put the accent a diphthong counts as one syllable.

When a word has two strong vowels in succession, e.g. <u>leo</u>, <u>marea</u>, <u>caos</u>, each vowel generates its own syllable. The three example words fall under Rule #1 above and are pronounced LE-o, ma-RE-a, and CA-os.

A written accent over the weak vowel of a diphthong dissolves the diphthong creating an additional syllable in the word. <u>Rio</u> is a one syllable word meaning 'he or she laughed;' <u>río</u> is a two syllable word meaning 'river' or the verb form 'I laugh.' <u>Seis</u> has one syllable, <u>país</u> has two.

Rare, especially in vosotros-less[39] New World Spanish, is the triphthong. The triphthong is a strong vowel flanked by weak vowels - Paraguay and the verb form cambiáis are examples. The triphthong generates just one syllable.

That's all there is, folks! Spanish has none of that free-floating English stress, slipping like quick-silver from syllable to syllable the way the pea jumps from cup to cup in the con-man's game. Any Spanish word can be pronounced correctly the first time, every time.

Questions may arise however, because now and then you will see an accent mark where none seems necessary. This is because the accent mark, or tilde, does something else besides indicate stress. It has a diacritical use, that is to say, it is used to distinguish between two grammatical functions of one word. For example, the verb form sé (from saber and ser) is distinguished from the reflexive pronoun se by means of the diacritical accent mark.

There is a pecking order that establishes which function is more important and therefore is the recipient of the tilde. Nouns and verbs come first, then personal pronouns, object pronouns, adjectives, adverbs, conjunctions and the lowly preposition.

Examples:

Ayer, **él** (personal pronoun) leyó **el** (adjective) cuento.
   Yesterday, **he** read **the** story.

Mi (adjective) casa es para **mí** (obj. pron.) solamente.
   My house is for **me** alone.

Ellos **te** (obj. pron.) sirvieron **té** (noun) de menta.
   They served **you** mint **tea**.

Tú (personal pron.) debes abrir **tu** (adjec.) regalo.
   You ought to open **your** present.

Quiero que me **dé** (verb) un poco **de** (prep.) vino.
   I want that you **give** me a bit **of** the wine.

Sí (adv.), lo hizo por **sí** (obj. pron.), **si** (conj.) quieres saber la verdad. (Si has three functions, the first two in rank carry the accent.)
   Yes, he did it for **him**self, **if** you want to know the truth.

Voy a decirles **más** (adv.), **mas** (conj.) no en este momento.
   I am going to tell them **more, but** not right now.

---

[39]The present tense endings for vosotros, -áis and -éis, begin with diphthongs and will generate triphthongs if the stem of the infinitive ends with a weak vowel, e.g. cambiar (see example above) and averiguar.

There are a few two-syllabled verb forms (como, para, entre, sobre) that also have a second grammatical function. The Academy did not deem it necessary that they be given a tilde.

Aun has an accent when it means 'still' or 'yet,' no accent when it means 'even.'

Goya dijo que **aun** en su vejez y ceguera aprendía **aún**.
　Goya said that **even** in his old age and blindness he was **still** learning.

The demonstrative adjectives - este, ese, aquel and their feminine and plural forms - become pronouns when carrying the tilde.

Bueno, **éste** dice que **este** carro es suyo.
　Well, **this one** (this man) says that **this** car is his.

Solo earns a tilde when it means solamente.

Voy al cine **solo sólo** si mi novia no quiere.
　I go to the movies **alone only** if my girl friend doesn't want to go.

All of the interrogative words serve dual grammatical functions. They are accented when used in their interrogative capacity.

¿**Qué** dijo el hombre **que** está sentado allí?
　What said the man **that** is sitting there.

¿**Cuándo** estarás aquí **cuando** yo te necesito?
　When will you be here **when** I need you?

The conjunction o is given a tilde when it occurs between numbers to eliminate possible confusion with zero.

Esperando la señal aquella noche histórica, Pablo Revere se preguntaba, "!Caray! ¿Es 1 ó 2 si por tierra?"

It has been almost one hundred years since the Academy ruled that nouns and verb forms that have only one syllable do not take an accent mark except for diacritical purposes. But here in my adopted home town one still sees the name of The Royal Town of the Holy Faith of Saint Francis of Assisi written Santa Fé. If done in ignorance it is a totally harmless error. If done on purpose it is probably intended to evoke images of simpler, gentler times - as do the long since abandoned 'e's of Olde Boston Towne.

An adjective that has a written accent retains the tilde when made into an adverb by the addition of the suffix -mente, (-ly). For example, the adjective fácil, (easy), becomes the adverb fácilmente, (easily).

The first element of a compound word retains a written accent if the two elements are joined in lexical bliss by a hyphen. It discards the accent mark if the two elements are united without benefit of this grammatical clergy. An example of the former is árabe-americano; and the latter, decimoquinto - décimo is 'tenth,' quinto is 'fifth,' put them together and you get 'fifteenth.'

Note: (not related to the use of the accent mark but a frequent question) a compound adjective like nuevomexicano, from Nuevo México, agrees with the noun it modifies only at the end of the word, not at the junction of the two elements. Las señoritas nuevomexicanas son encantadoras.

The use of the tilde is optional in cases where it would sit atop an upper case letter. In practice the option to omit is usually chosen. As a matter of fact, the computer I am using to write this does not even give me the option of putting a tilde over an upper case letter, neither for stress nor for the upper case 'ñ.' Newspaper headlines are probably the most common situation in which one must play "tilde, tilde, who's got the tilde?" This can create occasional ambiguity, especially given the telegram-like quality of many headlines.

PAPA DENUNCIA A SU HIJO LADRON

(He is not supposed to have children - just running the Catholic church is a more than full-time job).

For the native speaker the lack of accent marks in the upper case is seldom a problem. But how many times has a student of mine, applying Rule #1 about accentuation, pronounced the name of southern California's largest city as Los An-GE-les? It is Los AN-ge-les. However, as the first letters of proper names are capitalized the tilde is rarely there to guide the student in placing the stress on the correct syllable.

Caution: if the last letter of the stem of an infinitive is a weak vowel the diphthong created as the verb is conjugated in the present tense must be dealt with. Some verbs leave the diphthong intact, e.g. estudiar, yo estudio (es-TU-dio), tú estudias (es-TU-dias), etc.; others dissolve the diphthong, e.g. espiar, yo espío (es-PI-o), tú espías (es-PI-as), etc. These must be learned individually as you encounter them. Also keep in mind that if the stem of the infinitive ends with a strong vowel the two successive vowels that occur during conjugation of the verb are strong vowels. Therefore each generates a syllable and no tilde is needed; e.g. desear, yo deseo (de-SE-o), tú deseas (de-SE-as), etc.

****

We will finish with two exercises. The first is designed for students of all levels to check your ability to apply the rules of accentuation and syllabification. The second is more challenging, and is intended as entertainment as much as for education. The answers are at the end of the chapter.

First, write out the following schematized words in correct Spanish adding the tilde as needed. The bold upper case vowel indicates where the spoken emphasis falls.

lInea	aviOn	farmAcia	comunidAd	difIcil	continUa
japonEs	azUcar	pAjaro	hAblo	organicE	MarIa
superfIcie	trabajAr	atEo	Arbol	MartInez	

Second, supply the accent marks as needed in the following:

Un Dialogo Poco Probable: oido en algun bar sin nombre entre Che Guerrero and Gringo Gavin

Che - ¡Oye, tu, gringo! ¿Quien es el hombre mas fantastico, democratico, heroico, y tambien, simpatico que jamas ha puesto su pie sobre La Tierra?

Gringo - ¿Que fue lo que usted dijo? Y ¿Como sabe usted como me llamo yo? Mi nombre, que mi mama me dio a mi, si, es Gringo, pero si no nos conocemos ¿como sabia usted?

Che - Yo no se tu nombre, gringo. Ni tengo el menor interes en saberlo. Sabiendolo solo echaria a perder una celula de mi cerebro y no quiero que se desperdicie ni una sola celula por tan inutil razon. Solamente quiero oir de tus labios el nombre del gran heroe de este siglo, de el que inspira fe, quien predice la caida del Imperio Yanqui. Dimelo, rapidamente.

Gringo - Pero, ¿Quien es? En mi pais el heroe nacional es Jorge Guasinton porque lanzo un dolar de plata a traves del rio Potomac. Pero usted no esta hablando de este. Es necesario que usted me de una pista.

Che - Esta bien. Este señor tiene un hermano que se llama Raul. Dio la bendicion de la libertad a todos los cubanos. Ademas, es uno que en la batalla no sabe el significado del verbo 'huir.'

Gringo - Bueno, señor. Ya tengo una idea, pero dejeme pensarlo un poco mas y despues le envio mi respuesta por correo aereo. Creo que se refiere a uno que tiene teorias politico-economicas muy raras.

Che - ¡Sonrie cuando dices eso, gringo!

The answers:

First exercise –
>línea, avión, farmacia, comunidad, difícil, continúa,
>japonés, azúcar, pájaro, hablo, organicé, María,
>superf icie, trabajar, ateo, árbol, Martínez

Second exercise:

Un Diálogo Poco Probable: oído en algún bar sin nombre entre Che Guerrero y Gringo Gavin

Che - ¡Oye, tú, gringo! ¿Quién es el hombre más fantástico, democrático, heroico, y también, simpático que jamás ha puesto su pie sobre La Tierra?

Gringo - ¿Qué fue lo que usted dijo? Y, ¿Cómo sabe usted como me llamo yo? Mi nombre, que mi mamá me dio a mí, sí, es Gringo, pero si no nos conocemos, ¿cómo sabía usted?

Che - Yo no sé tu nombre, gringo, ni tengo el menor interés en saberlo. Sabiéndolo sólo echaría a perder una célula de mi cerebro y no quiero que se desperdicie ni una sola célula.

Solamente quiero oír de tus labios el nombre del gran héroe de este siglo, de él que inspira fe, quien predice la caída del Imperio Yanqui. Dímelo rápidamente.

Gringo - Pero, ¿quién es? En mi país el héroe nacional es Jorge Guásinton poque lanzó un dólar de plata a través del río Potomac. Pero usted no está hablando de éste. Es necesario que me dé una pista.

Che - Está bien. Este señor tiene un hermano que se llama Raúl. Dio la bendición de la libertad a todos los cubanos. Además, es uno que en la batalla no sabe el significado del verbo 'huir.'

Gringo - Bueno, señor. Ya tengo una idea. Pero déjeme pensarlo un poco más y después le envío mi respuesta por correo aéreo. Creo que se refiere a uno que tiene teorías político-económicas muy raras.

Che - ¡Sonríe cuando dices eso, gringo!

Chapter Eighteen

It Cleans, Fixes, and Gives Splendor

One summer evening I was playing the Spanish version of Trivial Pursuits with a few fellow teachers and some of our students. A throw of the die and up came the question, "¿Qué limpia, fija, y da esplendor?" This brought a collective, "Huh!?" from the group. It was obvious that no one was going to answer the question. The card was immediately flipped over. We read the answer. "La Real Academia de la Lengua Española." (The Royal Academy of the Spanish Language).

The question that so totally stumped us is the motto of the Academy. The Royal Academy was established in 1714. But the seed of the idea for such an institution was probably planted back in 1469 when Isabel, Queen of Castilla y Leon, married Ferdinand, King of Aragon. The happy couple set an example of equality of the sexes that few feminist/new-American-male unions of our time could match. They had identical thrones set at exactly the same height above the palace court. Neither one of them cooked or did the dishes.

Their marriage united the two most powerful kingdoms of Spain. Then, instead of going off on separate royal career tracks that might have generated competitive tensions and conflicting professional demands in their happy castle, they chose to do a job-sharing thing - that job being a concerted effort to bring the entire Iberian peninsula under their sway.

Their strategy was three pronged - military, religious and linguistic.

On the military front their biggest obstacle was the Kingdom of Granada, the last Moorish stronghold after almost 800 years of Moslem presence (with its accompanying turf warfare) in Spain. Finally, in January, 1492, the Moors abandoned Spain for good, retreating back to North Africa. They departed Spain at a massive rock formation with the Arabic name Jebel-al-Tarik, Tarik's Mountain, for it was at this same place that Tarik had first led the Moors into Spain in the year 711. It is still called Tarik's Mountain today, but the pronunciation has gotten somewhat garbled over the years and it now comes out Gibraltar. The Moors left behind some magnificent architecture and thousands of words that are still part of every Spanish-speaker's vocabulary.

1492! Surely a bell went off in your head. Was that not the year that "Columbus sailed the ocean blue?"

Yes, of course, and it is no coincidence. The victory over the Moors meant the end of a large military operation. That in turn meant the end of a tremendous financial drain on the limited resources of our struggling young couple. Thus it was that Ferdinand and Isabel had some discretionary duros available later that year to bet on the wacky ideas of an obscure Italian who believed that he could reach the fabled East by sailing west. And when else in history has such a small wager paid off so handsomely?

The religious part of their royal equally-highnesses' unification strategy was quite simple - Catholicism.

When one uses modern ethical standards to condemn historical decisions and acts one runs the risk of seeming a moral poseur or outright hypocrite. But from a post-World War II perspective it certainly is hard other than to boo and hiss the royal decree of that same fateful year, 1492, expelling the Jews from Spain. Actually Spanish Jews were given the choice of converting to Catholicism or leaving the country. Unlike the Moors who had arrived in Spain on a wave of Islamic militancy, the Jews were peaceful immigrants. They represented a disproportionately large percentage of the small part of the population that was educated and they had served their sovereigns well.

Many Jews left. Those who stayed at the least had to go through all the motions of being Catholic. As the generations passed many of these families ended up genuinely Catholic.

In recent years, here in New Mexico, historian/scholars are inquiring among some of the oldest Hispanic Catholic families. There are family traditions among them which, unbeknownst to the people themselves, may be the vestiges of Jewish worship practiced in secret by their ancestors in 'all-Catholic' Spain.

This is a fascinating bit of historical trivia and perhaps of considerable interest to some of the families involved.

Some historians have suggested that the expulsion of the Jews by los reyes católicos constituted a serious loss of administrative and money managing skills (the drain in Spain was mainly of the brain!). It might 'elp explain 'ow Spain went from being the wealthiest country in Europe in the 16th century to one of its poorest at the start of the twentieth century.

The third prong of their strategy bears most directly on the question of the Royal Academy.

15th century Spain was very fragmented linguistically. For more than a century before Christ and into the fifth century of the Christian era Spain, or Iberia, as it was called at the time, was part of the Roman Empire. Then followed a series of invasions by peoples from northern Europe. Of these peoples the Visigoths were to have the greatest long term influence. In the 8th century the Moors entered the picture precipitating seven more centuries of intermittent warfare.

The political result of all this was not Spain, rather an Iberian Peninsula divided into a number of rival kingdoms. The linguistic result was that by the time of Ferdinand and Isabel, the Latin of Iberia was evolving into regional dialects with less and less in common.

Ferdinand and Isabel realized that to unify and rule effectively, the disparate parts of the kingdom would need a common language. Thus it was by the will of this ambitious couple that the Spanish spoken in the Kingdom of Castile became the dominant language of the peninsula. And that is why you will hear the language called 'Castilian Spanish' or simply castellano in Spanish.

The importance of language as a unifying agent should not be underestimated. Even today the dream of Spanish unification is not fully realized. More than five centuries after the marriage of Ferdinand and Isabel there are still separatist movements within Spain, especially in Catalonia and the Basque country. Use of their traditional language is one of the rallying points for both of these movements.

The importance of the role of language in shaping a modern nation state led to the establishment in 1714 of La Real Academia de la Lengua Española. We have no equivalent institution in the English-speaking world. The Academy is the arbiter and final authority over all questions relating to the Spanish language. It decides what is right and what is wrong, what is acceptable and what is not. The existence and acceptance of such an institution is reflected in a respect for their language prevalent in Spanish-speaking countries that I have not observed in the English-speaking world. Misuse of and disrespect for the language in Spain would provoke reactions more akin to (but not as heated as) American feelings about desecration of the flag.[40]

I have witnessed this custodial concern for their language on a number of occasions. A fine example occurred in Spain in the winter of 1966. That was when the United States accomplished the first soft landing of a spacecraft on the moon. Many years later this is my recollection of what happened then.

The event itself generated some interest in Madrid. But the terminology used by the newspaper that first reported the event created even more public interest. The paper

---

[40]In making these observations about the respect for their language that one finds in Spanish-speaking countries I do not wish to create uncalled for alarm among Spanish students who are thinking about traveling abroad. You might at this point be thinking, "Will my pathetic attempt to speak their language offend people?"

My experience, and that of every student who has ever reported back to me, has been without exception the same. Everywhere in the Spanish-speaking world, at whatever linguistic level you are operating, people will be very appreciative of your effort to speak their language. You will have praise heaped upon you. You will be told repeatedly how well you speak the language. All very nice, but there is a downside to this. No matter how often you ask, you will find very few people willing to point out your errors so that you can improve linguistically. To call attention to any inadequacies in your Spanish would display both rudeness and ingratitude.

announced, "Una nave espacial aterriza en la luna!" (A spacecraft lands on the moon!) The verb aterrizar has as its stem terr- which relates to tierra which means both 'earth' and 'Earth' in Spanish. So the verb literally means 'to come to Earth (or land).'

A rival paper quickly raised the question, "How can you come to Earth on the moon?" The Earth is the Earth and the moon is the moon, and never the twain shall meet (we certainly hope!). You cannot make un aterrizaje (a landing or 'earthing') on the moon, you must make un alunizaje on the moon. And this also necessitates a new verb, alunizar. (A seaplane can not even 'land' on water in Spanish - the terms are contradictory - that is another verb, amarizar.)

All this discussion was carried on in featured editorials in the major newspapers of Madrid. The logic of the case made for alunizar carried the day. All the papers began using it in reporting on the event. But that was not the end of the discussion about terminology. What, one editor asked, was to happen when those space-crazy Americans inevitably one day reach Mars, (Marte)? Must we create another verb, amartizar, and another noun, amartizaje?

Here the split between the rival papers became permanent. One paper stayed with the logic that you cannot come to Earth anywhere except on Earth. Another pointed out that with all the possible future landing sites out there in space this line of thinking would place on the Spanish language the burden of eventually having to create hundreds of new verbs and nouns. This paper took the position that the moon, as our closest celestial neighbor, deserved a verb of its own. Beyond that the phraseology un aterrizaje en Marte, un aterrizaje en Venus, should be used. A third paper pointed out that all this argument was academic, meaning exactly the opposite, that it was not 'academic.' The Royal Academy would in due time deliberate these weighty questions and announce its decision. That would be that.[41]

Compare all this concern for language with the linguistic free-for-all that we get in the American print media. Can you imagine the Chicago Tribune locked in editorial combat with the Boston Globe over a verb form? During that year-long press party called Watergate we were gleefully given 'stonewall' as a verb, the 'modified total hangout' was legitimized as both language and behavior, and 'deepthroat' moved uptown from the marquees of X-rated movie houses to the front pages of our most prestigious newspapers.

This is not written to make the case that one approach to language is better than the other. Rather the intent is simply to point out differing cultural attitudes about how one's language should be treated.

---

[41]The most recent edition of the dictionary of the Royal Academy, 1992, includes both alunizar and alunizaje. There have been landings on Mars but the dictionary does not list amartizar. However, the definition of aterrizar makes no reference to extra-terrestrial bodies. So the larger question remains unresolved.

A more personal encounter with this linguistic protectiveness happened a few years back at a wedding reception. One of the guests was an old man from Spain. As he spoke no English I was asked to make an effort to keep him from feeling left out. Thus it came to pass that I spent several hours in his company.

He was a small trim erect figure with the demeanor of a professor <u>emeritus</u> and the weathered face and hands of genteel European peasantry. He must have been at least 70 years old, he could have been 95. He wore a dark suit and tie with an immaculate white shirt and a beret. There were no frills to his attire. One might have thought that he had absolutely no vanity about his personal appearance. But the beret gave him away. Not the beret itself which was black and devoid of ornamentation. The tipoff was the very precise angle at which it was set upon his close-cropped dome. That tilt was no accident. I suspect that he had a series of very carefully calibrated settings - one angle for funerals, another for Easter Sunday, a third when in the company of a <u>señorita</u>, etc.

He would have blended right in with the crowd in a pub in County Cork (the Celts were in Spain as well as Ireland). But this was a leprechaun with an attitude. This was a Spaniard! His opinions matched his attire perfectly - black and white and no frills.

Our conversation inevitably came around to the Spanish language itself. He had no kind words for the Spanish spoken in the New World, full of <u>barbarismos</u> and <u>neologismos</u> in combination with <u>una pronunciación viciosa</u>.

At this point it must be explained that one of the significant differences between the Spanish spoken in the Western Hemisphere and the mother tongue of Spain is found in the pronunciation of the 'c,' 's,' and 'z.' In the Americas there is no difference in the pronunciation of 'sa' and 'za,' or 'ce' and 'se.' The same is true of 'ci' and 'si,' 'so' and 'zo,' and 'su' and 'zu.' In all of these instances the consonant is pronounced as a sibilant 's.' In peninsular Spanish the 's' is sibilant but in the combinations 'za,' 'ce,' 'ci,' 'zo,' and 'zu' the consonant sounds 'th.' This does result in occasional ambiguities in American Spanish.

My newfound friend sternly rebuked the New World for this defect of speech. His tone was that of a collector of beautiful antiques who discovers his grandchildren using a 19th century silver teapot and some fine china cups to prepare and serve grape kool-aid.

"When they want you to close the door," he scolded, "they ask you to please saw the door in half!" <u>Cerrar</u> 'to close' and <u>serrar</u> 'to saw' are pronounced the same in the Americas, both start with a sibilant 's' sound; but for the Spaniard there is a significant difference between "<u>cierre</u> [thierre] <u>la puerta por favor</u>" and "<u>sierre la puerta</u>."

"And what," he demanded, "is the chef supposed to do when a patron of his restaurant asks to have his sirloin steak nicely stitched up?" <u>Bien cocido</u> is the usual term for 'well done,' but the Spaniard must hear [cothido] so as not to confuse <u>cocer</u> [cother] 'to cook' with <u>coser</u> 'to sew.'

In spite of his indignation at this mistreatment of "the language of Christianity" he did show some unexpected delicacy in regard to my feelings. He went on at length about what 'they' are doing to el castellano on this side of the Atlantic. But it was clearly understood by both of us that the 'they' that he kept referring to included me.

For most English-speakers the language is a very handy tool that has the additional virtue of being a tool that requires absolutely no maintenance.

The language is a vital tool for the Spanish-speaker as well, but it is a tool whose handle should be kept smooth and polished and whose blade should be sharpened and oiled frequently. I do not know if the Academy exists because Spaniards felt this way about their language or if Spanish speakers take this proprietary interest in their language because the Academy has created and promoted a focus of concern for the language.

However, the existence of such an institution as the Royal Academy does not mean that the language is monolithic and unchanging. Every language is a living thing that grows and changes and eventually may even die. Spanish is rich in regional dialects, slang and many forms unacceptable to the Academy. But the fact that there is a standard upheld by the Academy, a 'correct' Spanish, may be the reason why a language spoken for so many centuries over a large part of the globe is still a viable means of communication between residents of Toledo, Texas, and Tierra del Fuego.

The present day speaker of English who wishes to learn Spanish should be grateful for the existence of this venerable institution. During its almost three centuries-long history it has lived up to its motto. It has removed impurities from the language, it has made things firm and certain, and it has given the language a luster. It has clarified, standardized, and imposed order on the language. And in doing so it has made Spanish the easiest of all the major languages of the world to learn.

And two final words: **paciencia, persistencia.**

About the Author

James Gavin started learning Spanish as a Peace Corps volunteer in Venezuela. Since then, pursuing parallel careers as an artist and Spanish-speaker-for-hire (teacher, translator, interpreter, language evaluator and advisor) he has lived in Puerto Rico, *Nueva* York, and Costa Rica. He has also worked and traveled extensively in Spain, Mexico, Honduras, Panama and the Dominican Republic. He now lives, happily surrounded by Spanish-speakers, in northern New Mexico.

The linguistic insights accumulated during his forty years of diverse experiences as a learner, speaker and teacher of Spanish are gathered together in *Gramática Apasionada*. This is a philosophical grammar book, a grammar *con alma*.

Printed in the United States
80815LV00001B/114